AVENGERS PRIME

WRITER	**BRIAN MICHAEL BENDIS**
PENCILER	**ALAN DAVIS**
INKER	**MARK FARMER**
COLORIST	**JAVIER RODRIGUEZ**
LETTERER	**CHRIS ELIOPOULOS**
ASSOCIATE EDITOR	**LAUREN SANKOVITCH**
EDITOR	**TOM BREVOORT**

Collection Editor: JENNIFER GRÜNWALD
Editorial Assistants: JAMES EMMETT & JOE HOCHSTEIN
Assistant Editors: ALEX STARBUCK & NELSON RIBEIRO
Editor, Special Projects: MARK D. BEAZLEY
Senior Editor, Special Projects: JEFF YOUNGQUIST
Senior Vice President of Sales: DAVID GABRIEL
Book Design: JEFF POWELL

Editor in Chief: AXEL ALONSO
Chief Creative Officer: JOE QUESADA
Publisher: DAN BUCKLEY
Executive Producer: ALAN FINE

AVENGERS
PRIME

NGERS PRIME. Contains material originally published in magazine form as AVENGERS PRIME #1-5. First printing 2011. Hardcover ISBN# 978-0-7851-4725-1. Softcover ISB
shed by MARVEL WORLDWIDE, INC., a subsidiary of MARVEL ENTERTAINMENT, LLC. OFFICE OF PUBLICATION: 135 West 50th Street, New York, NY 10020. Copyright © 2010 and
All rights reserved. Hardcover: $24.99 per copy in the U.S. and $27.99 in Canada (GST #R127032852). Softcover: $16.99 per copy in the U.S. and $18.99 in Canada (GST
ement #40668537. All characters featured in this issue and the distinctive names and likenesses thereof, and all related indicia are trademarks of Marvel Characters, Inc. N
e names, characters, persons, and/or institutions in this magazine with those of any living or dead person or institution is intended, and any such similarity which may ex
ted in the U.S.A. ALAN FINE, EVP - Office of the President, Marvel Worldwide, Inc. and EVP & CMO Marvel Characters B.V.; DAN BUCKLEY, Publisher & President - Print, Anim
QUESADA, Chief Creative Officer; JIM SOKOLOWSKI, Chief Operating Officer; DAVID BOGART, SVP of Business Affairs & Talent Management; TOM BREVOORT, SVP of Publishing
or & Content Development; DAVID GABRIEL, SVP of Publishing Sales & Circulation; MICHAEL PASCIULLO, SVP of Brand Planning & Communications; JIM O'KEEFE, VP of Op
Executive Director of Publishing Technology; JUSTIN F. GABRIE, Director of Publishing & Editorial Operations; SUSAN CRESPI, Editorial Operations Manager; ALEX MORALI
ger; STAN LEE, Chairman Emeritus. For information regarding advertising in Marvel Comics or on Marvel.com, please contact Ron Stern, VP of Business Development, at rstern
cription inquiries, please call 800-217-9158. Manufactured between 2/21/2011 and 3/21/2011 (hardcover), and 2/21/2011 and 9/19/2011 (softcover), by R.R. DONNELLEY

87654321

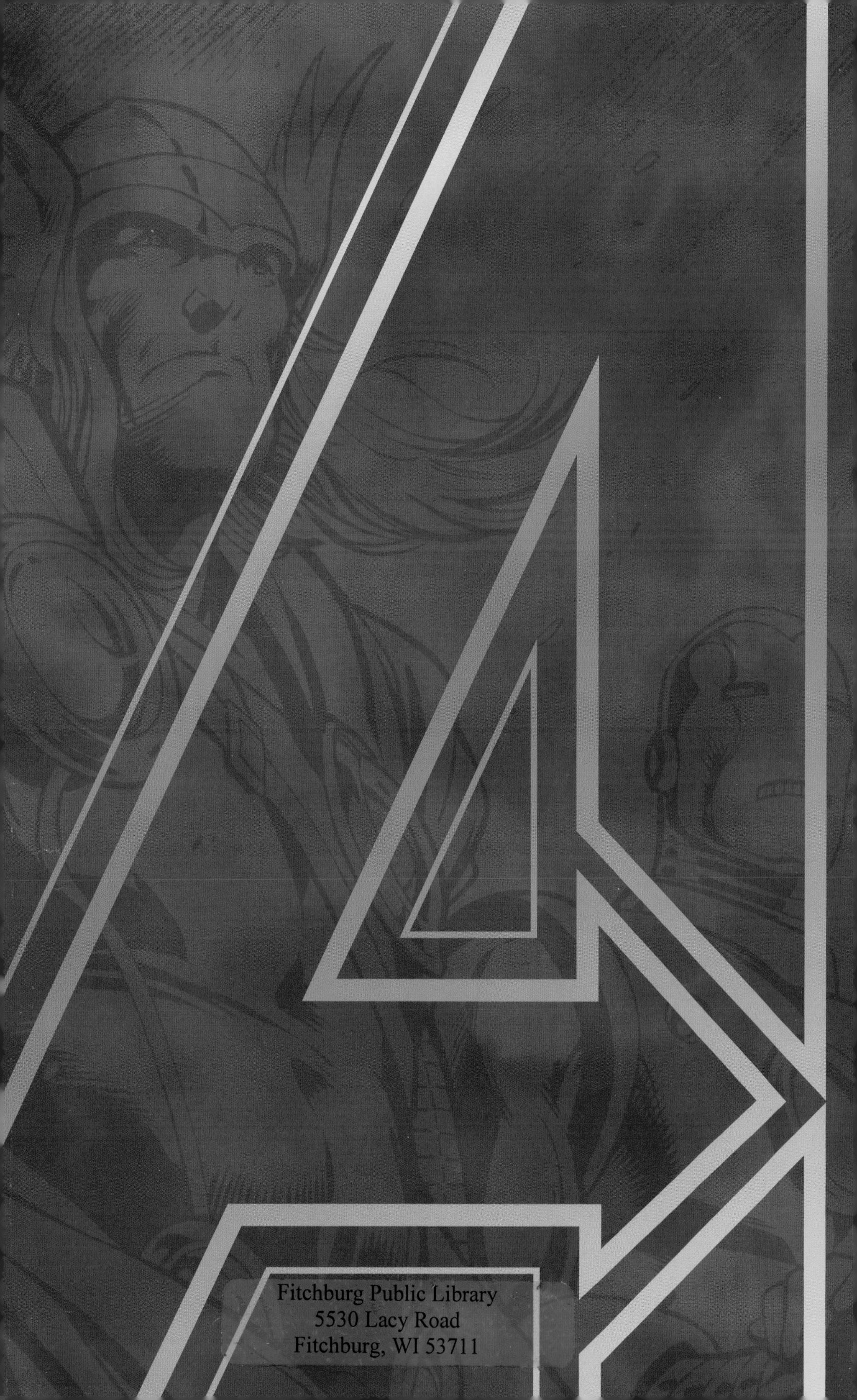

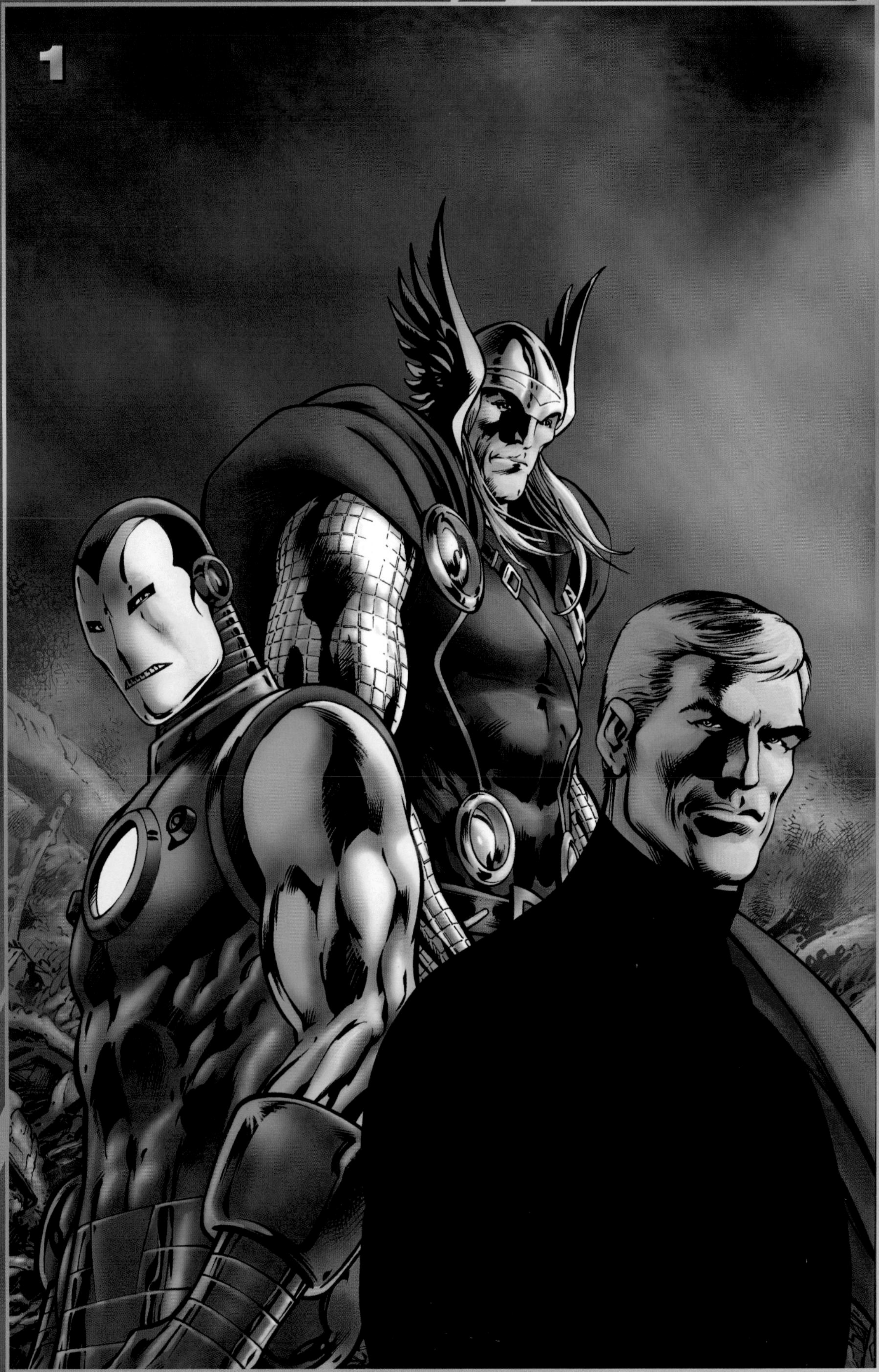
1

EARTH'S MIGHTIEST HEROES, UNITED AGAINST A COMMON THREAT! ON THAT DAY THE AVENGERS WERE BORN, TO FIGHT FOES THAT NO SINGLE HERO COULD WITHSTAND!

SIEGE: AFTERMATH
AVENGERS PRIME

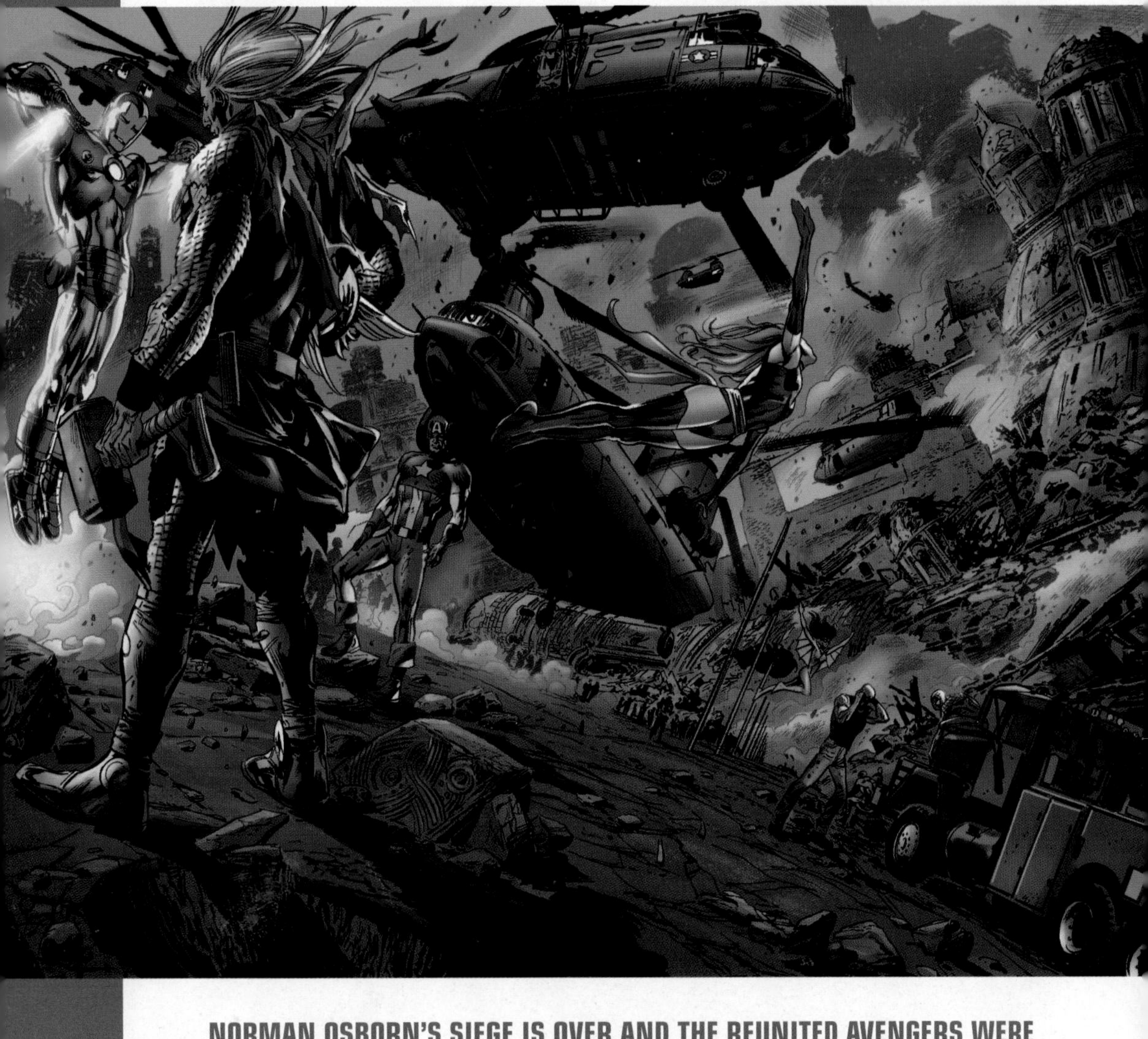

NORMAN OSBORN'S SIEGE IS OVER AND THE REUNITED AVENGERS WERE TRIUMPHANT. STEVE ROGERS, THE MAN WHO WAS CAPTAIN AMERICA, IS NOW IN CHARGE OF THE UNITED STATES' SECURITY.

BUT ALL THIS WAS NOT WITHOUT COST. THE GREAT CITY OF ASGARD HAS FALLEN.

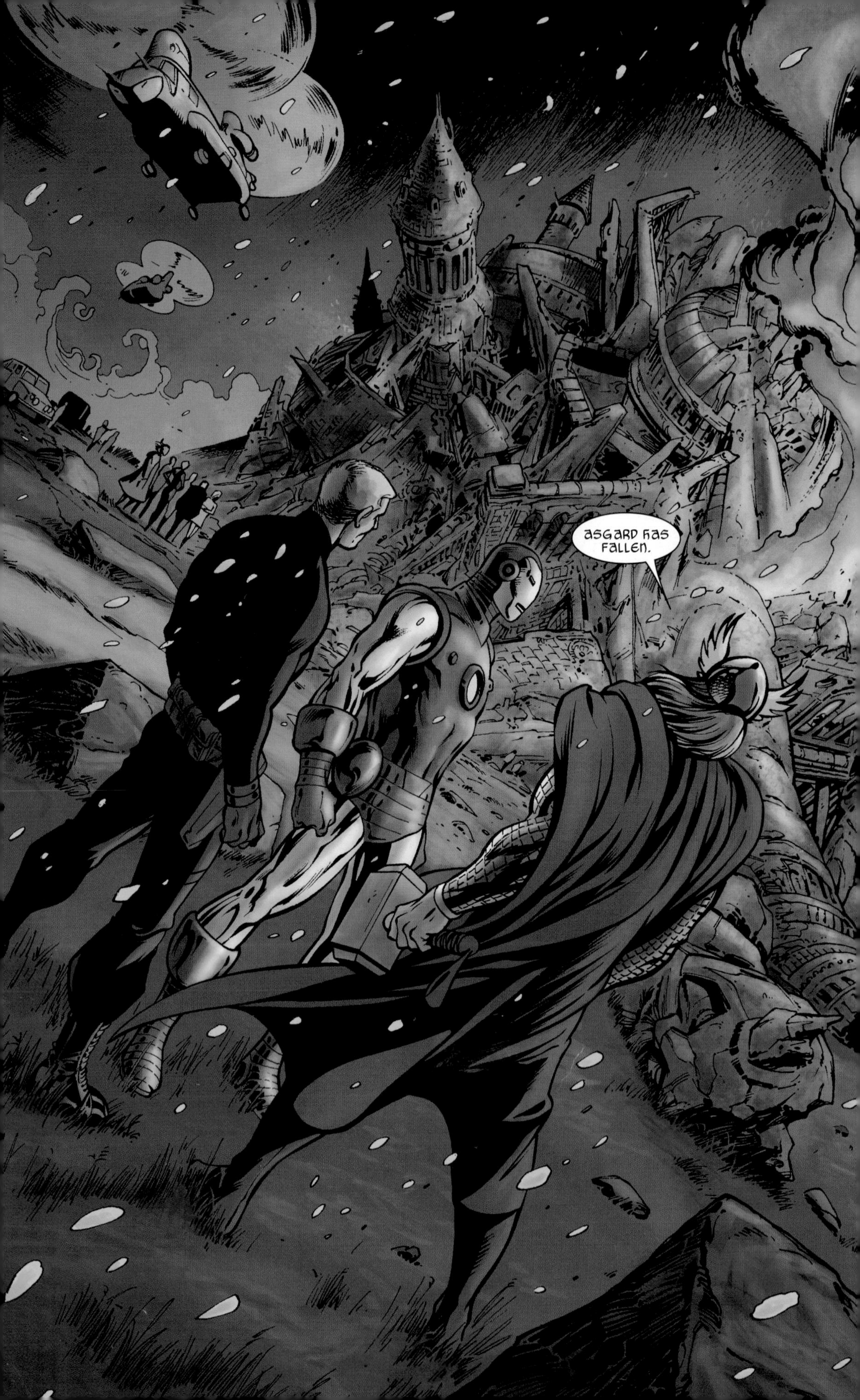
ASGARD HAS FALLEN.

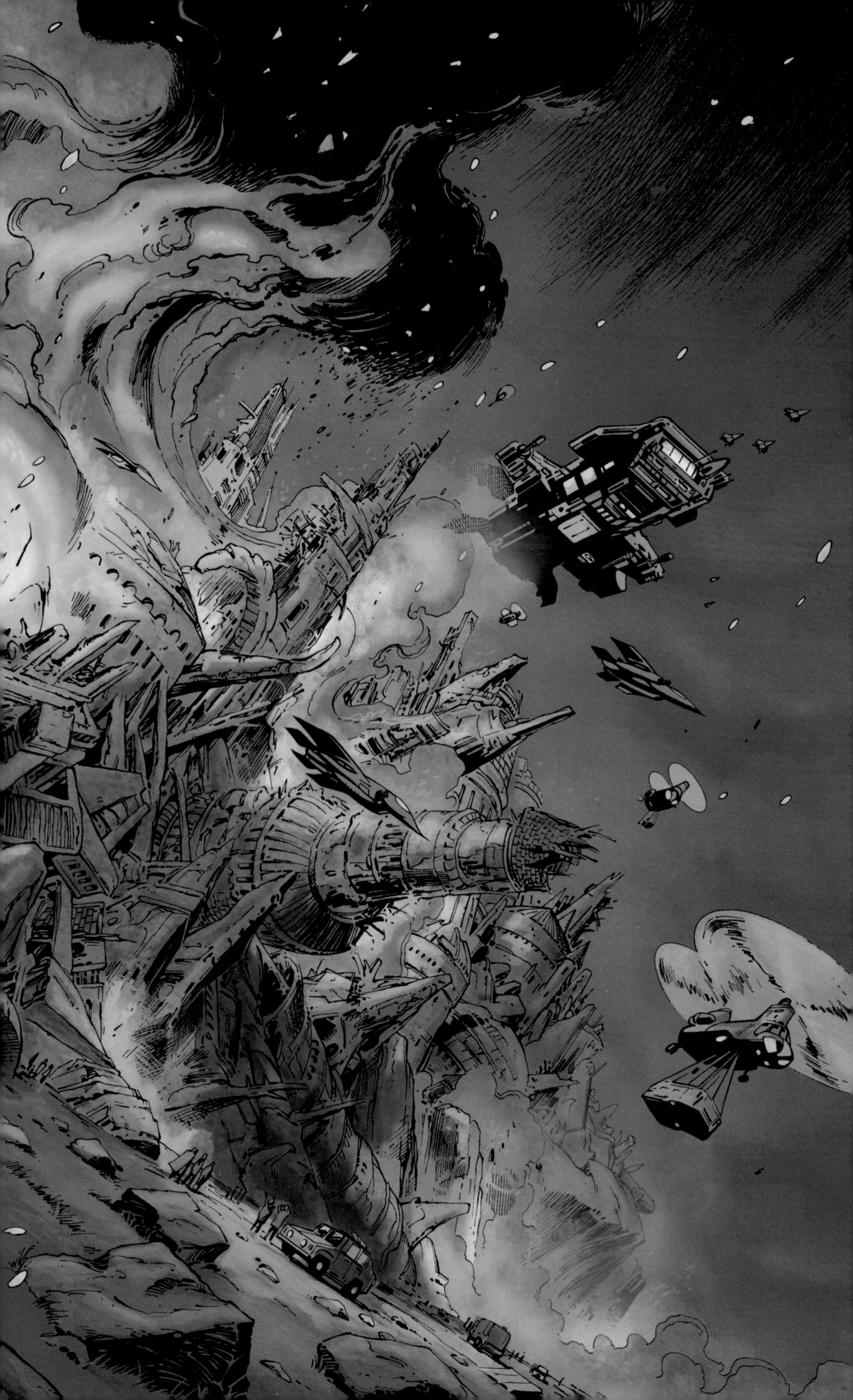

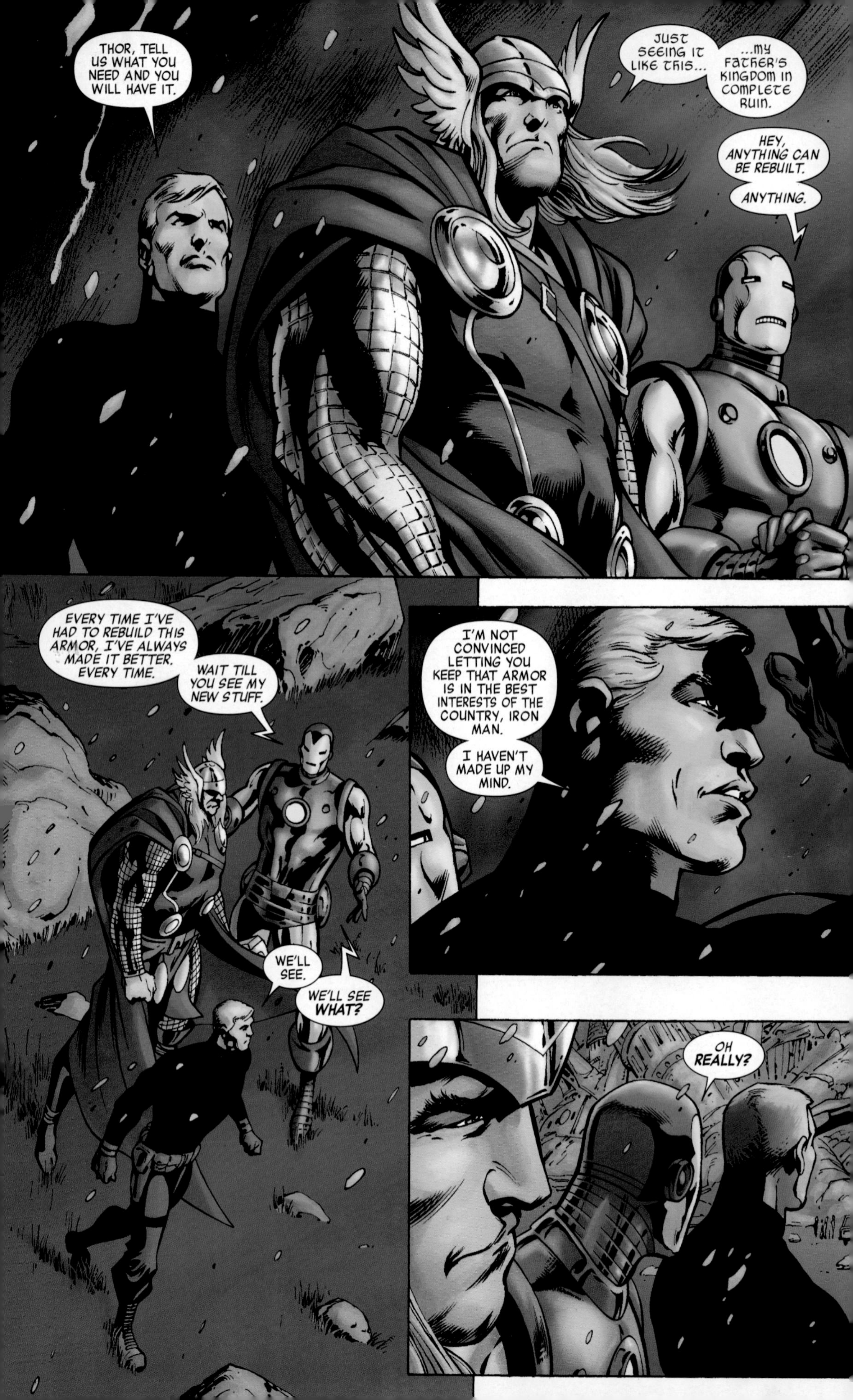
THOR, TELL US WHAT YOU NEED AND YOU WILL HAVE IT.
JUST SEEING IT LIKE THIS...
...MY FATHER'S KINGDOM IN COMPLETE RUIN.
HEY, ANYTHING CAN BE REBUILT.
ANYTHING.
EVERY TIME I'VE HAD TO REBUILD THIS ARMOR, I'VE ALWAYS MADE IT BETTER. EVERY TIME.
WAIT TILL YOU SEE MY NEW STUFF.
WE'LL SEE.
WE'LL SEE WHAT?
I'M NOT CONVINCED LETTING YOU KEEP THAT ARMOR IS IN THE BEST INTERESTS OF THE COUNTRY, IRON MAN.
I HAVEN'T MADE UP MY MIND.
OH REALLY?

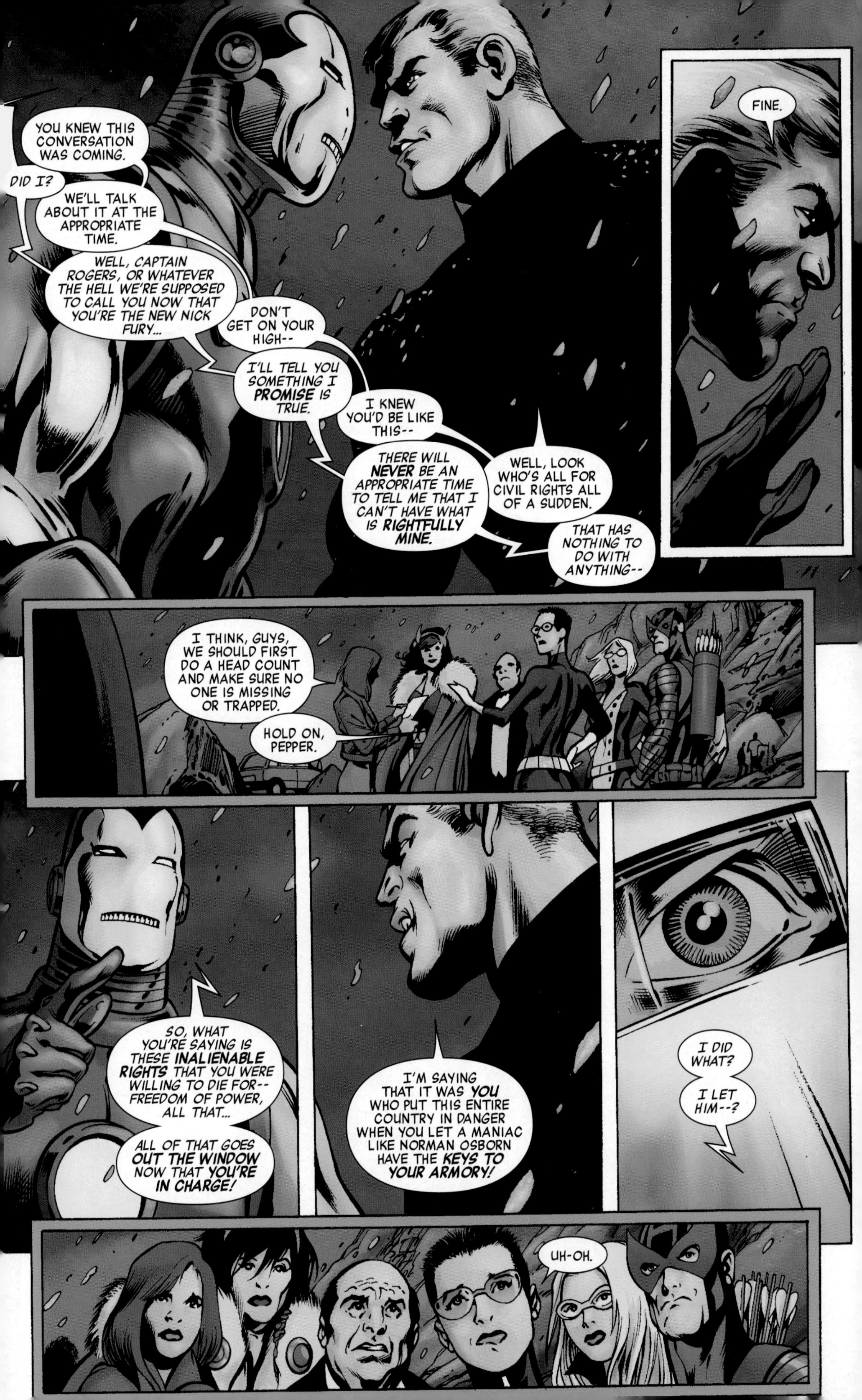

YOU KNEW THIS CONVERSATION WAS COMING.
DID I?
WE'LL TALK ABOUT IT AT THE APPROPRIATE TIME.
WELL, CAPTAIN ROGERS, OR WHATEVER THE HELL WE'RE SUPPOSED TO CALL YOU NOW THAT YOU'RE THE NEW NICK FURY...
DON'T GET ON YOUR HIGH--
I'LL TELL YOU SOMETHING I PROMISE IS TRUE.
I KNEW YOU'D BE LIKE THIS--
THERE WILL NEVER BE AN APPROPRIATE TIME TO TELL ME THAT I CAN'T HAVE WHAT IS RIGHTFULLY MINE.
WELL, LOOK WHO'S ALL FOR CIVIL RIGHTS ALL OF A SUDDEN.
THAT HAS NOTHING TO DO WITH ANYTHING--
FINE.
I THINK, GUYS, WE SHOULD FIRST DO A HEAD COUNT AND MAKE SURE NO ONE IS MISSING OR TRAPPED.
HOLD ON, PEPPER.
SO, WHAT YOU'RE SAYING IS THESE INALIENABLE RIGHTS THAT YOU WERE WILLING TO DIE FOR-- FREEDOM OF POWER, ALL THAT...
ALL OF THAT GOES OUT THE WINDOW NOW THAT YOU'RE IN CHARGE!
I'M SAYING THAT IT WAS YOU WHO PUT THIS ENTIRE COUNTRY IN DANGER WHEN YOU LET A MANIAC LIKE NORMAN OSBORN HAVE THE KEYS TO YOUR ARMORY!
I DID WHAT?
I LET HIM--?
UH-OH.

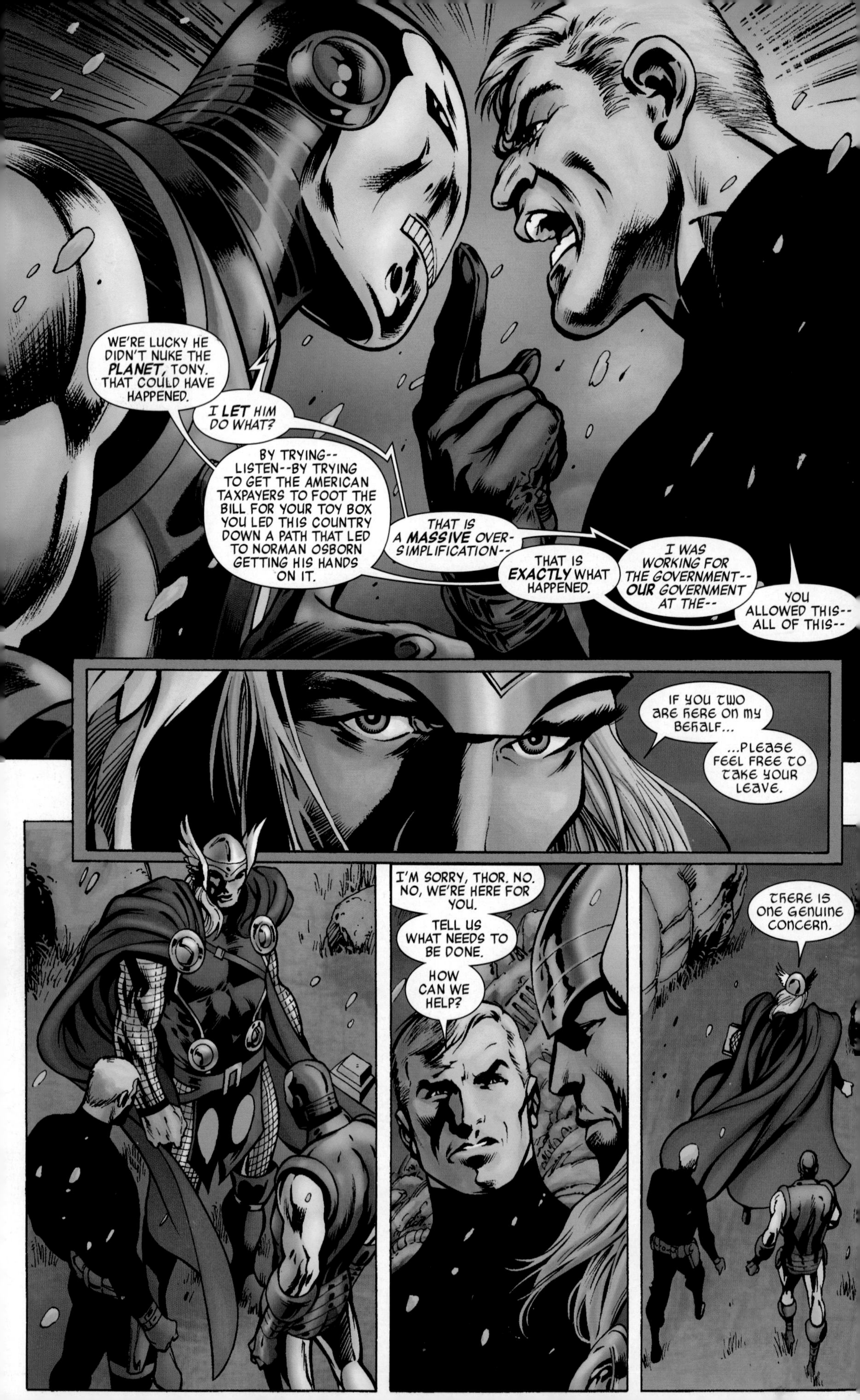

WE'RE LUCKY HE DIDN'T NUKE THE PLANET, TONY. THAT COULD HAVE HAPPENED.
I LET HIM DO WHAT?
BY TRYING--LISTEN--BY TRYING TO GET THE AMERICAN TAXPAYERS TO FOOT THE BILL FOR YOUR TOY BOX YOU LED THIS COUNTRY DOWN A PATH THAT LED TO NORMAN OSBORN GETTING HIS HANDS ON IT.
THAT IS A MASSIVE OVER-SIMPLIFICATION--
THAT IS EXACTLY WHAT HAPPENED.
I WAS WORKING FOR THE GOVERNMENT--OUR GOVERNMENT AT THE--
YOU ALLOWED THIS--ALL OF THIS--
IF YOU TWO ARE HERE ON MY BEHALF...
...PLEASE FEEL FREE TO TAKE YOUR LEAVE.
I'M SORRY, THOR. NO. NO, WE'RE HERE FOR YOU.
TELL US WHAT NEEDS TO BE DONE.
HOW CAN WE HELP?
THERE IS ONE GENUINE CONCERN.

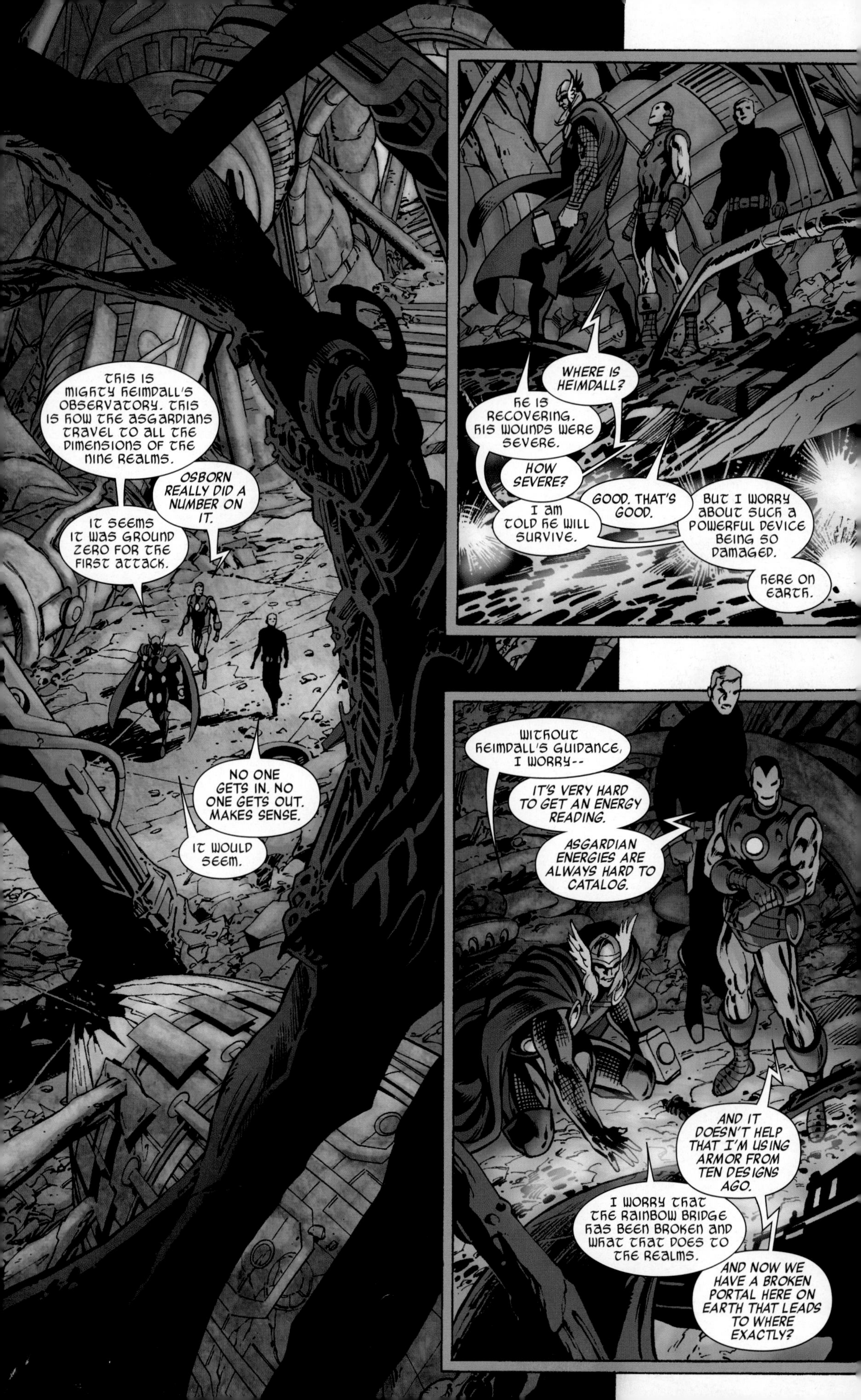
THIS IS MIGHTY HEIMDALL'S OBSERVATORY. THIS IS HOW THE ASGARDIANS TRAVEL TO ALL THE DIMENSIONS OF THE NINE REALMS.
OSBORN REALLY DID A NUMBER ON IT.
IT SEEMS IT WAS GROUND ZERO FOR THE FIRST ATTACK.
NO ONE GETS IN. NO ONE GETS OUT. MAKES SENSE.
IT WOULD SEEM.
WHERE IS HEIMDALL?
HE IS RECOVERING. HIS WOUNDS WERE SEVERE.
HOW SEVERE?
I AM TOLD HE WILL SURVIVE.
GOOD. THAT'S GOOD.
BUT I WORRY ABOUT SUCH A POWERFUL DEVICE BEING SO DAMAGED.
HERE ON EARTH.
WITHOUT HEIMDALL'S GUIDANCE, I WORRY--
IT'S VERY HARD TO GET AN ENERGY READING.
ASGARDIAN ENERGIES ARE ALWAYS HARD TO CATALOG.
AND IT DOESN'T HELP THAT I'M USING ARMOR FROM TEN DESIGNS AGO.
I WORRY THAT THE RAINBOW BRIDGE HAS BEEN BROKEN AND WHAT THAT DOES TO THE REALMS.
AND NOW WE HAVE A BROKEN PORTAL HERE ON EARTH THAT LEADS TO WHERE EXACTLY?

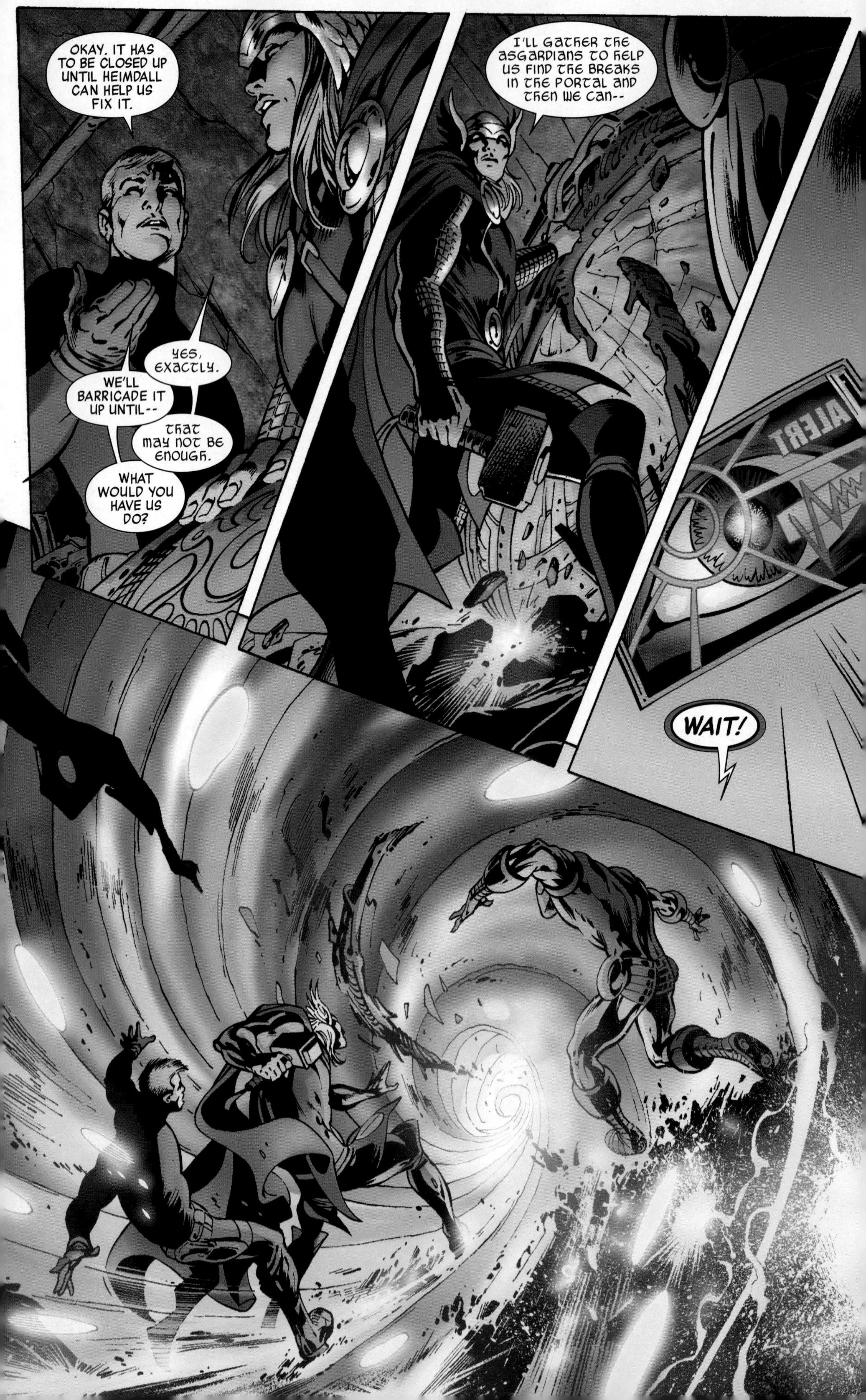

OKAY. IT HAS TO BE CLOSED UP UNTIL HEIMDALL CAN HELP US FIX IT.
YES, EXACTLY.
WE'LL BARRICADE IT UP UNTIL--
THAT MAY NOT BE ENOUGH.
WHAT WOULD YOU HAVE US DO?
I'LL GATHER THE ASGARDIANS TO HELP US FIND THE BREAKS IN THE PORTAL AND THEN WE CAN--
ALERT
WAIT!

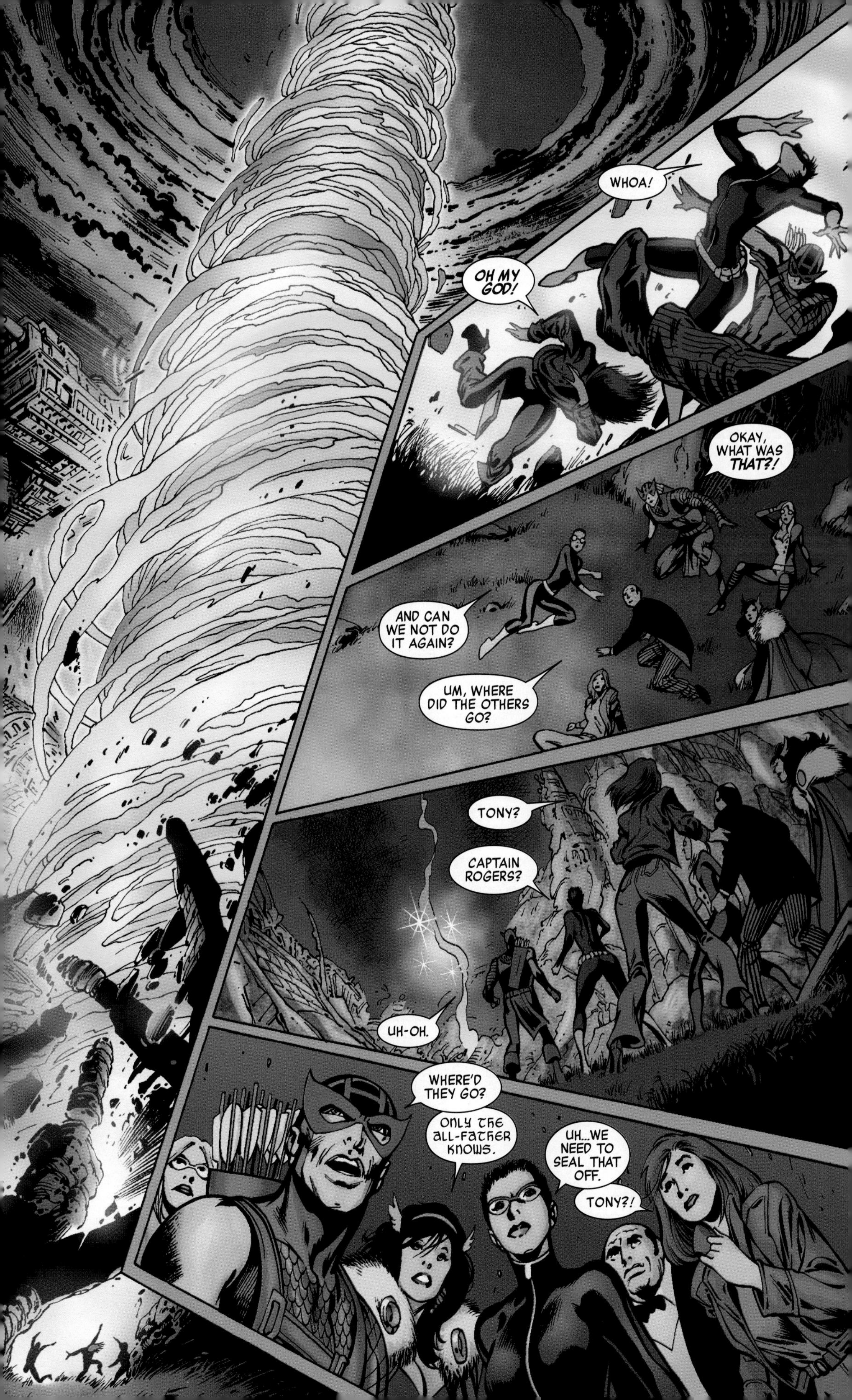
WHOA!
OH MY GOD!
OKAY, WHAT WAS THAT?!
AND CAN WE NOT DO IT AGAIN?
UM, WHERE DID THE OTHERS GO?
TONY?
CAPTAIN ROGERS?
UH-OH.
WHERE'D THEY GO?
ONLY THE ALL-FATHER KNOWS.
UH...WE NEED TO SEAL THAT OFF.
TONY?!

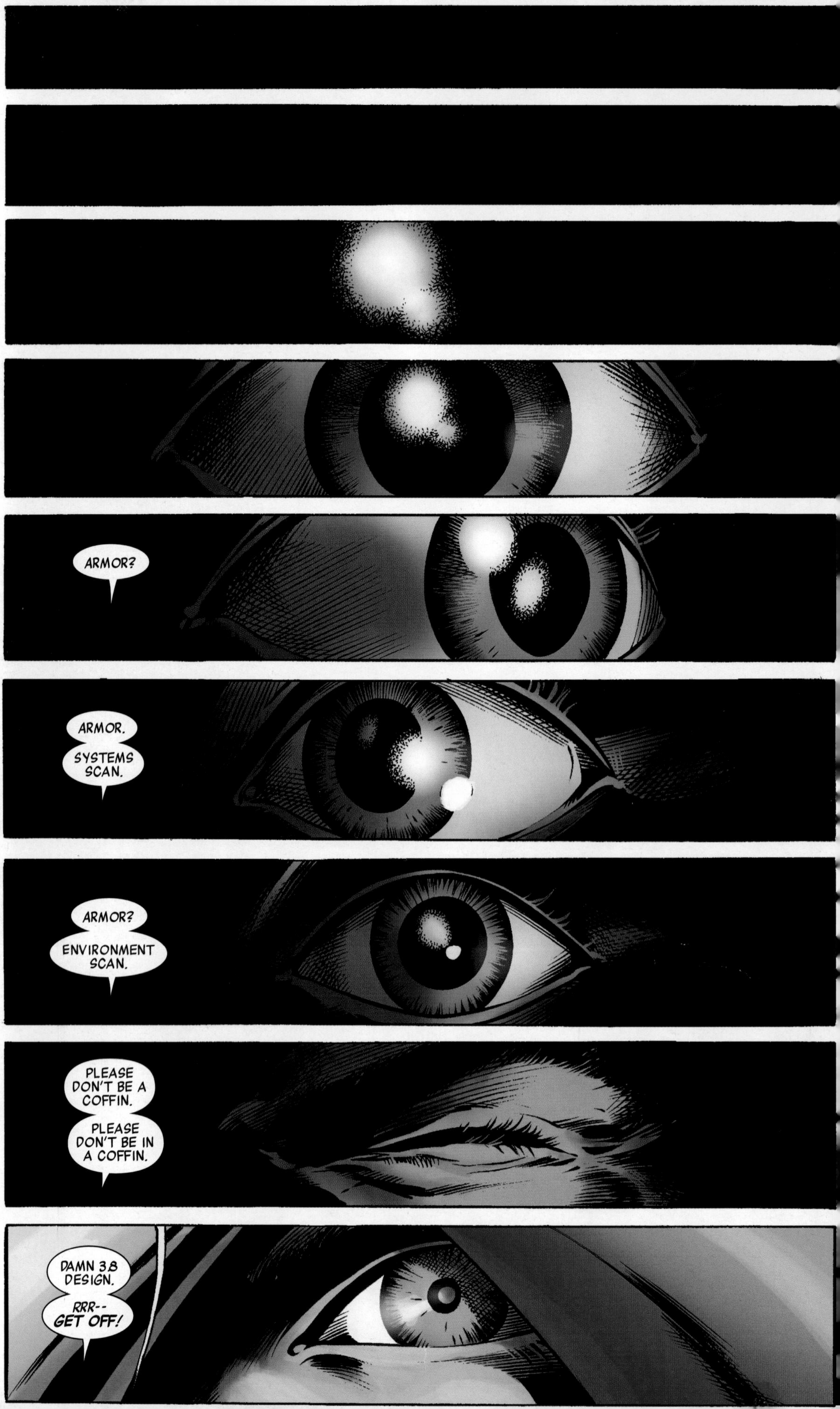
ARMOR?
ARMOR.
SYSTEMS SCAN.
ARMOR?
ENVIRONMENT SCAN.
PLEASE DON'T BE A COFFIN.
PLEASE DON'T BE IN A COFFIN.
DAMN 3.8 DESIGN.
RRR-- GET OFF!

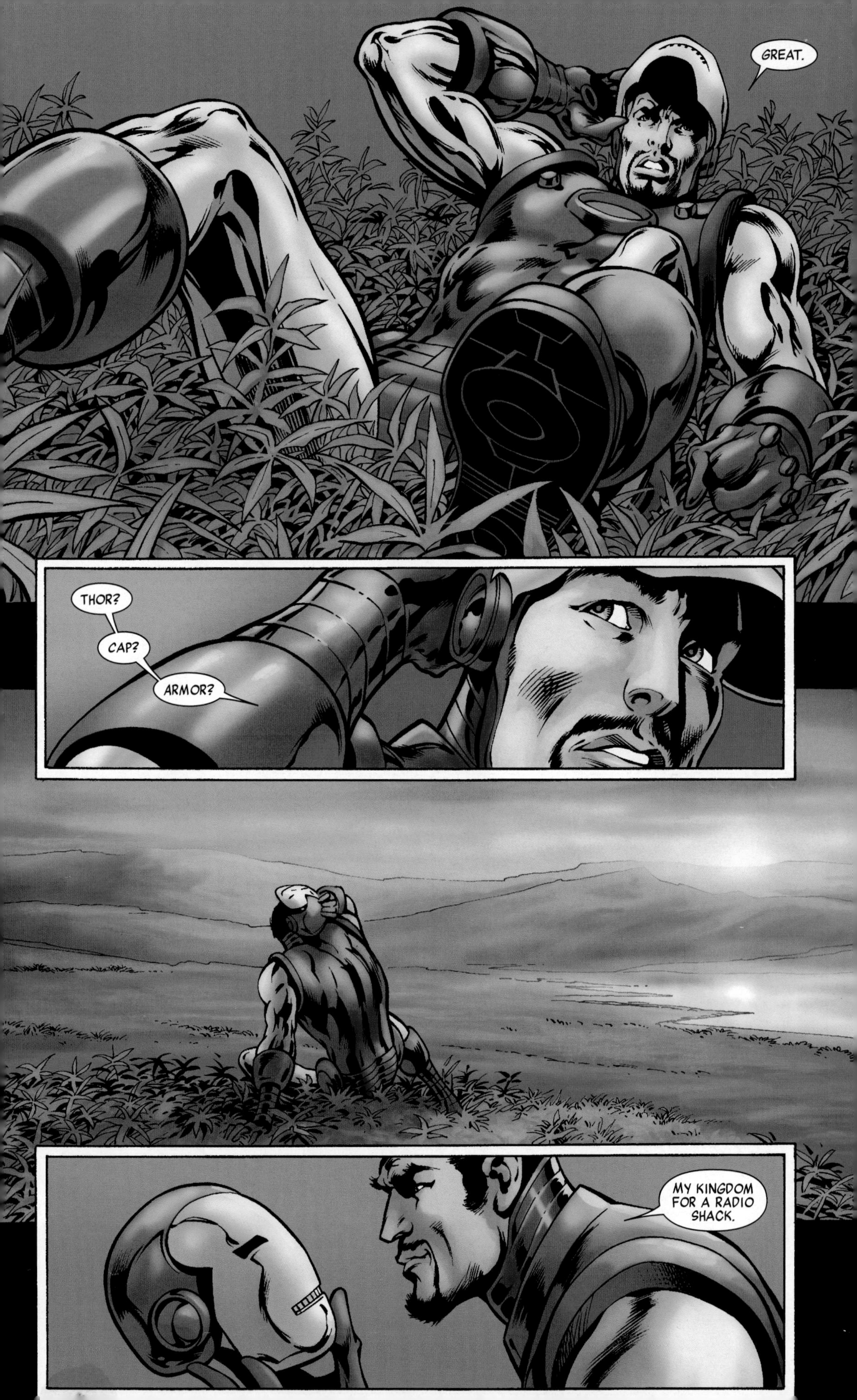
GREAT.
THOR?
CAP?
ARMOR?
MY KINGDOM FOR A RADIO SHACK.

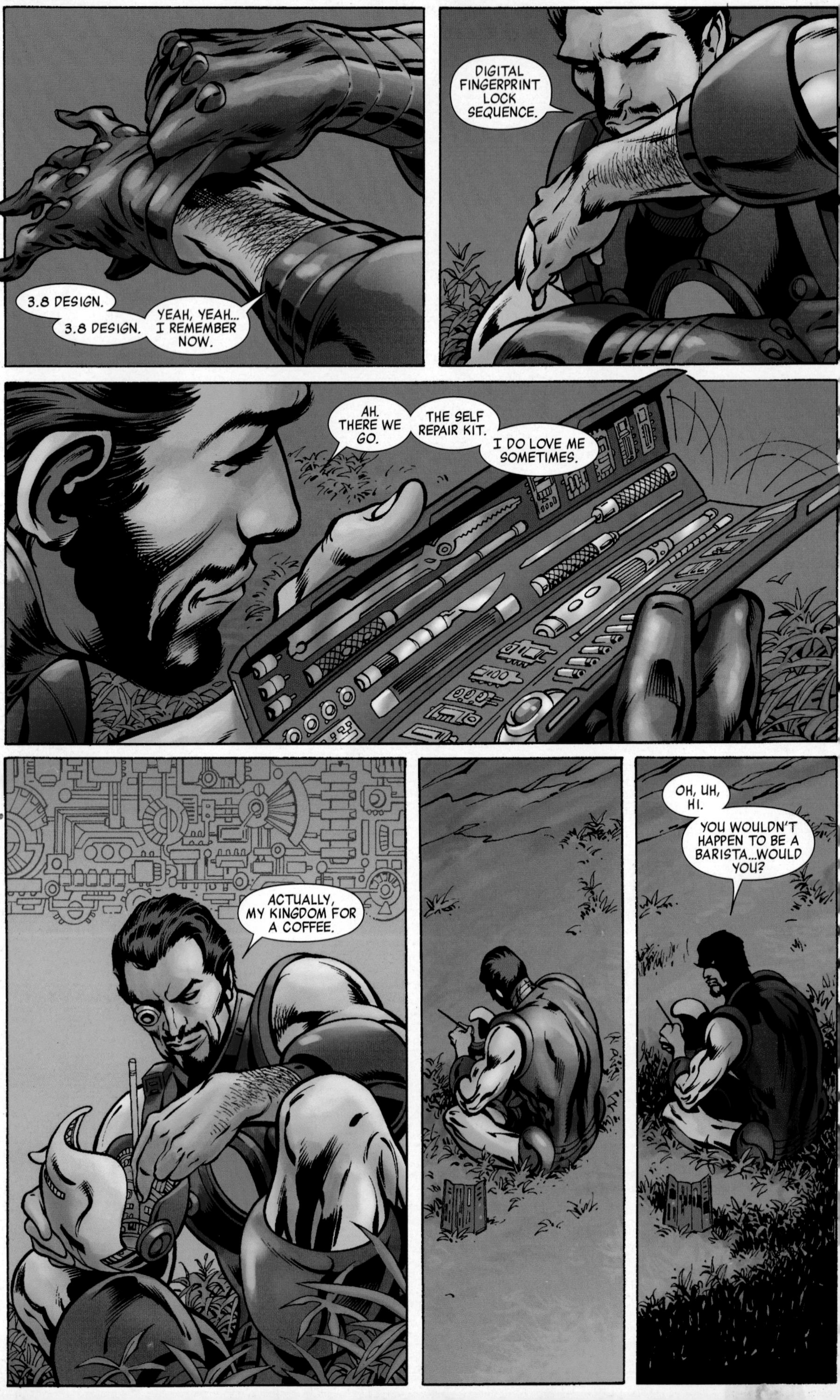
3.8 DESIGN.
3.8 DESIGN.
YEAH, YEAH... I REMEMBER NOW.
DIGITAL FINGERPRINT LOCK SEQUENCE.
AH. THERE WE GO.
THE SELF REPAIR KIT.
I DO LOVE ME SOMETIMES.
ACTUALLY, MY KINGDOM FOR A COFFEE.
OH, UH, HI.
YOU WOULDN'T HAPPEN TO BE A BARISTA...WOULD YOU?

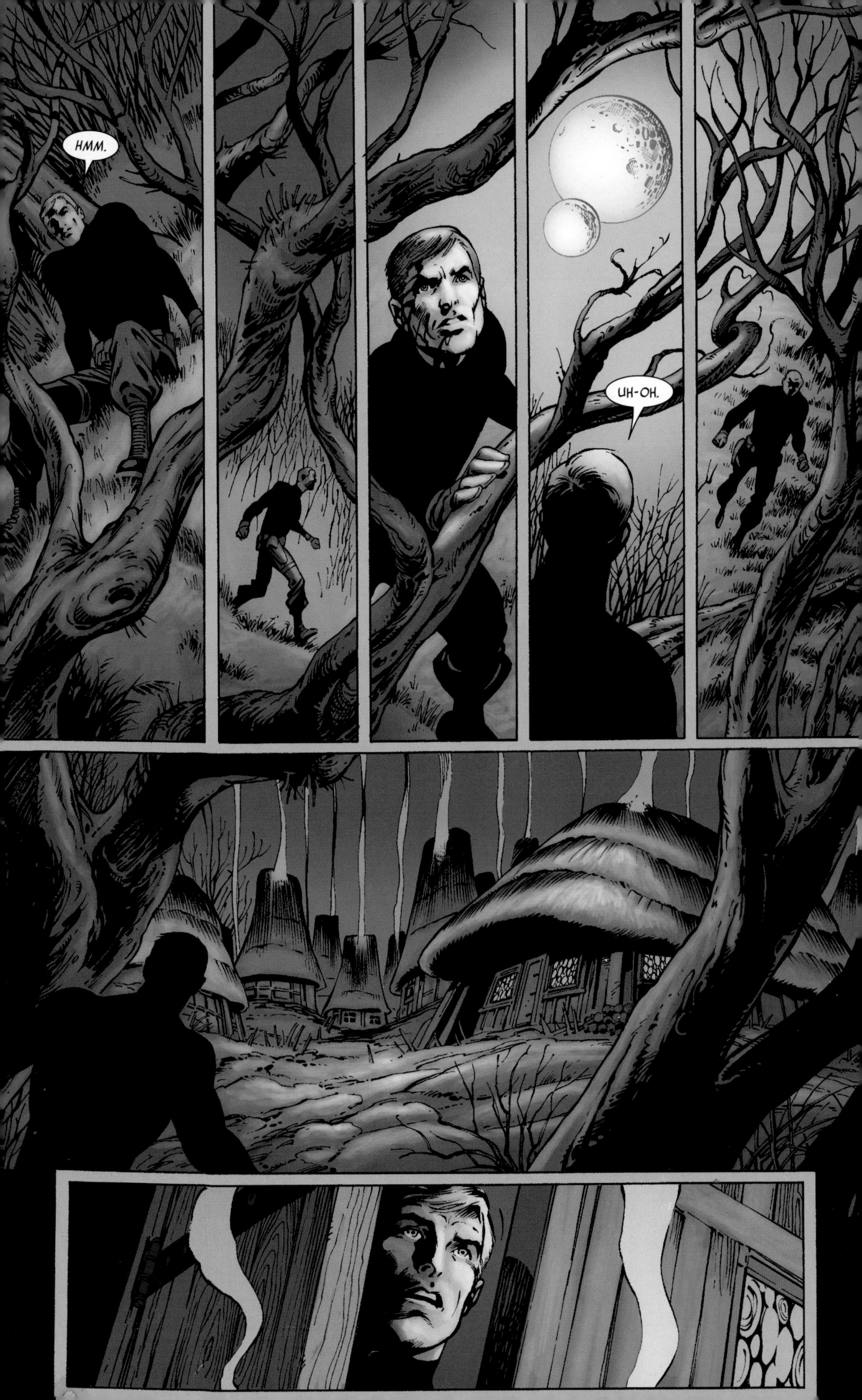
HMM.
UH-OH.

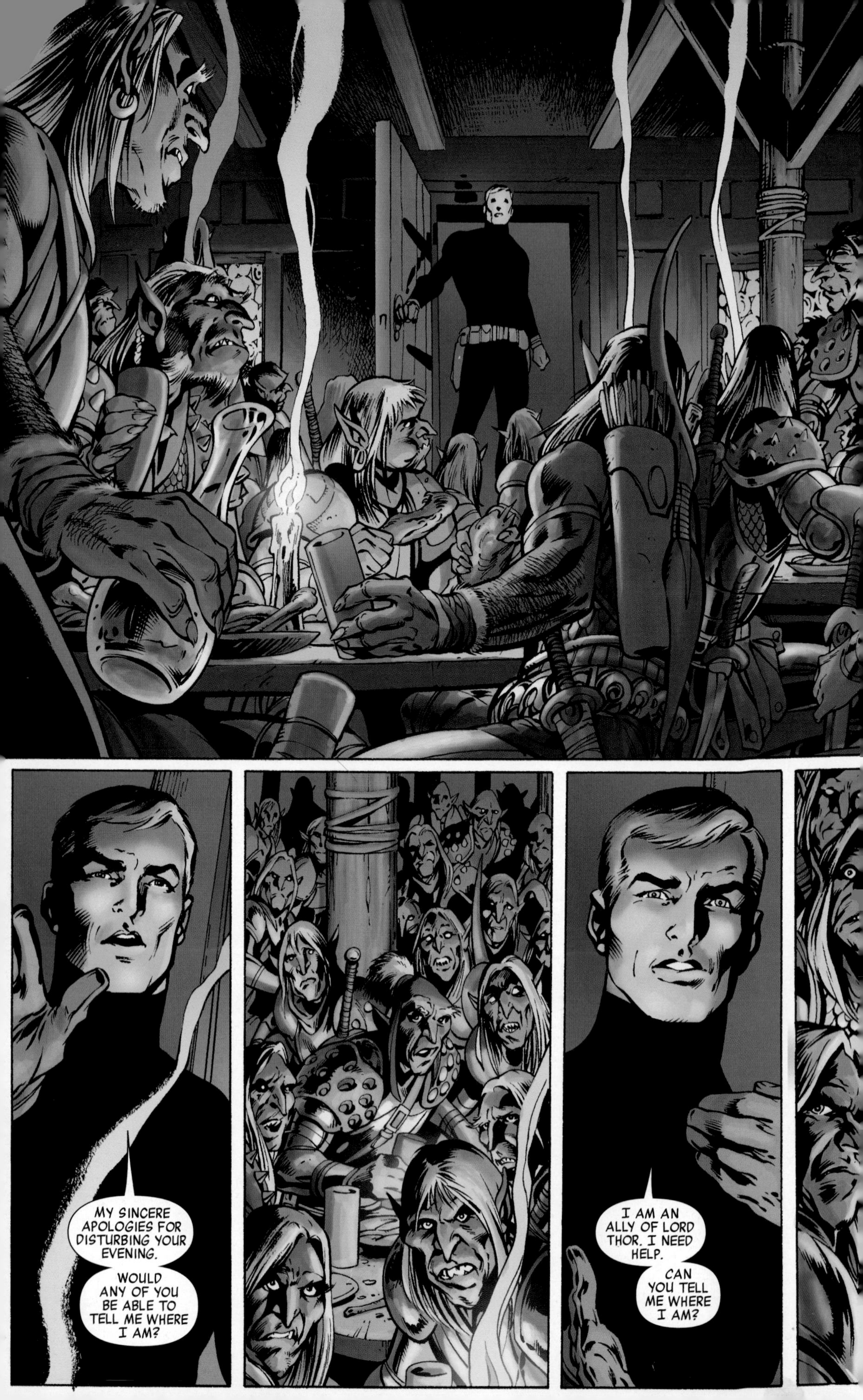
MY SINCERE APOLOGIES FOR DISTURBING YOUR EVENING.
WOULD ANY OF YOU BE ABLE TO TELL ME WHERE I AM?
I AM AN ALLY OF LORD THOR. I NEED HELP.
CAN YOU TELL ME WHERE I AM?

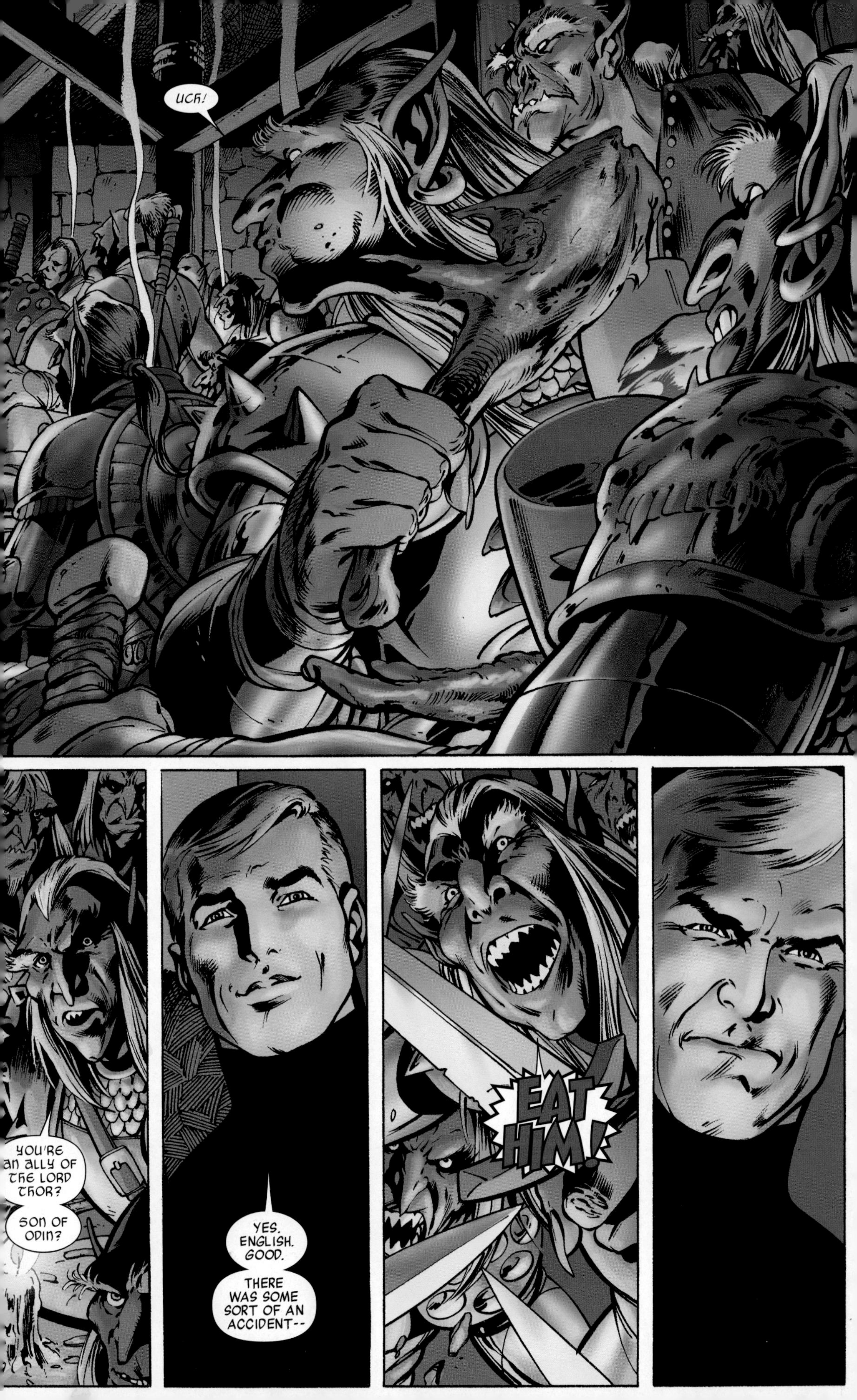
UGH!
YOU'RE AN ALLY OF THE LORD THOR?
SON OF ODIN?
YES. ENGLISH. GOOD.
THERE WAS SOME SORT OF AN ACCIDENT--
EAT HIM!

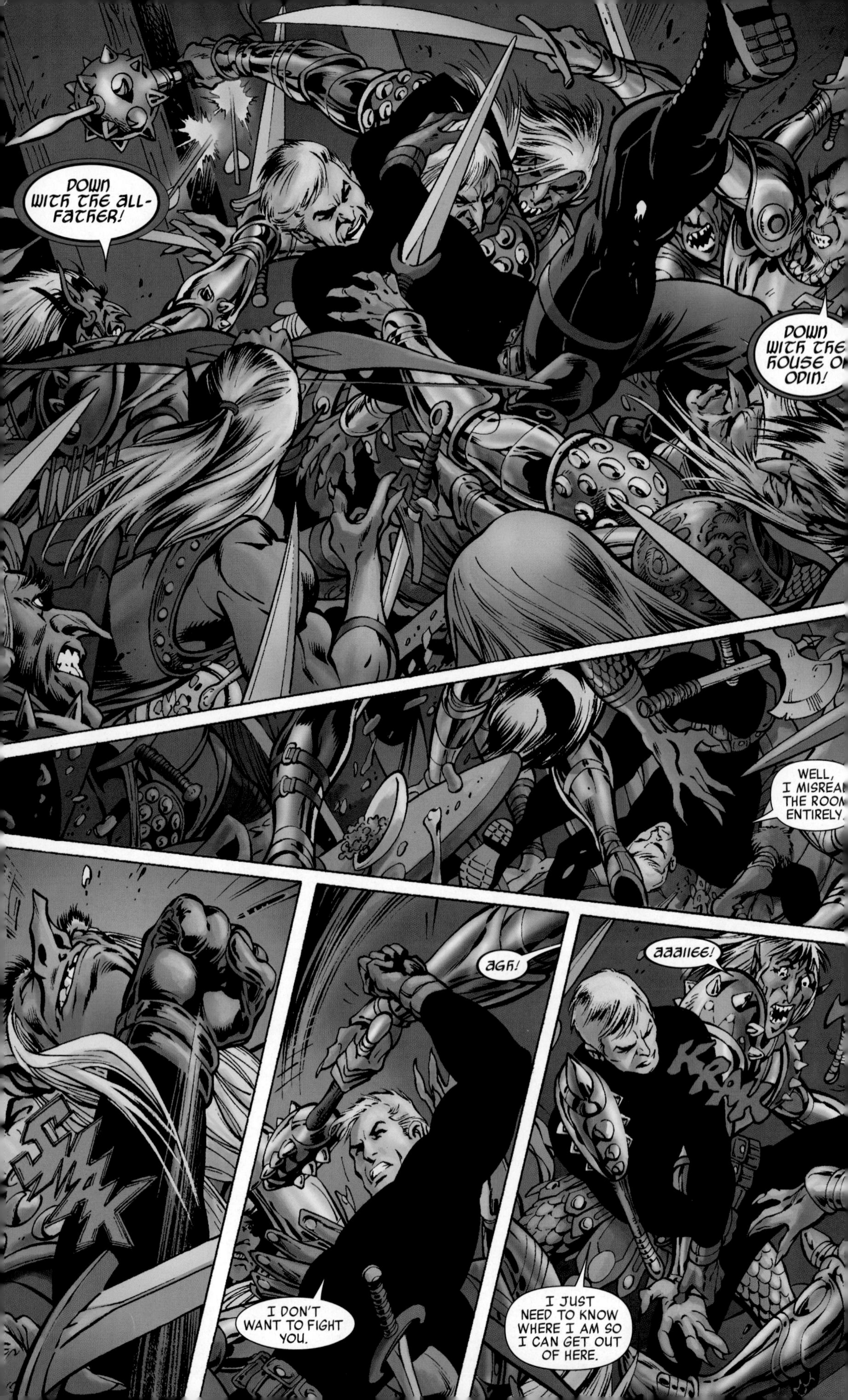
DOWN WITH THE ALL-FATHER!
DOWN WITH THE HOUSE OF ODIN!
WELL, I MISREAD THE ROOM ENTIRELY.
AGH!
AAAIIEE!
KRAK
I DON'T WANT TO FIGHT YOU.
I JUST NEED TO KNOW WHERE I AM SO I CAN GET OUT OF HERE.

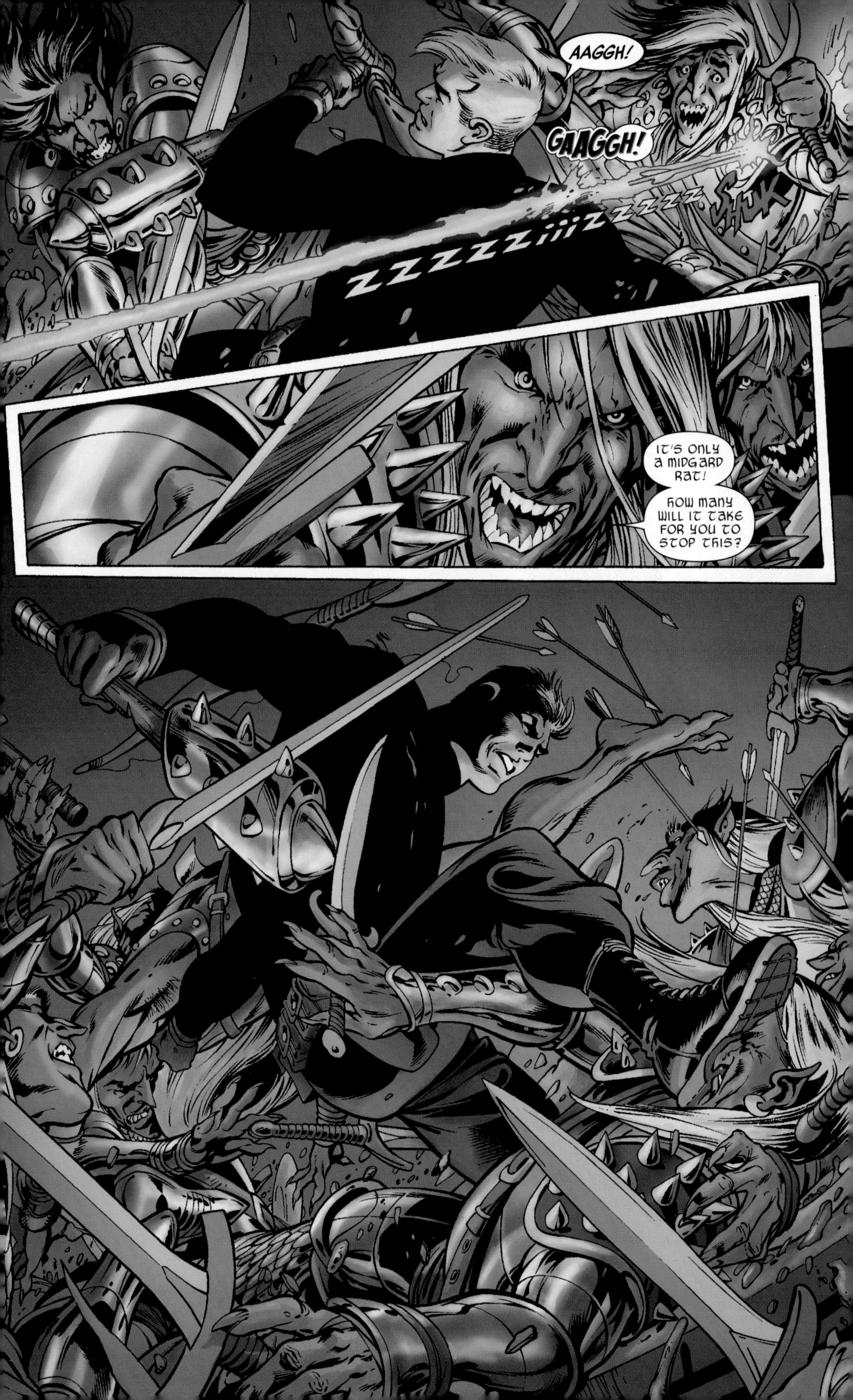

AAGGH!
GAAGGH!
SHUK
ZZZZZZiiiiZZZZZZZ
IT'S ONLY A MIDGARD RAT!
HOW MANY WILL IT TAKE FOR YOU TO STOP THIS?

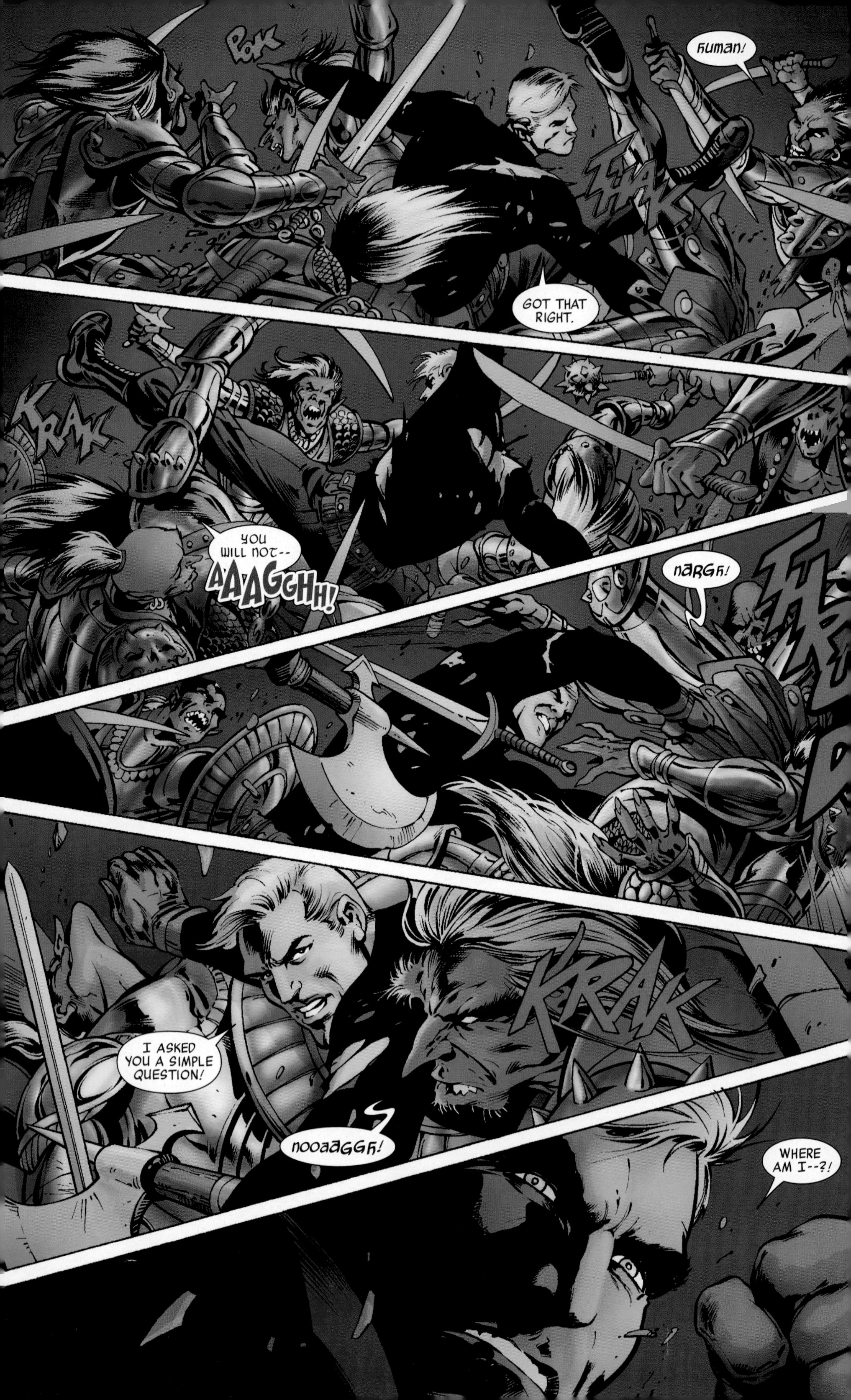
POK
HUMAN!
THAK
GOT THAT RIGHT.
KRAK
YOU WILL NOT--
AAAGGHHH!
NARGH!
I ASKED YOU A SIMPLE QUESTION!
KRAK
NOOAAGGH!
WHERE AM I--?!

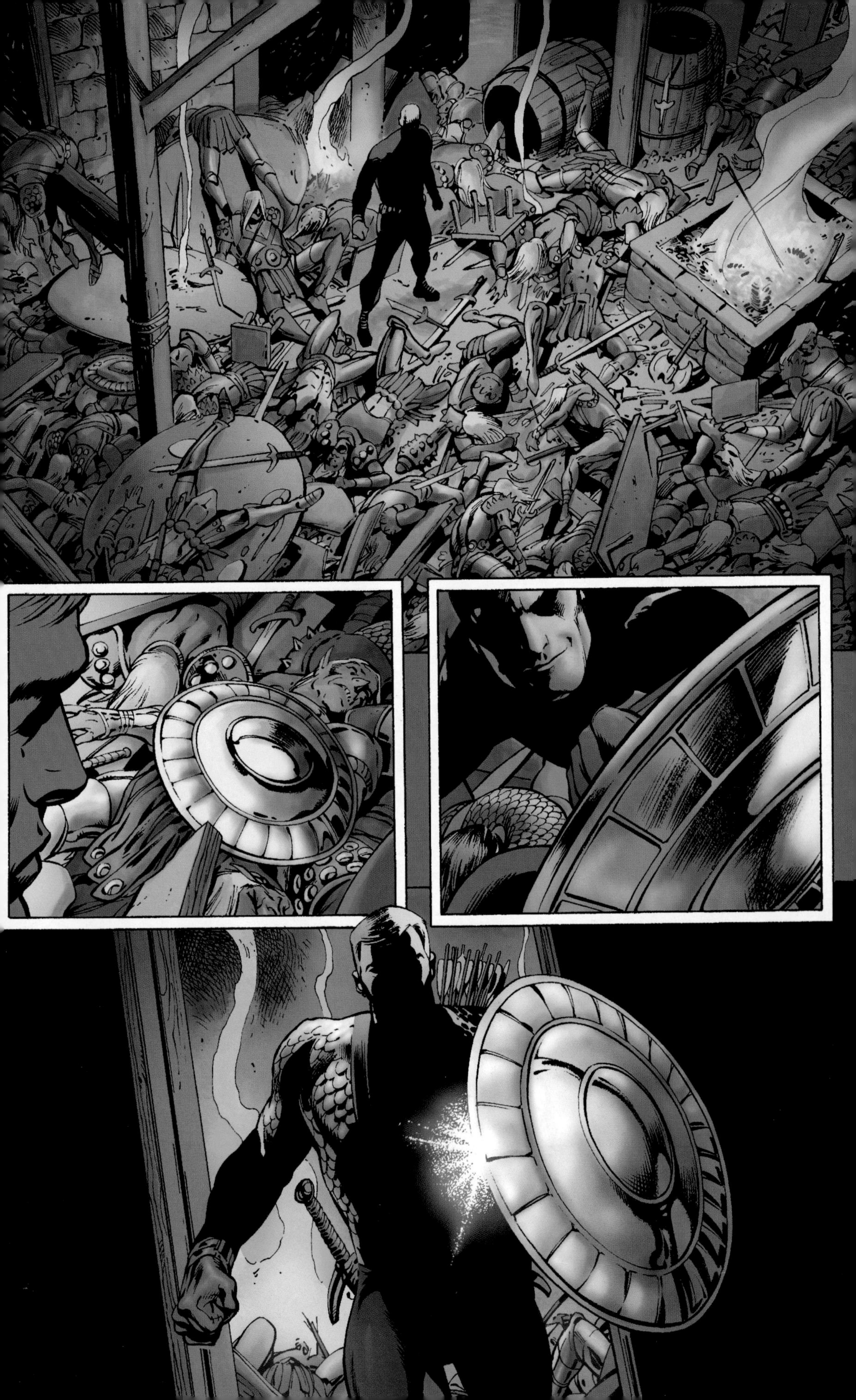

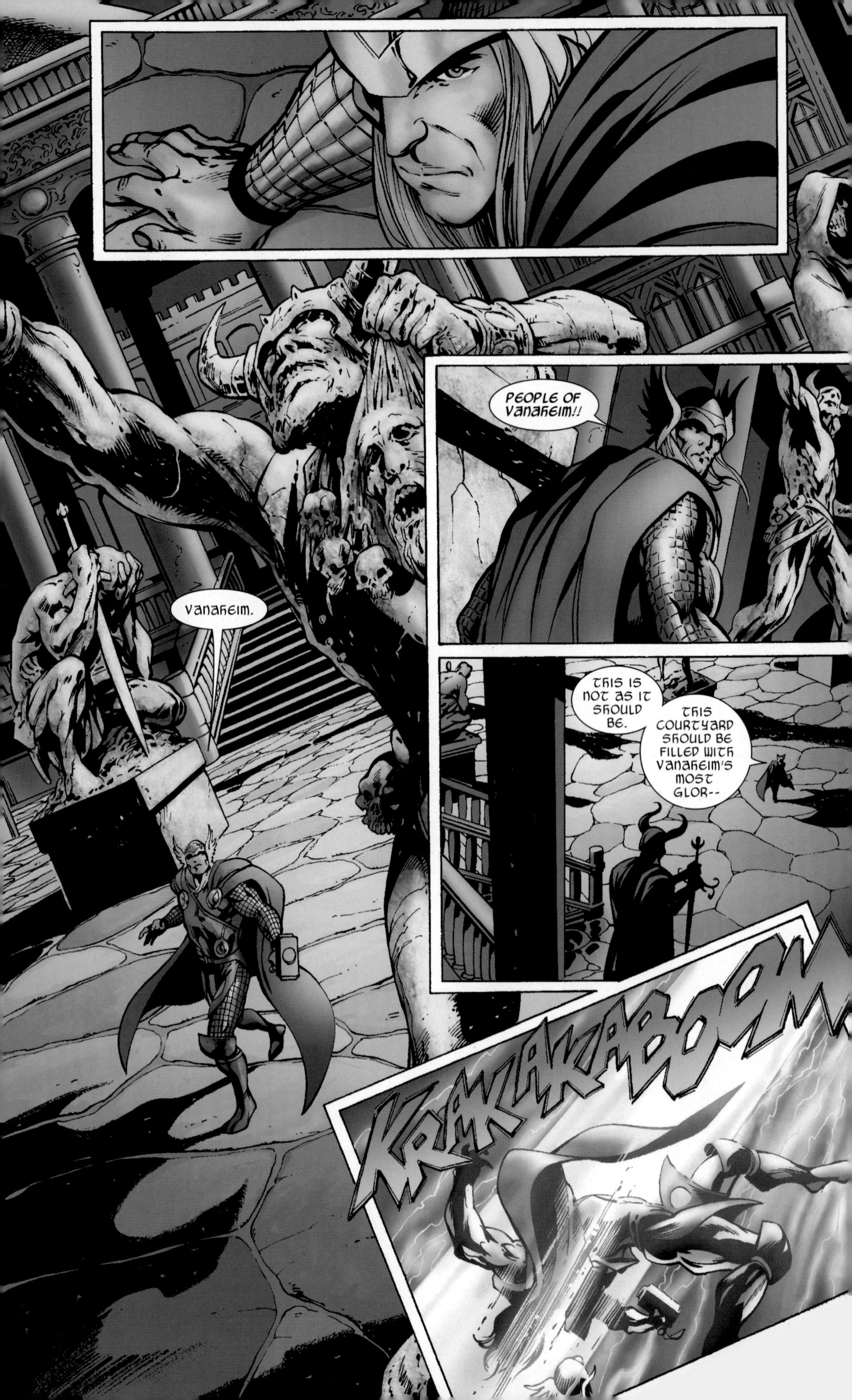
VANAHEIM.
PEOPLE OF VANAHEIM!!
THIS IS NOT AS IT SHOULD BE.
THIS COURTYARD SHOULD BE FILLED WITH VANAHEIM'S MOST GLOR--
KRAKAKABOOM

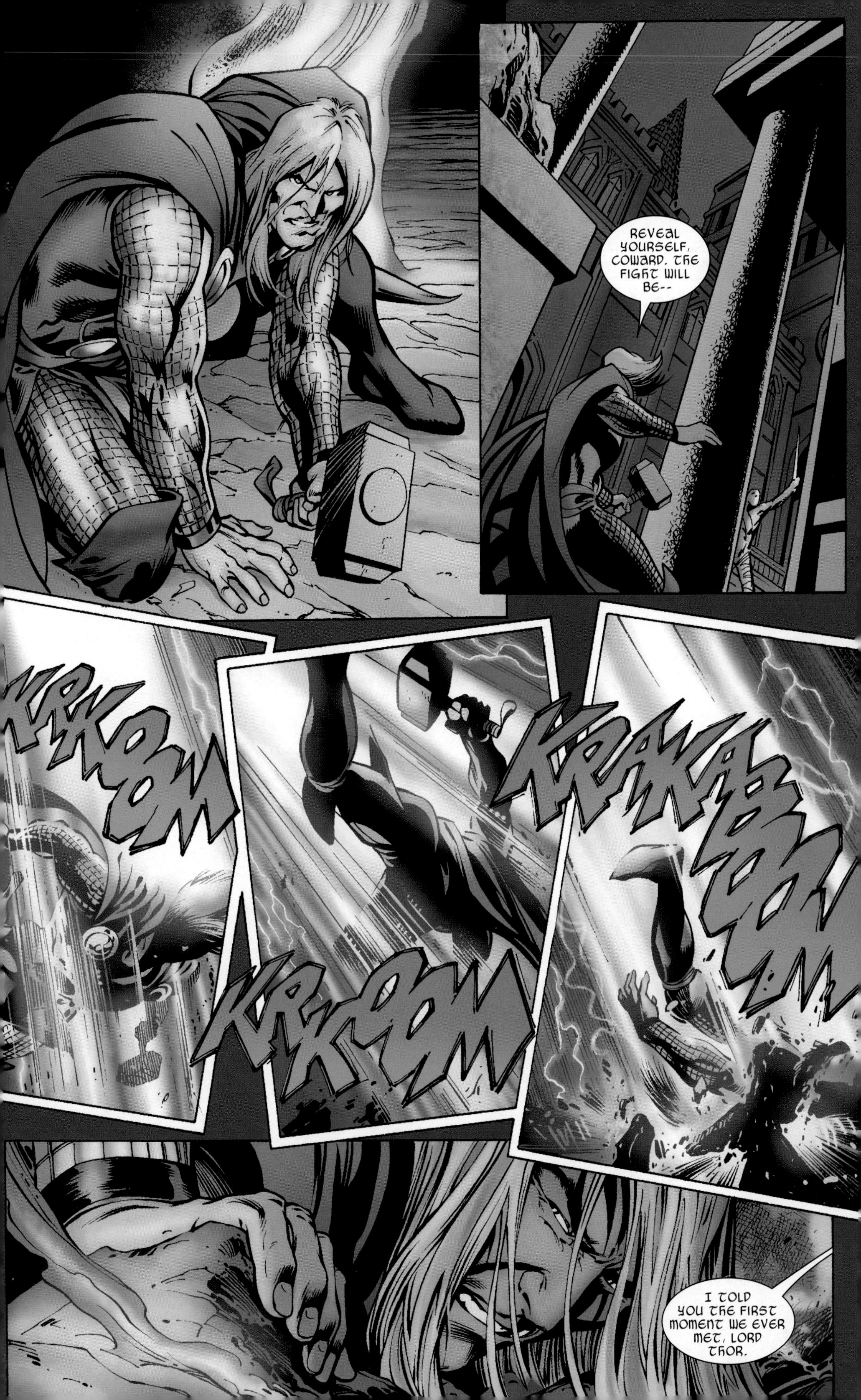
REVEAL YOURSELF, COWARD. THE FIGHT WILL BE--
KRKOOM
KRKOOM
KRAKABOOM
I TOLD YOU THE FIRST MOMENT WE EVER MET, LORD THOR.

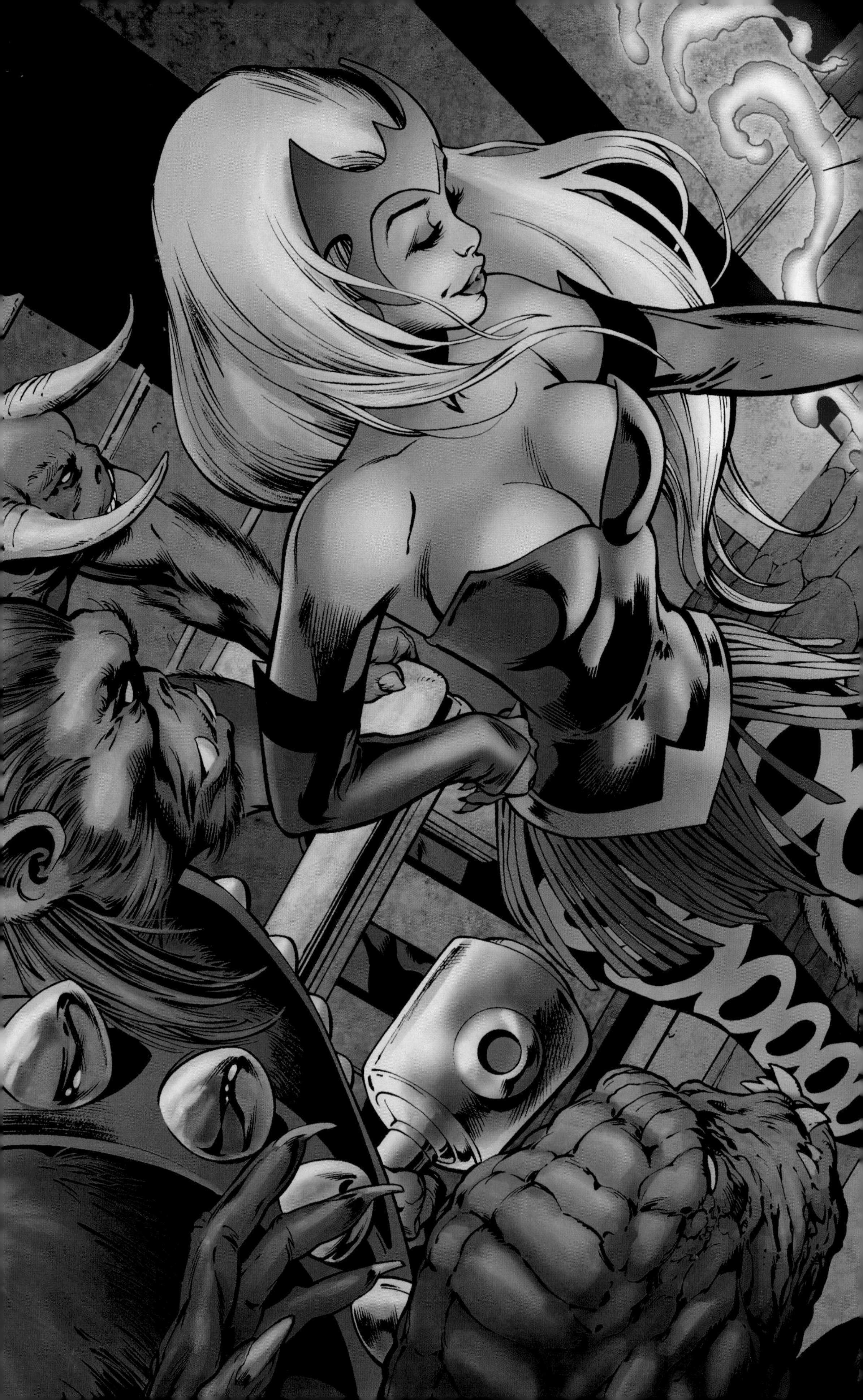

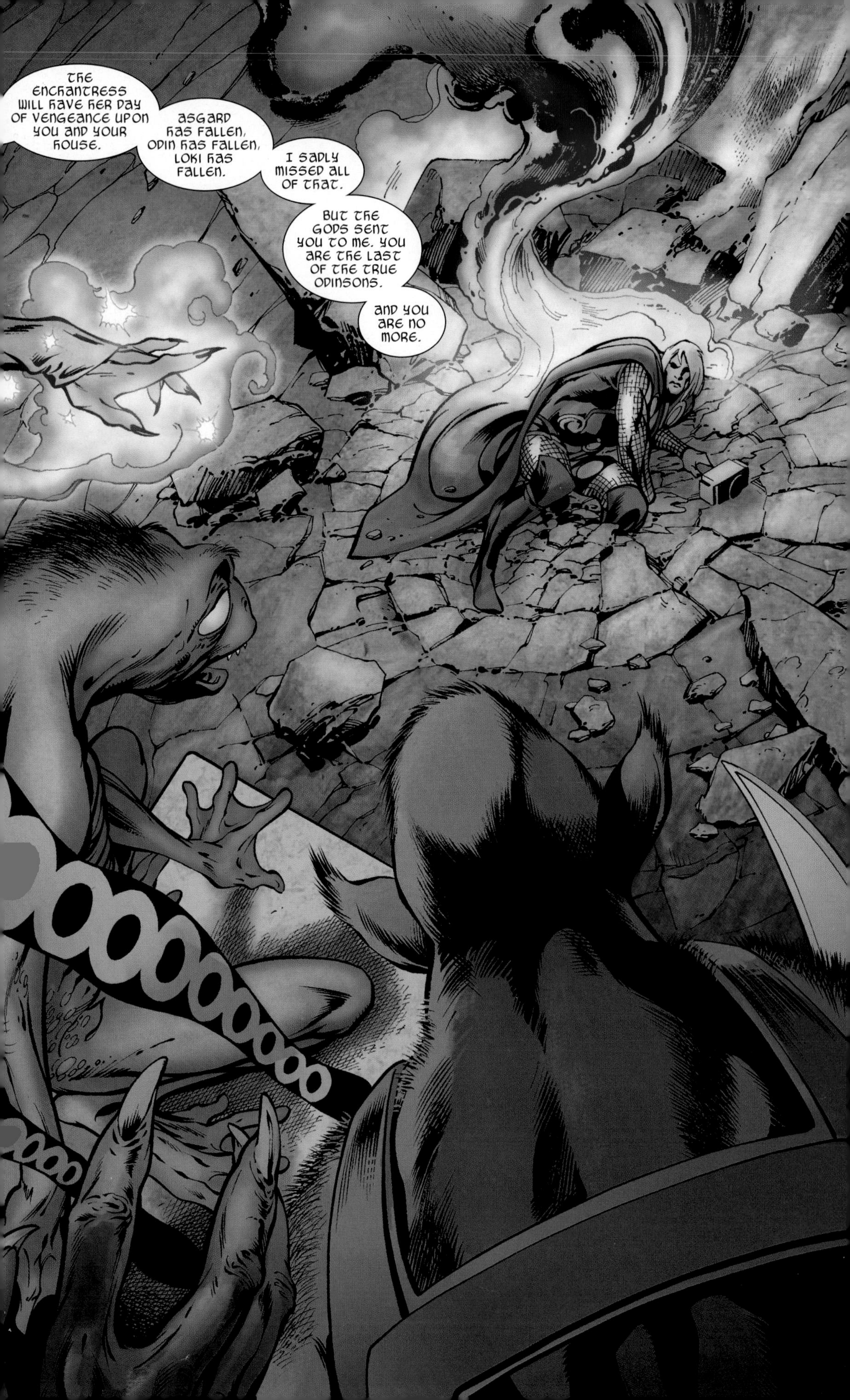
THE ENCHANTRESS WILL HAVE HER DAY OF VENGEANCE UPON YOU AND YOUR HOUSE.
ASGARD HAS FALLEN, ODIN HAS FALLEN, LOKI HAS FALLEN.
I SADLY MISSED ALL OF THAT.
BUT THE GODS SENT YOU TO ME. YOU ARE THE LAST OF THE TRUE ODINSONS.
AND YOU ARE NO MORE.

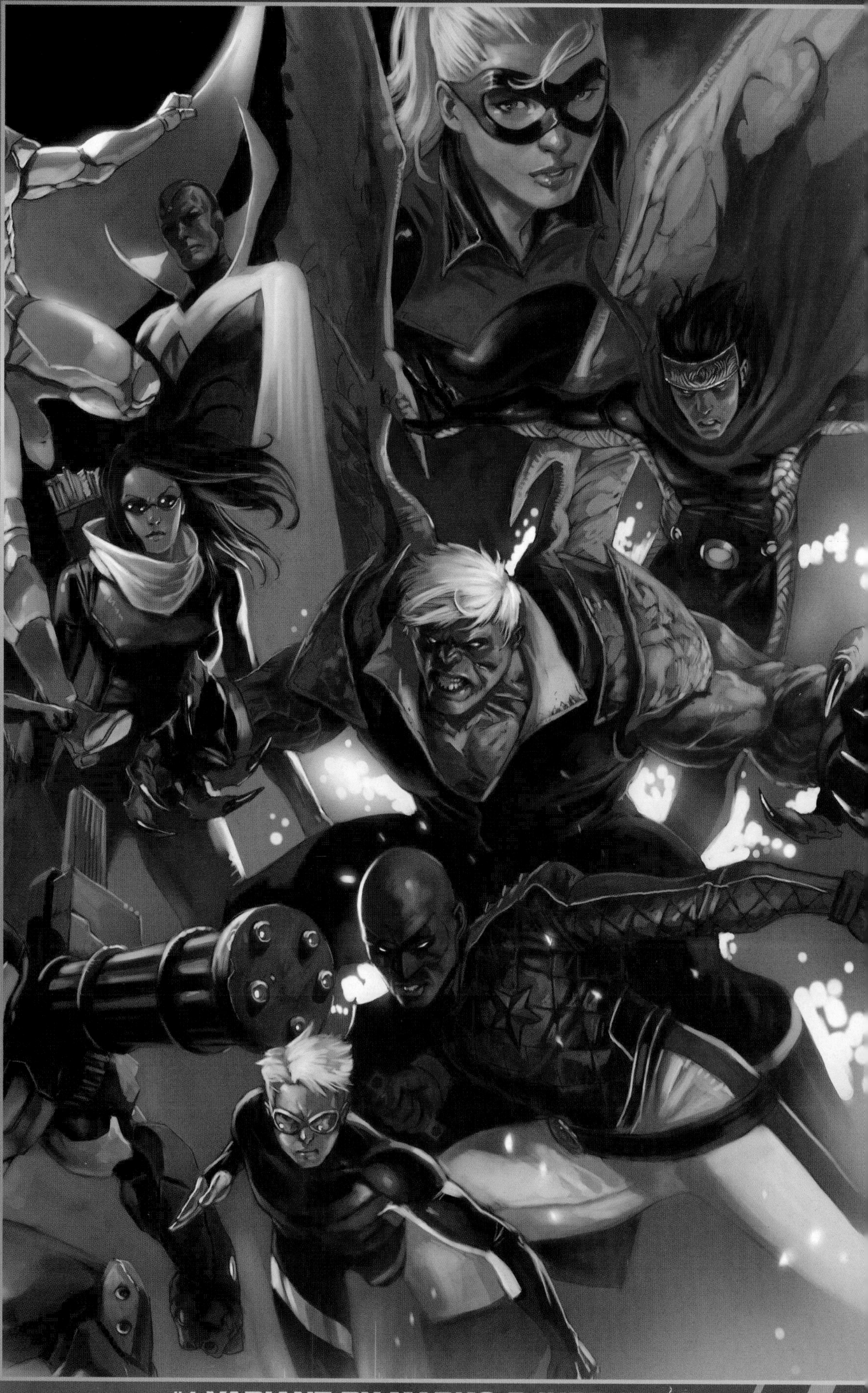

#1 VARIANT BY MARKO DJURDJEVIĆ

2

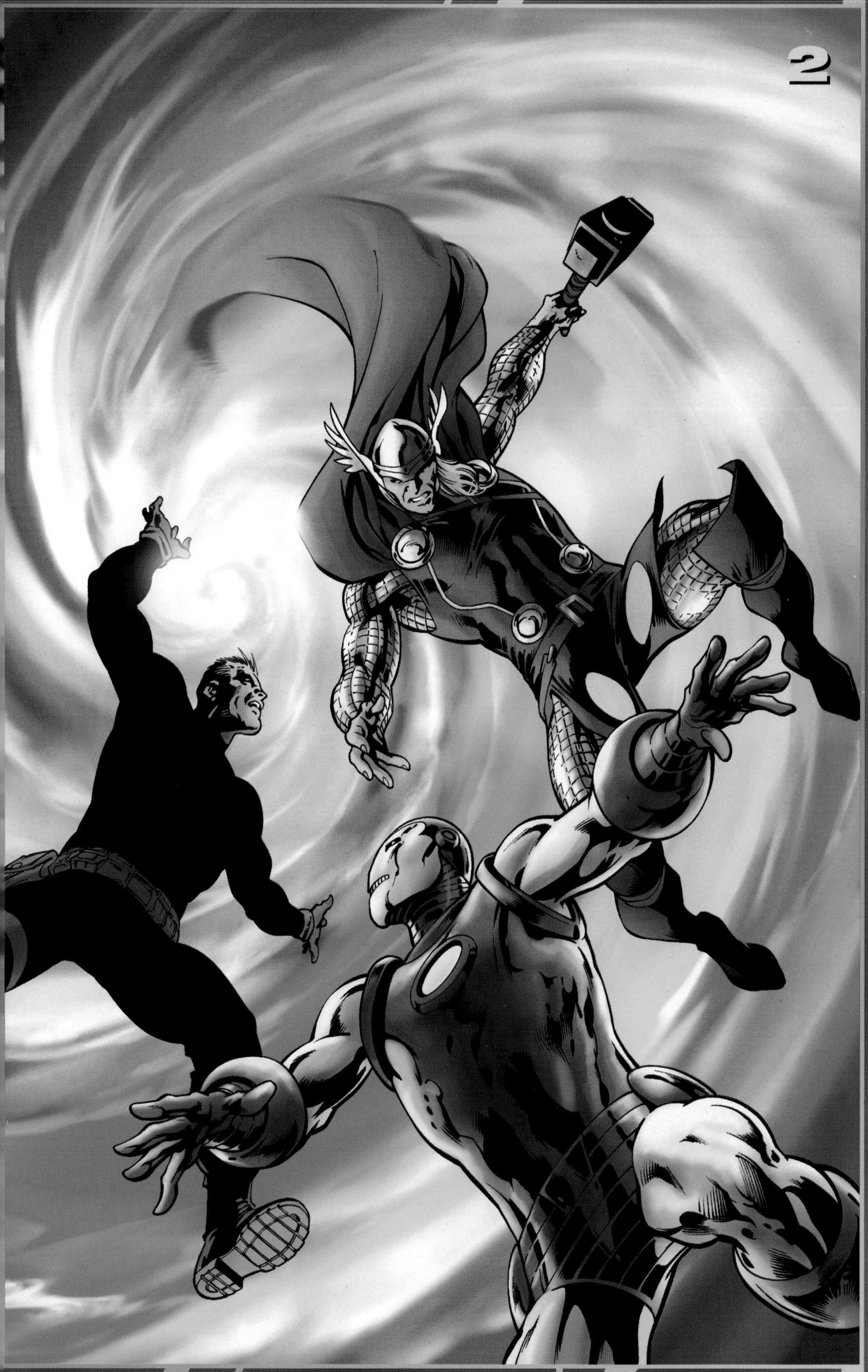

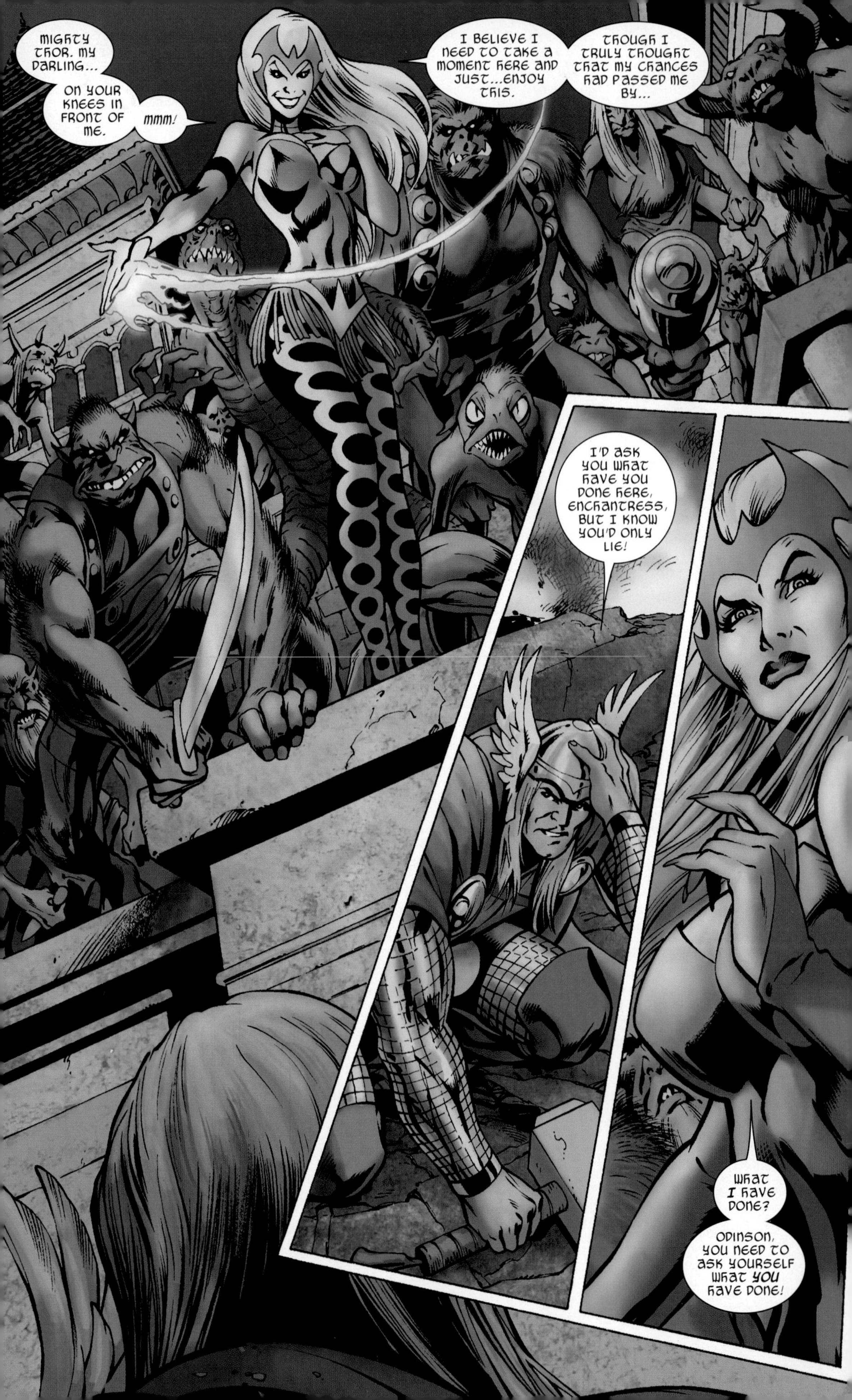
MIGHTY THOR. MY DARLING...
ON YOUR KNEES IN FRONT OF ME.
MMM!
I BELIEVE I NEED TO TAKE A MOMENT HERE AND JUST...ENJOY THIS.
THOUGH I TRULY THOUGHT THAT MY CHANCES HAD PASSED ME BY...
I'D ASK YOU WHAT HAVE YOU DONE HERE, ENCHANTRESS, BUT I KNOW YOU'D ONLY LIE!
WHAT I HAVE DONE?
ODINSON, YOU NEED TO ASK YOURSELF WHAT YOU HAVE DONE!

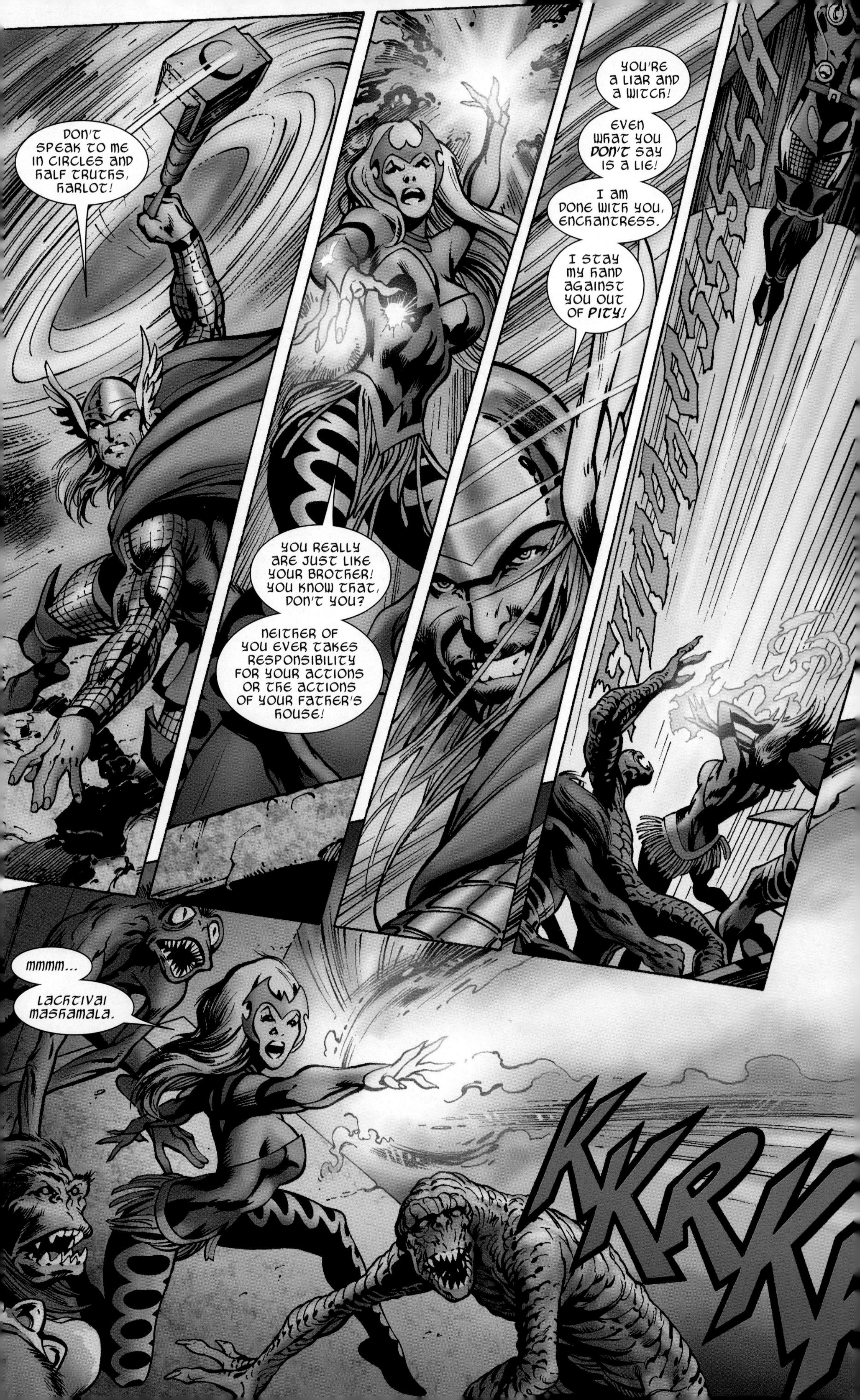
DON'T SPEAK TO ME IN CIRCLES AND HALF TRUTHS, HARLOT!
YOU REALLY ARE JUST LIKE YOUR BROTHER! YOU KNOW THAT, DON'T YOU?
NEITHER OF YOU EVER TAKES RESPONSIBILITY FOR YOUR ACTIONS OR THE ACTIONS OF YOUR FATHER'S HOUSE!
YOU'RE A LIAR AND A WITCH!
EVEN WHAT YOU DON'T SAY IS A LIE!
I AM DONE WITH YOU, ENCHANTRESS.
I STAY MY HAND AGAINST YOU OUT OF PITY!
THWOOOSSSH
MMMM...
LACHTIVAI MASHAMALA.
KKRKK

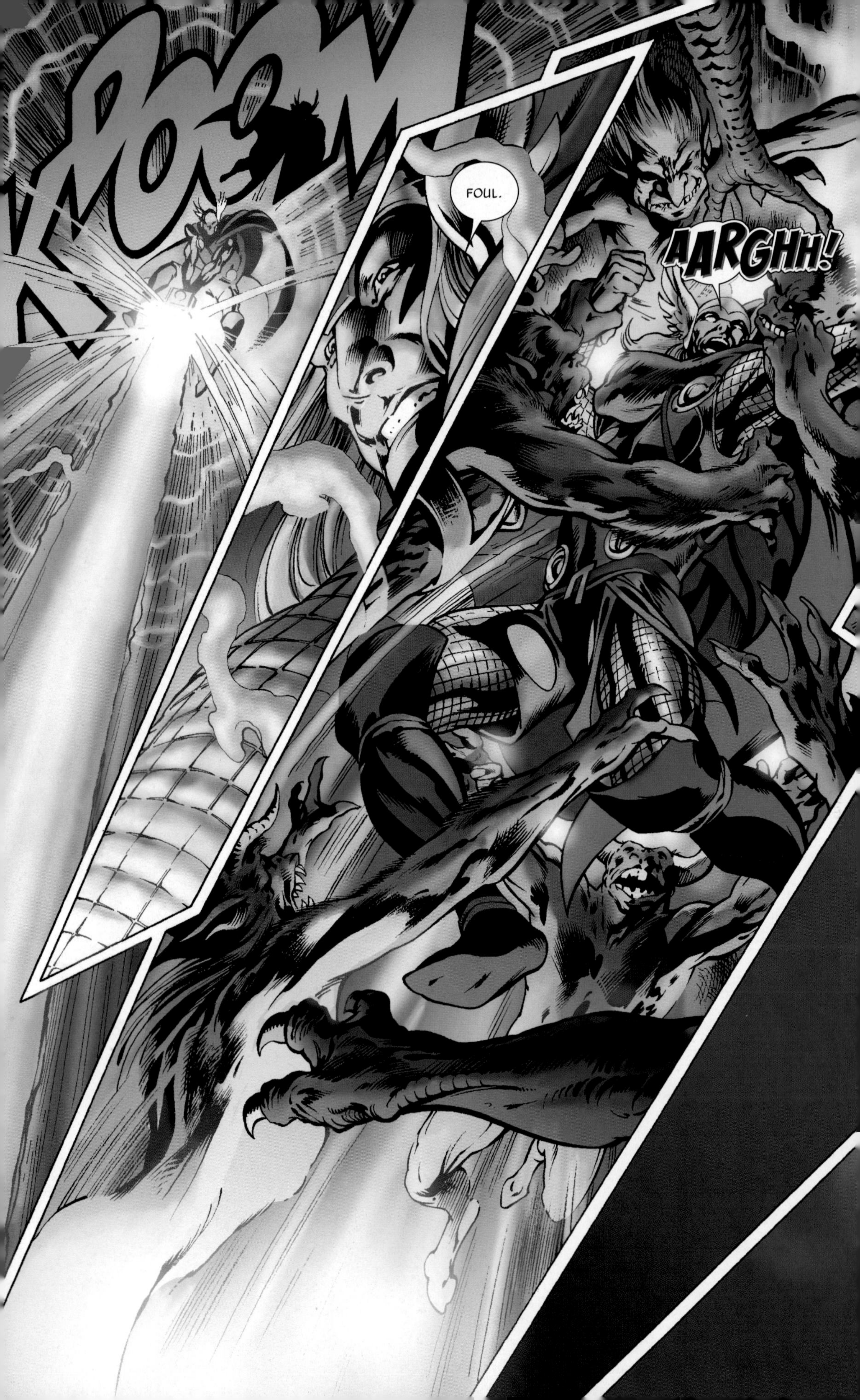

VOOOM!
FOUL.
AARGHH!

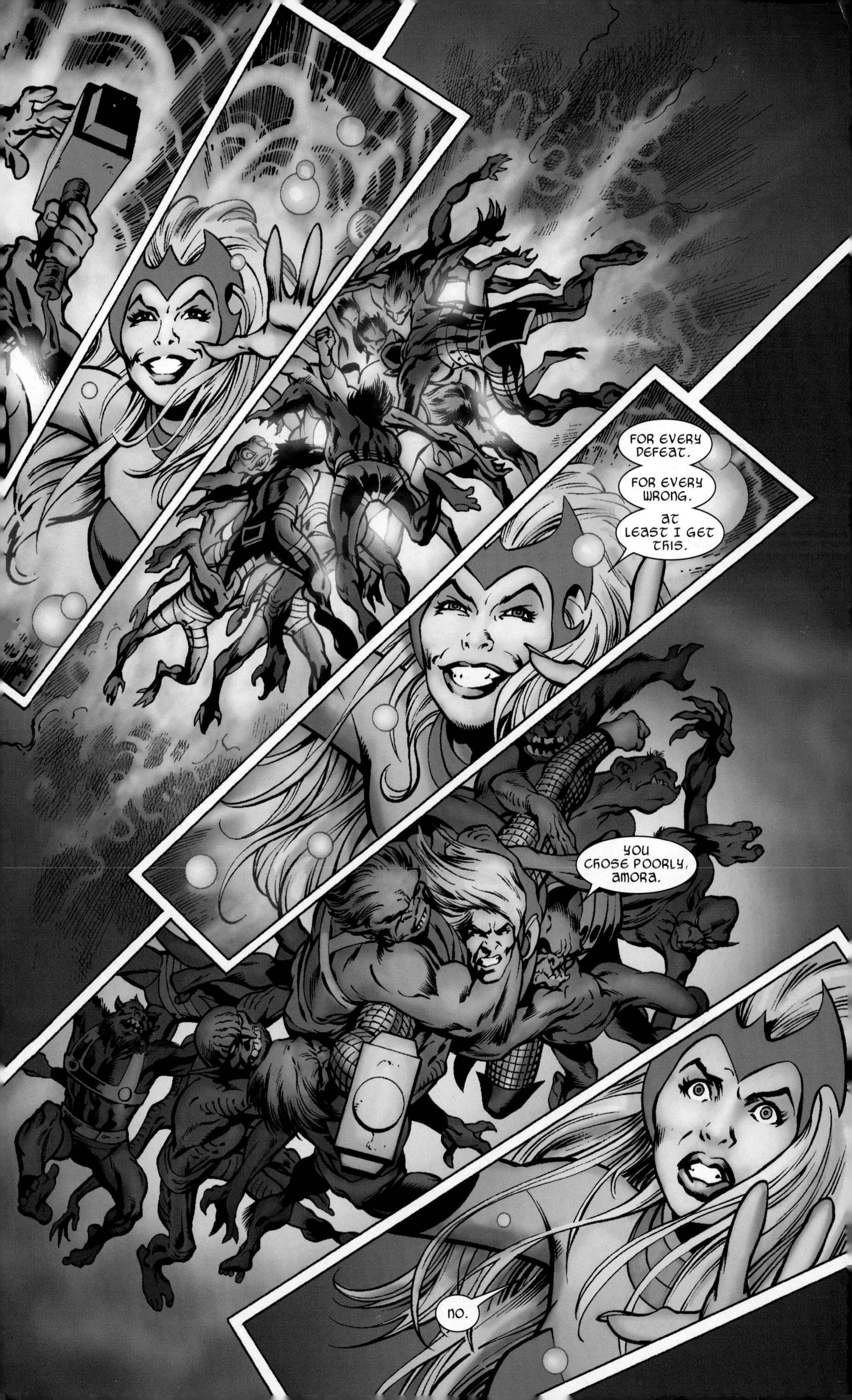
FOR EVERY DEFEAT.
FOR EVERY WRONG.
AT LEAST I GET THIS.
YOU CHOSE POORLY, AMORA.
NO.

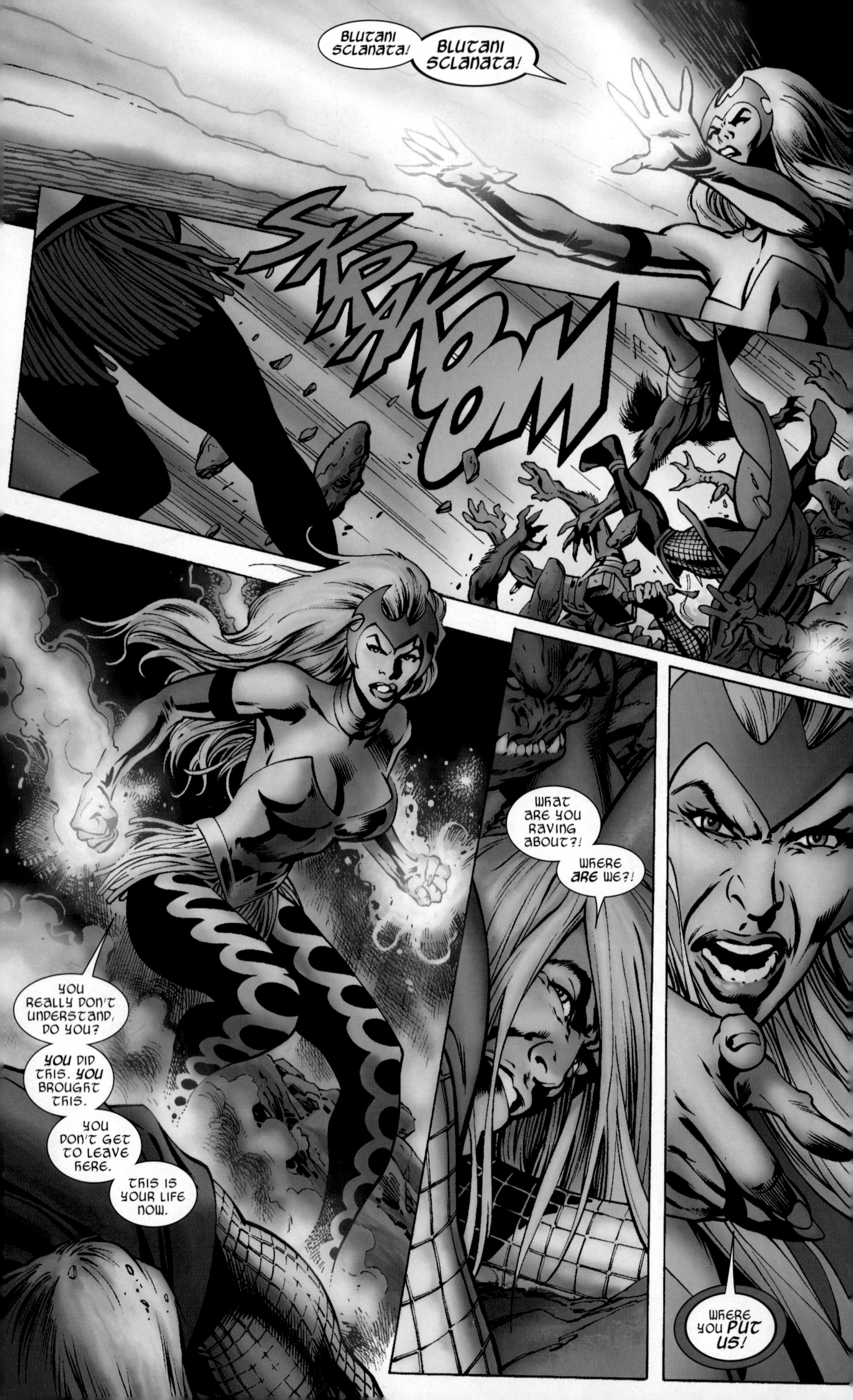
BLUTANI SCLANATA!
BLUTANI SCLANATA!
SKRAKOOM
YOU REALLY DON'T UNDERSTAND, DO YOU?
YOU DID THIS. YOU BROUGHT THIS.
YOU DON'T GET TO LEAVE HERE.
THIS IS YOUR LIFE NOW.
WHAT ARE YOU RAVING ABOUT?!
WHERE ARE WE?!
WHERE YOU PUT US!

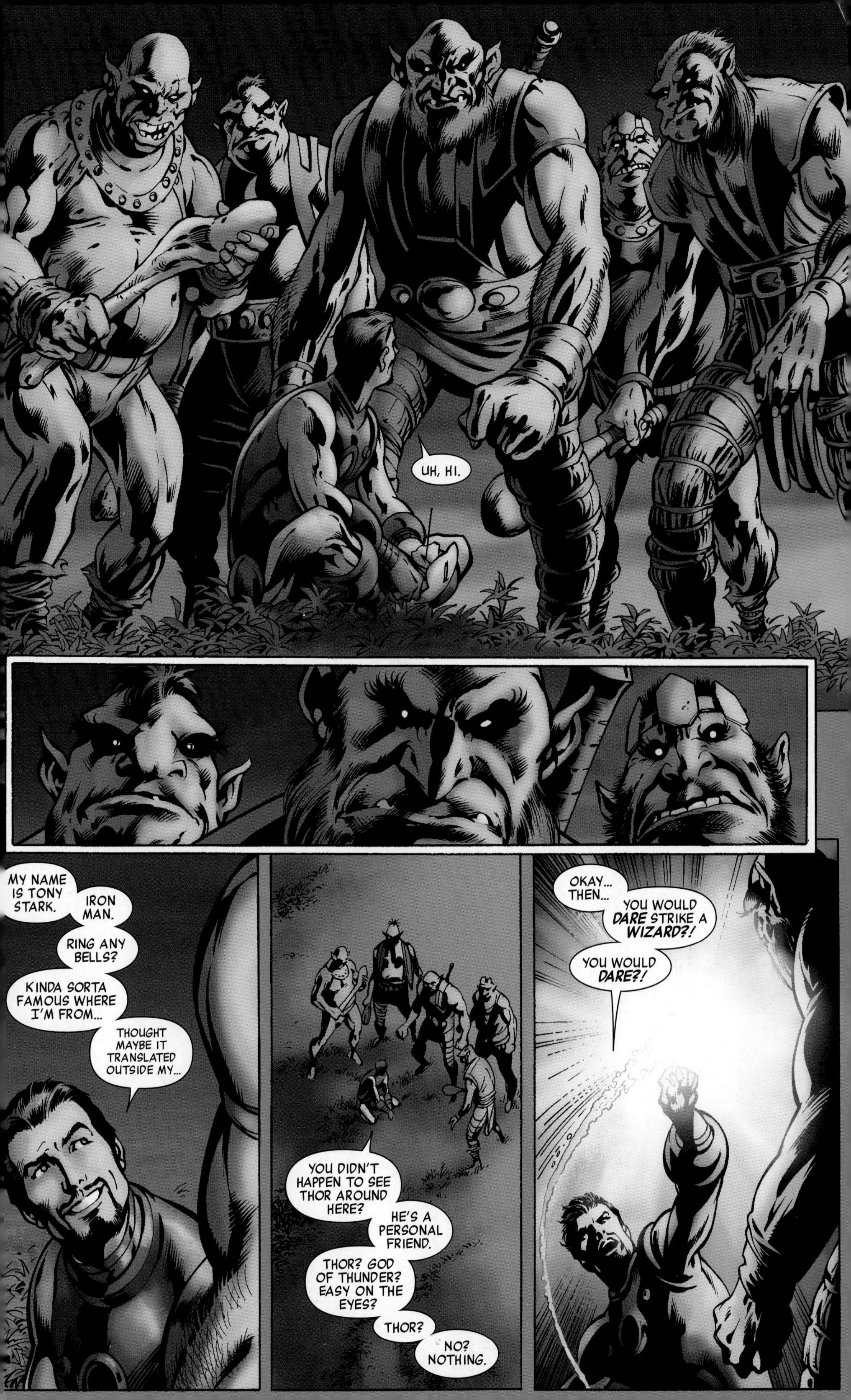
UH, HI.
MY NAME IS TONY STARK.
IRON MAN.
RING ANY BELLS?
KINDA SORTA FAMOUS WHERE I'M FROM...
THOUGHT MAYBE IT TRANSLATED OUTSIDE MY...
YOU DIDN'T HAPPEN TO SEE THOR AROUND HERE?
HE'S A PERSONAL FRIEND.
THOR? GOD OF THUNDER? EASY ON THE EYES?
THOR?
NO? NOTHING.
OKAY... THEN...
YOU WOULD DARE STRIKE A WIZARD?!
YOU WOULD DARE?!

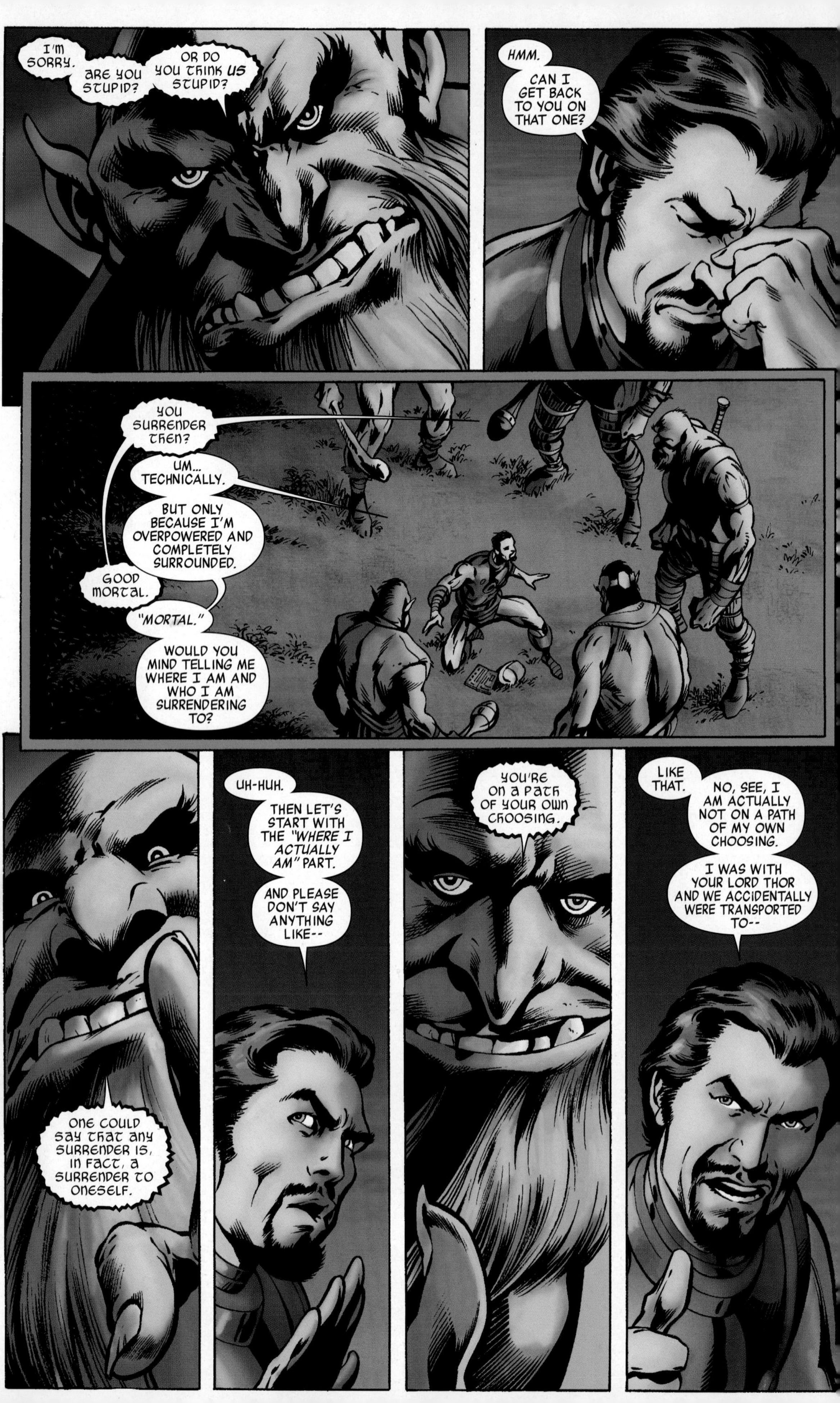
I'M SORRY.
ARE YOU STUPID?
OR DO YOU THINK US STUPID?
HMM.
CAN I GET BACK TO YOU ON THAT ONE?
YOU SURRENDER THEN?
UM... TECHNICALLY.
BUT ONLY BECAUSE I'M OVERPOWERED AND COMPLETELY SURROUNDED.
GOOD MORTAL.
"MORTAL."
WOULD YOU MIND TELLING ME WHERE I AM AND WHO I AM SURRENDERING TO?
ONE COULD SAY THAT ANY SURRENDER IS, IN FACT, A SURRENDER TO ONESELF.
UH-HUH.
THEN LET'S START WITH THE "WHERE I ACTUALLY AM" PART.
AND PLEASE DON'T SAY ANYTHING LIKE--
YOU'RE ON A PATH OF YOUR OWN CHOOSING.
LIKE THAT.
NO, SEE, I AM ACTUALLY NOT ON A PATH OF MY OWN CHOOSING.
I WAS WITH YOUR LORD THOR AND WE ACCIDENTALLY WERE TRANSPORTED TO--

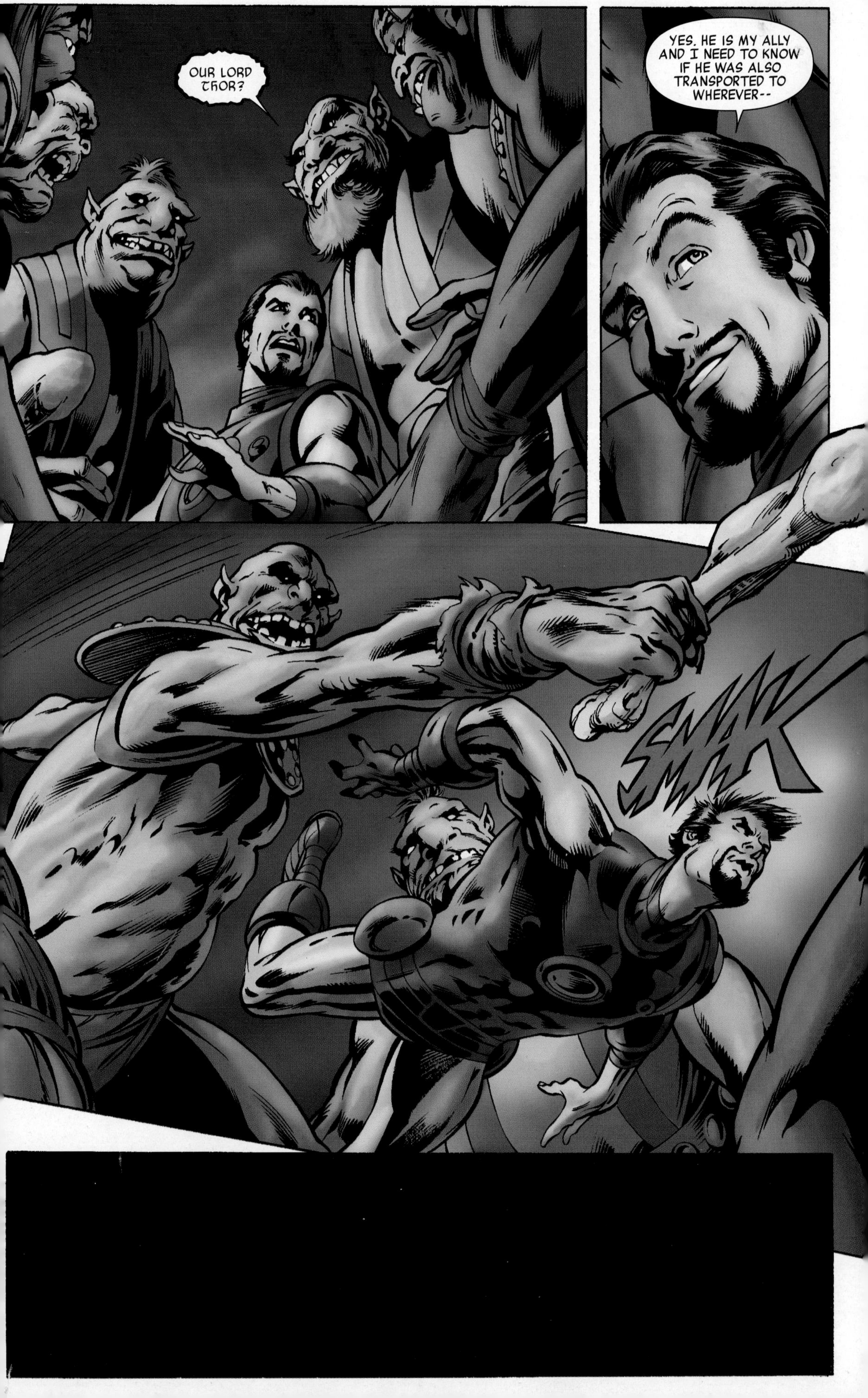
OUR LORD THOR?
YES. HE IS MY ALLY AND I NEED TO KNOW IF HE WAS ALSO TRANSPORTED TO WHEREVER--
SMAK

[redacted]

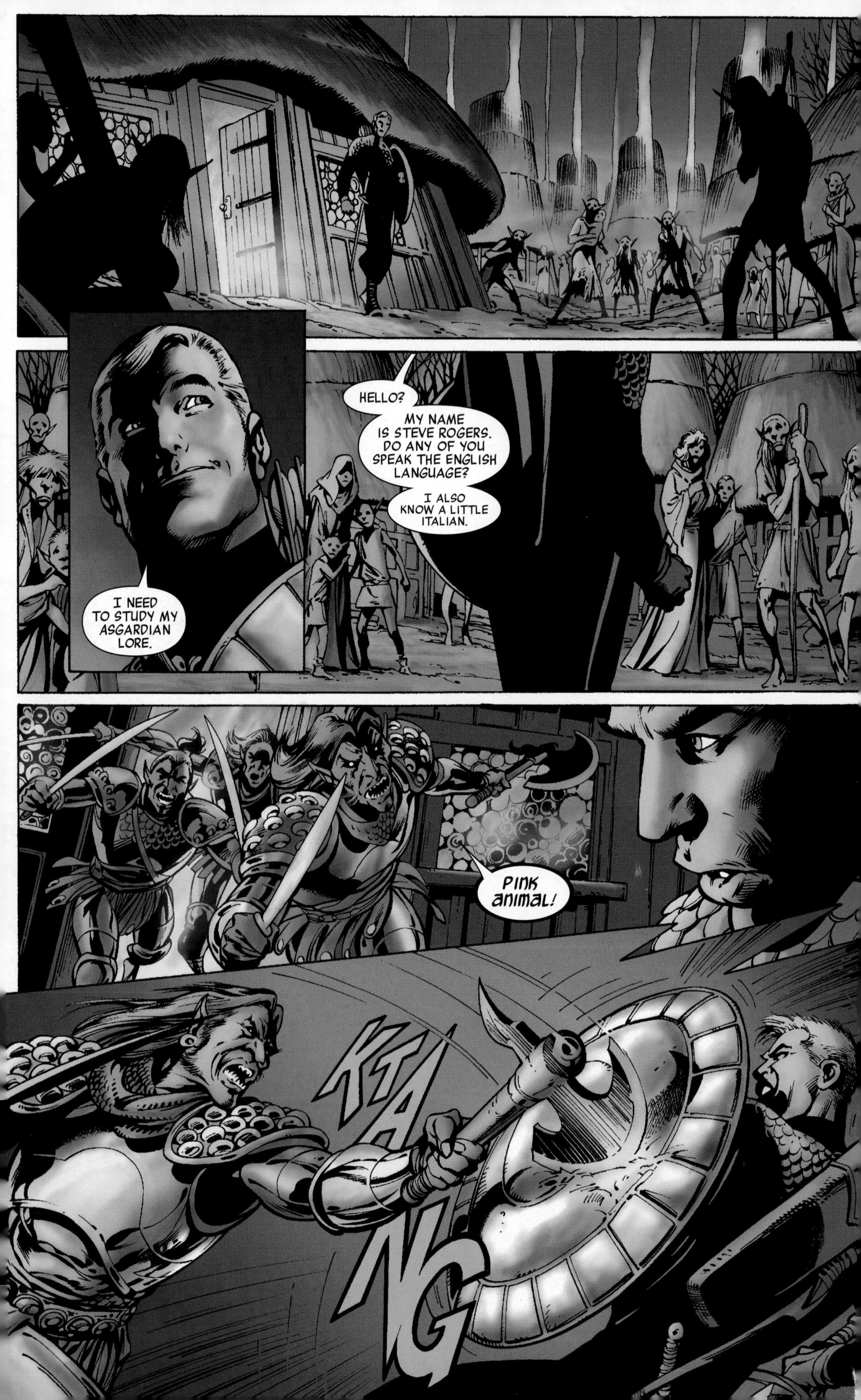
I NEED TO STUDY MY ASGARDIAN LORE.
HELLO?
MY NAME IS STEVE ROGERS. DO ANY OF YOU SPEAK THE ENGLISH LANGUAGE?
I ALSO KNOW A LITTLE ITALIAN.
PINK animal!
KTANG

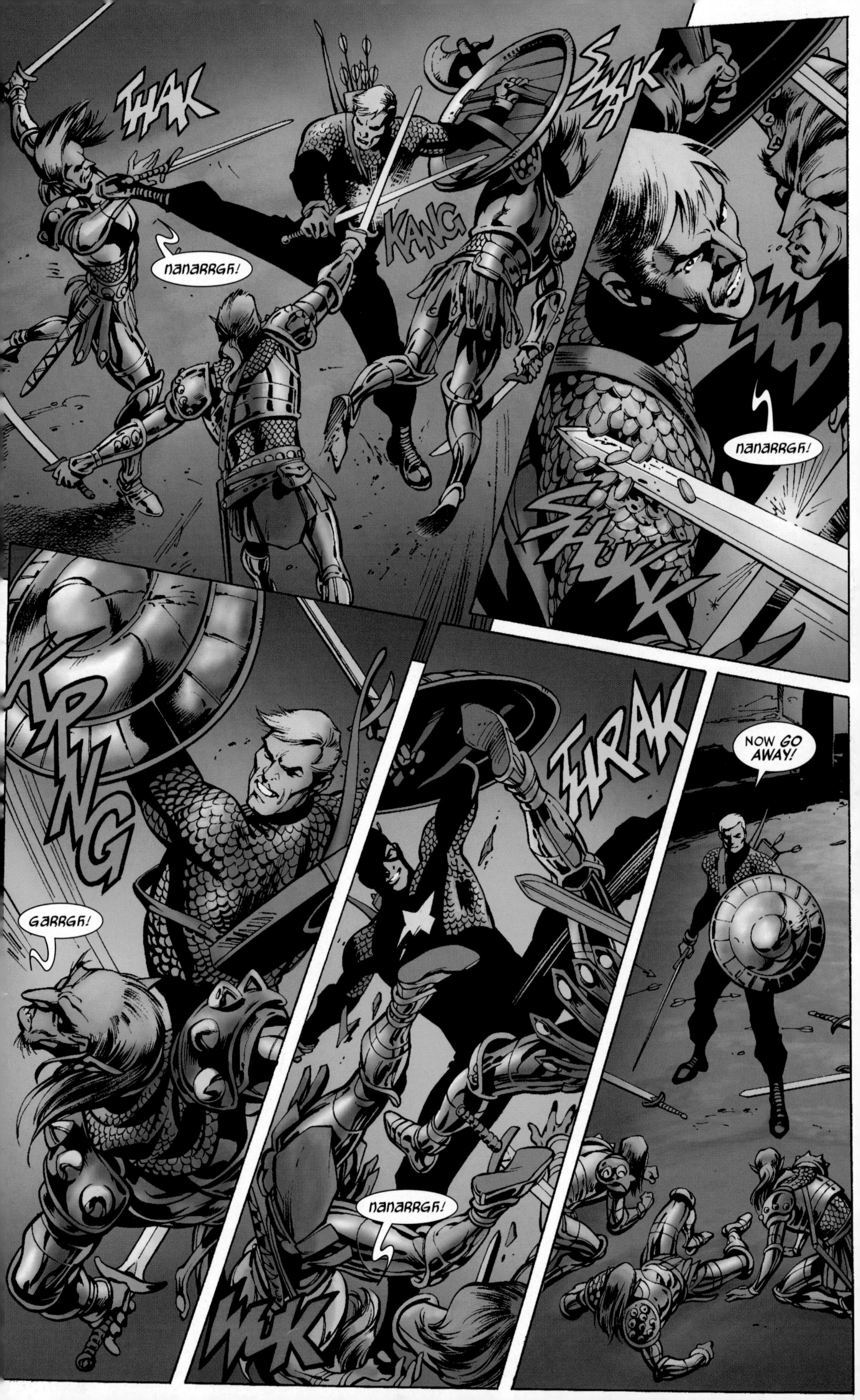
THAK
NANARRGH!
KANG
NANARRGH!
GARRGH!
THRAK
NANARRGH!
NOW GO AWAY!

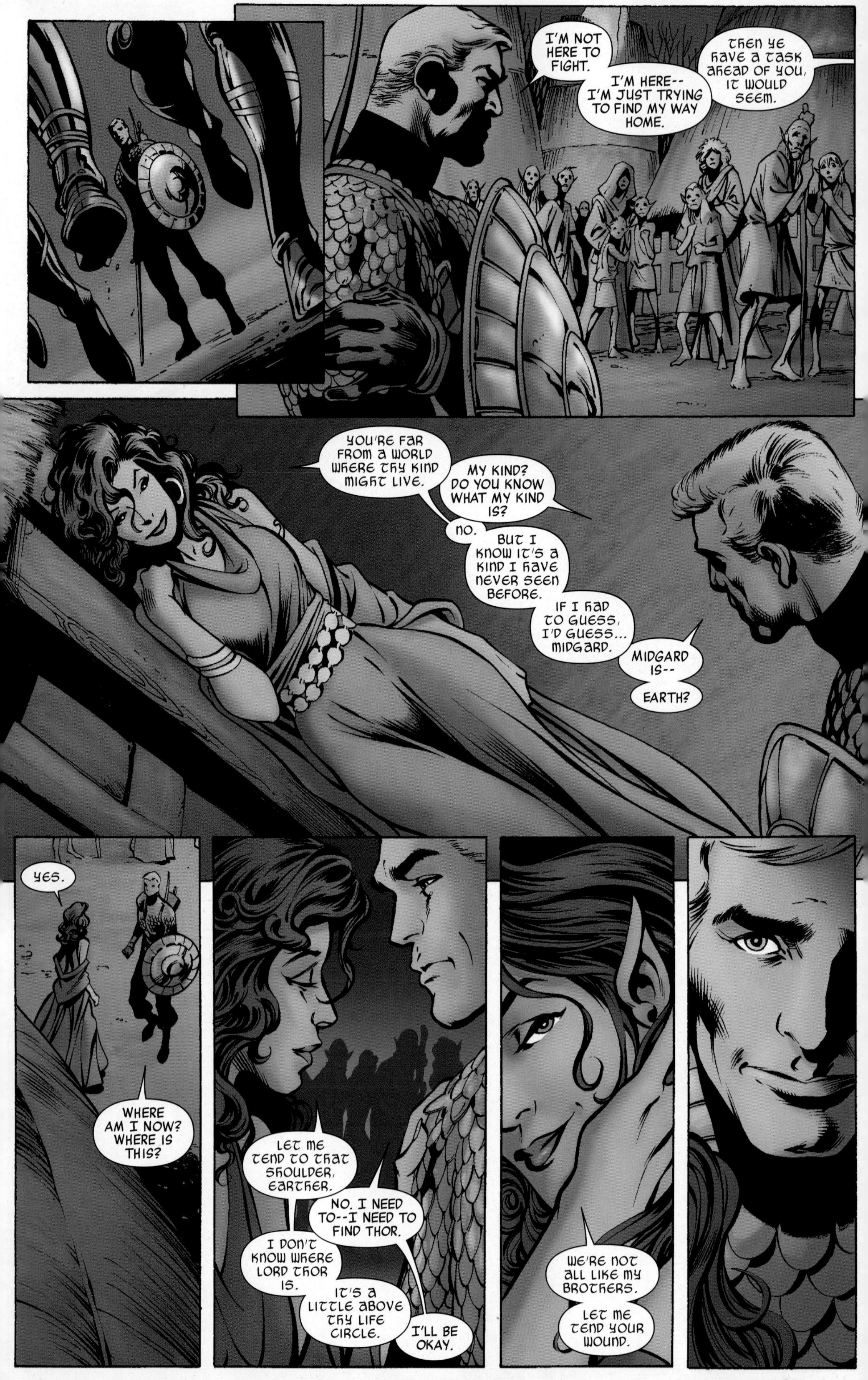
I'M NOT HERE TO FIGHT.
I'M HERE-- I'M JUST TRYING TO FIND MY WAY HOME.
THEN YE HAVE A TASK AHEAD OF YOU, IT WOULD SEEM.
YOU'RE FAR FROM A WORLD WHERE THY KIND MIGHT LIVE.
MY KIND? DO YOU KNOW WHAT MY KIND IS?
NO.
BUT I KNOW IT'S A KIND I HAVE NEVER SEEN BEFORE.
IF I HAD TO GUESS, I'D GUESS... MIDGARD.
MIDGARD IS--
EARTH?
YES.
WHERE AM I NOW? WHERE IS THIS?
LET ME TEND TO THAT SHOULDER, EARTHER.
NO. I NEED TO--I NEED TO FIND THOR.
I DON'T KNOW WHERE LORD THOR IS.
IT'S A LITTLE ABOVE THY LIFE CIRCLE.
I'LL BE OKAY.
WE'RE NOT ALL LIKE MY BROTHERS.
LET ME TEND YOUR WOUND.

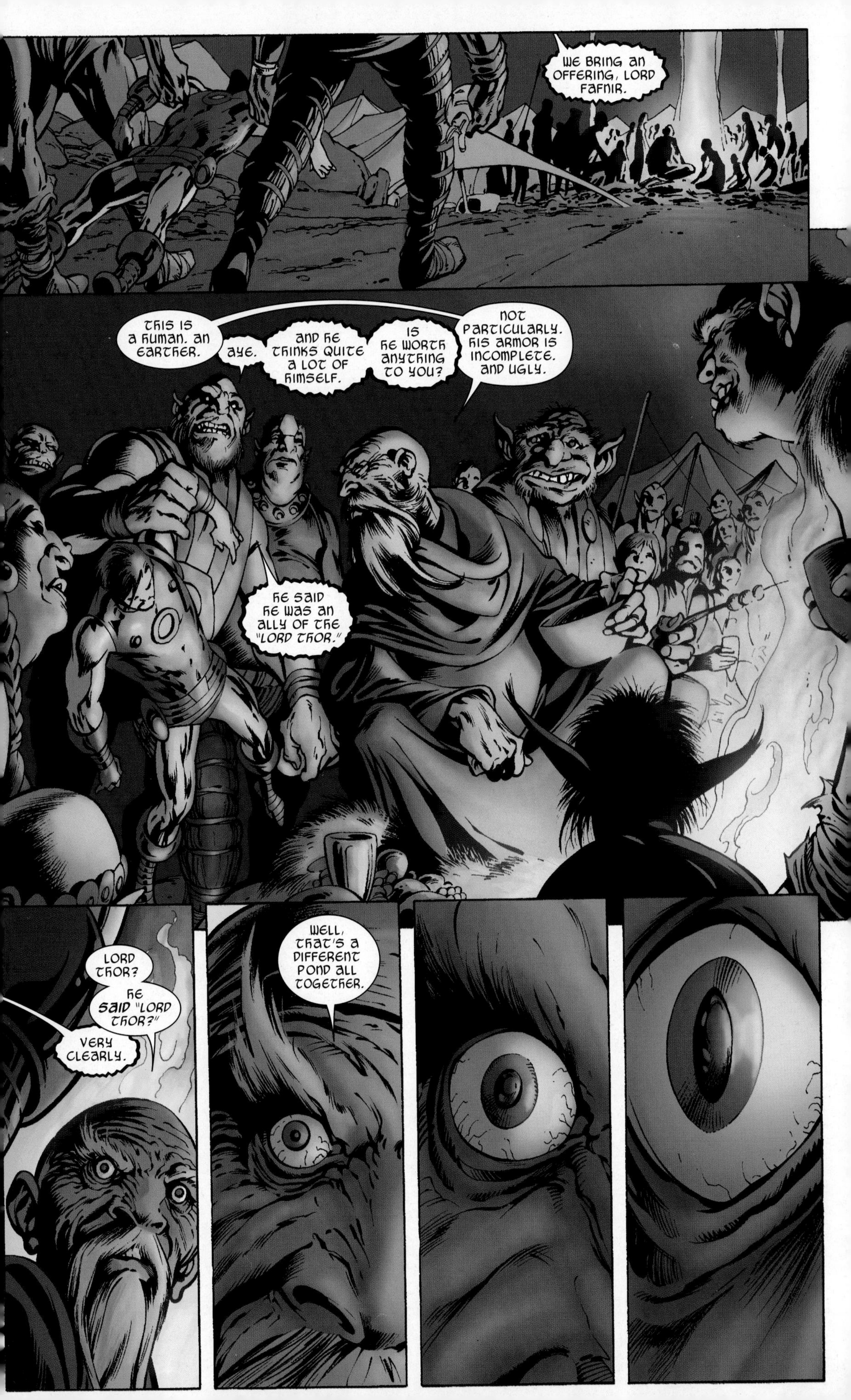
WE BRING AN OFFERING, LORD FAFNIR.
THIS IS A HUMAN. AN EARTHER.
AYE.
AND HE THINKS QUITE A LOT OF HIMSELF.
IS HE WORTH ANYTHING TO YOU?
NOT PARTICULARLY. HIS ARMOR IS INCOMPLETE. AND UGLY.
HE SAID HE WAS AN ALLY OF THE "LORD THOR."
LORD THOR?
HE SAID "LORD THOR?"
VERY CLEARLY.
WELL, THAT'S A DIFFERENT POND ALL TOGETHER.

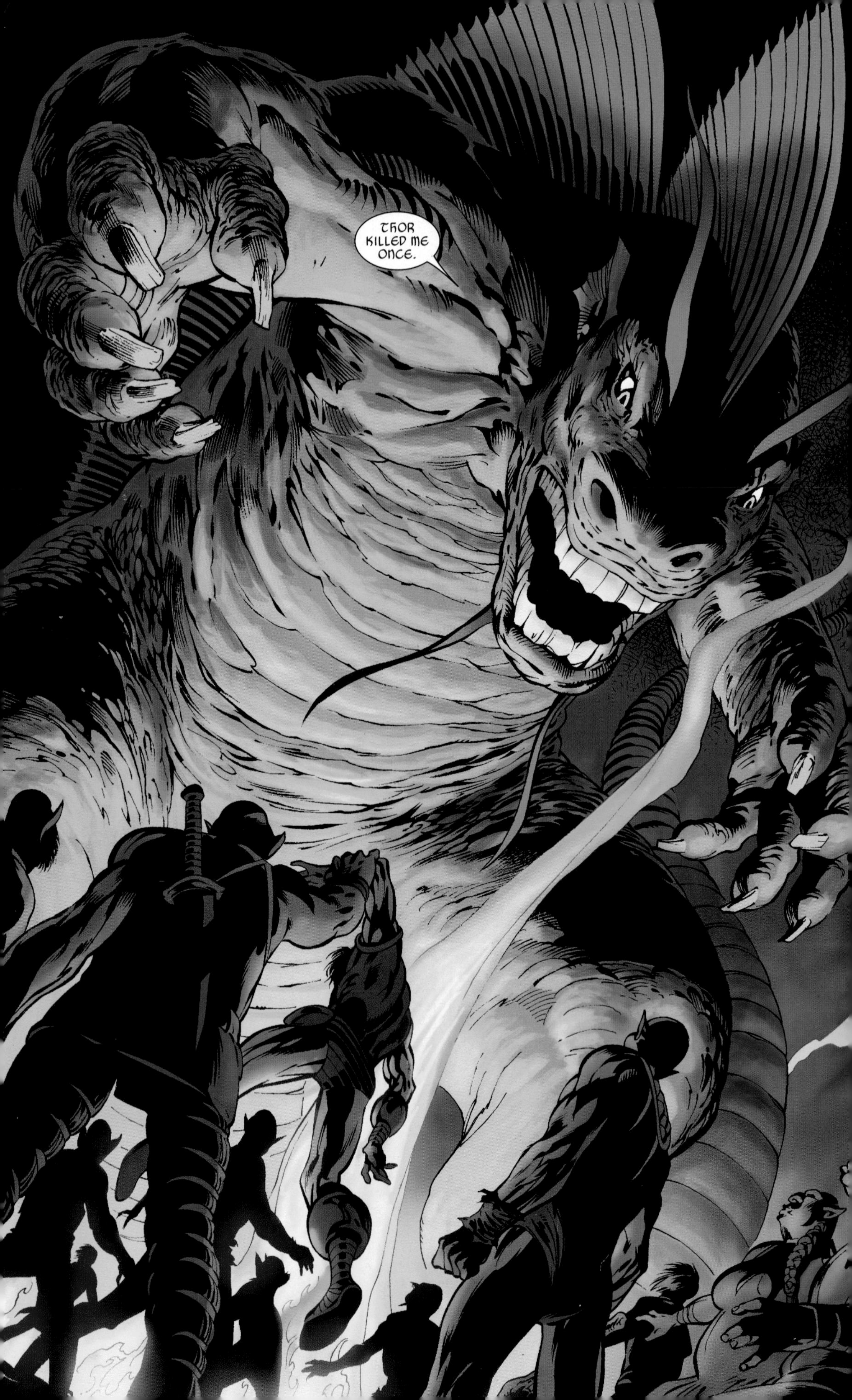
THOR KILLED ME ONCE.

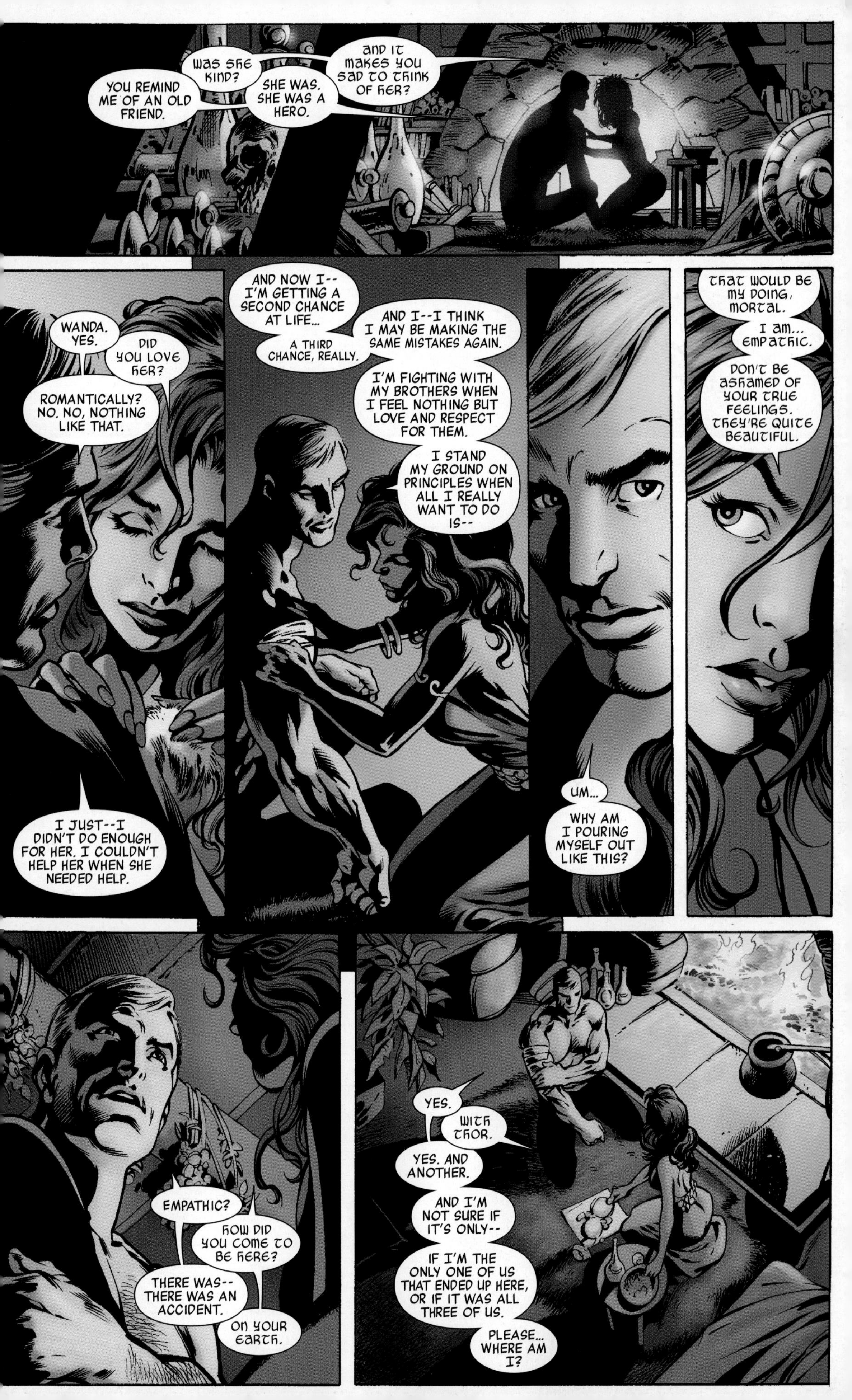
YOU REMIND ME OF AN OLD FRIEND.
WAS SHE KIND?
SHE WAS. SHE WAS A HERO.
AND IT MAKES YOU SAD TO THINK OF HER?
WANDA. YES.
DID YOU LOVE HER?
ROMANTICALLY? NO. NO, NOTHING LIKE THAT.
I JUST--I DIDN'T DO ENOUGH FOR HER. I COULDN'T HELP HER WHEN SHE NEEDED HELP.
AND NOW I-- I'M GETTING A SECOND CHANCE AT LIFE...
A THIRD CHANCE, REALLY.
AND I--I THINK I MAY BE MAKING THE SAME MISTAKES AGAIN.
I'M FIGHTING WITH MY BROTHERS WHEN I FEEL NOTHING BUT LOVE AND RESPECT FOR THEM.
I STAND MY GROUND ON PRINCIPLES WHEN ALL I REALLY WANT TO DO IS--
UM...
WHY AM I POURING MYSELF OUT LIKE THIS?
THAT WOULD BE MY DOING, MORTAL.
I AM... EMPATHIC.
DON'T BE ASHAMED OF YOUR TRUE FEELINGS. THEY'RE QUITE BEAUTIFUL.
EMPATHIC?
HOW DID YOU COME TO BE HERE?
THERE WAS-- THERE WAS AN ACCIDENT.
ON YOUR EARTH.
YES.
WITH THOR.
YES. AND ANOTHER.
AND I'M NOT SURE IF IT'S ONLY--
IF I'M THE ONLY ONE OF US THAT ENDED UP HERE, OR IF IT WAS ALL THREE OF US.
PLEASE... WHERE AM I?

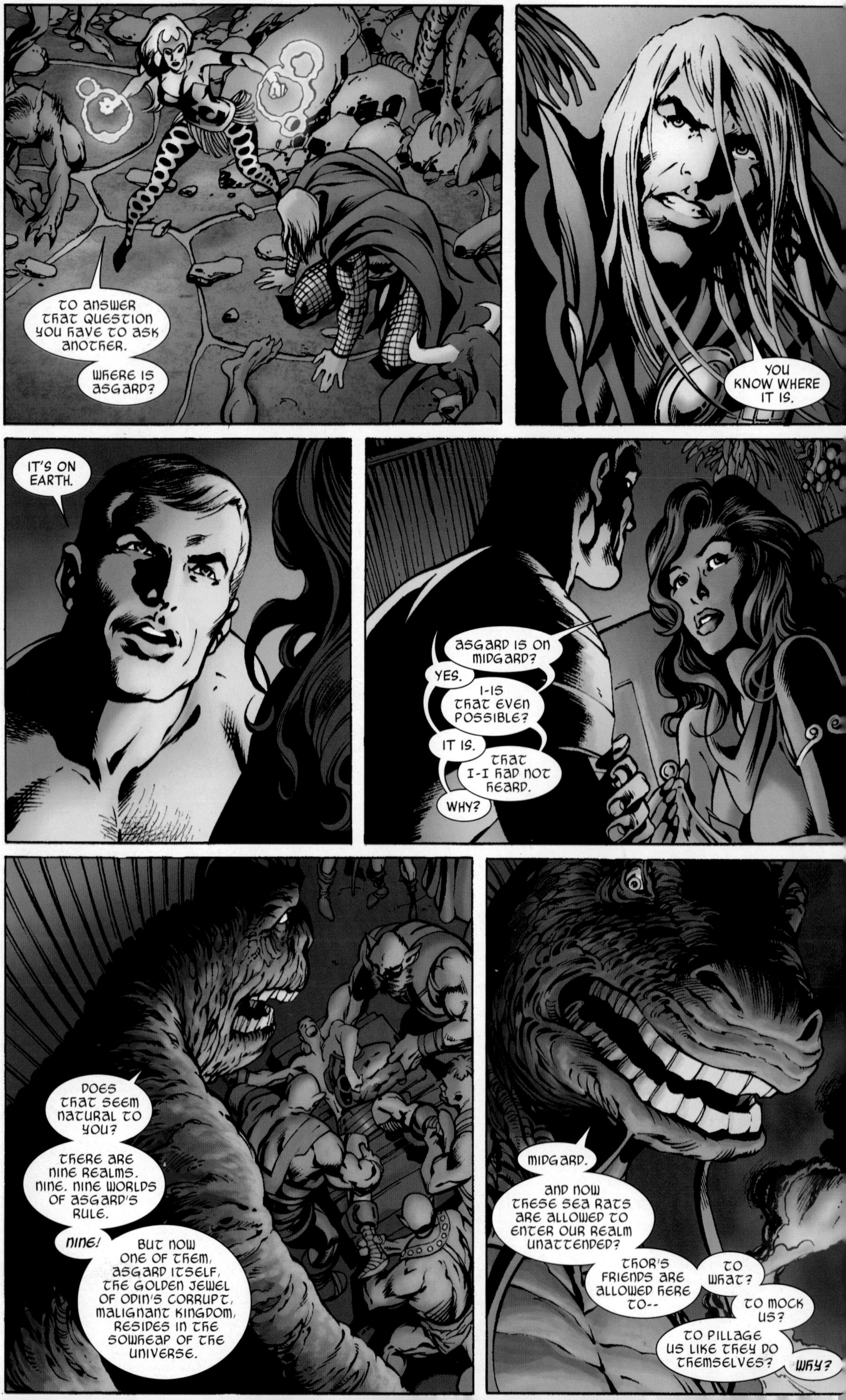
TO ANSWER THAT QUESTION YOU HAVE TO ASK ANOTHER.
WHERE IS ASGARD?
YOU KNOW WHERE IT IS.
IT'S ON EARTH.
ASGARD IS ON MIDGARD?
YES.
I-IS THAT EVEN POSSIBLE?
IT IS.
THAT I-I HAD NOT HEARD.
WHY?
DOES THAT SEEM NATURAL TO YOU?
THERE ARE NINE REALMS. NINE. NINE WORLDS OF ASGARD'S RULE.
NINE!
BUT NOW ONE OF THEM, ASGARD ITSELF, THE GOLDEN JEWEL OF ODIN'S CORRUPT, MALIGNANT KINGDOM, RESIDES IN THE SOWHEAP OF THE UNIVERSE.
MIDGARD.
AND NOW THESE SEA RATS ARE ALLOWED TO ENTER OUR REALM UNATTENDED?
THOR'S FRIENDS ARE ALLOWED HERE TO--
TO WHAT?
TO MOCK US?
TO PILLAGE US LIKE THEY DO THEMSELVES?
WHY?

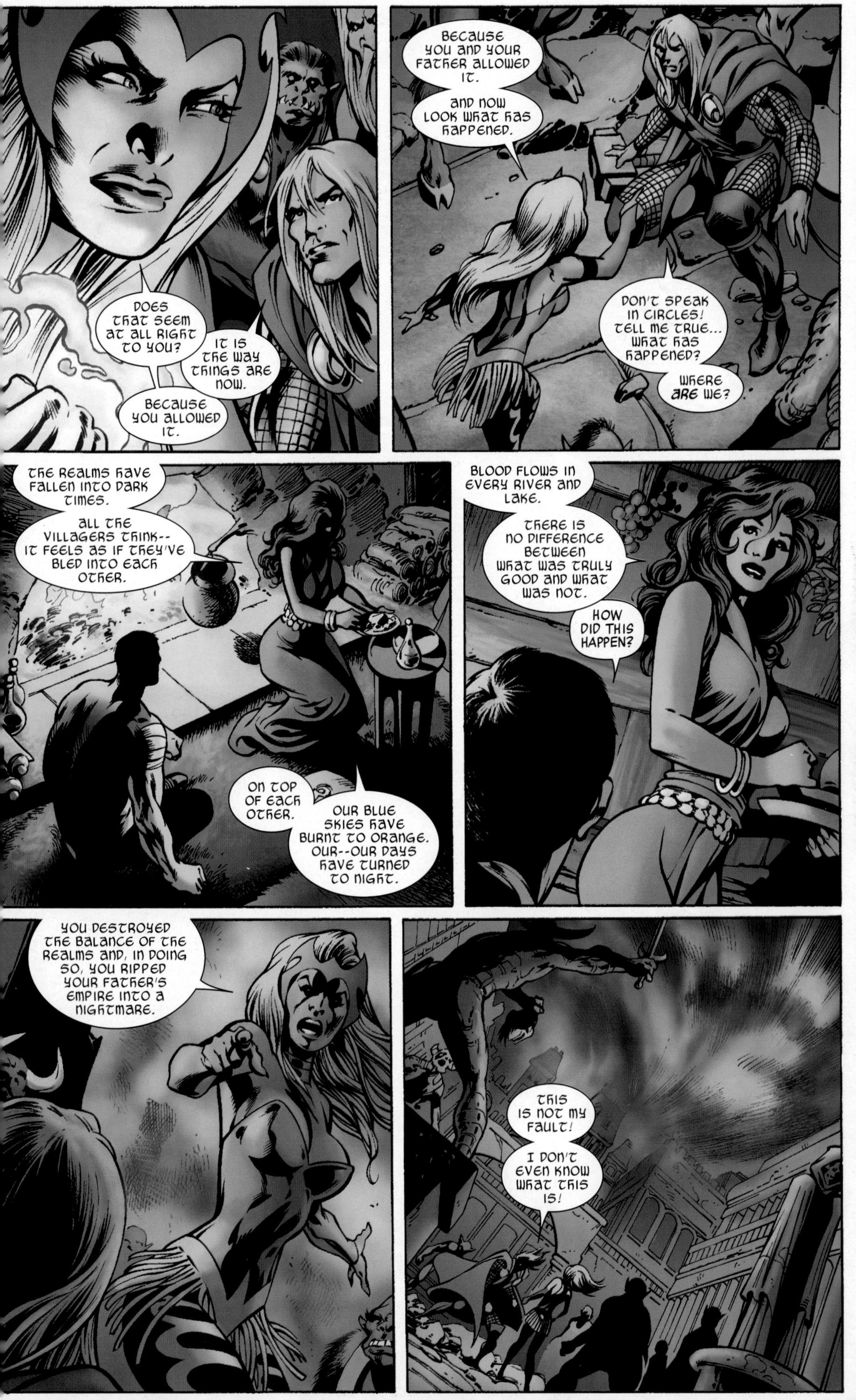
DOES THAT SEEM AT ALL RIGHT TO YOU?
IT IS THE WAY THINGS ARE NOW.
BECAUSE YOU ALLOWED IT.
BECAUSE YOU AND YOUR FATHER ALLOWED IT.
AND NOW LOOK WHAT HAS HAPPENED.
DON'T SPEAK IN CIRCLES! TELL ME TRUE... WHAT HAS HAPPENED?
WHERE ARE WE?
THE REALMS HAVE FALLEN INTO DARK TIMES.
ALL THE VILLAGERS THINK-- IT FEELS AS IF THEY'VE BLED INTO EACH OTHER.
ON TOP OF EACH OTHER.
OUR BLUE SKIES HAVE BURNT TO ORANGE. OUR--OUR DAYS HAVE TURNED TO NIGHT.
BLOOD FLOWS IN EVERY RIVER AND LAKE.
THERE IS NO DIFFERENCE BETWEEN WHAT WAS TRULY GOOD AND WHAT WAS NOT.
HOW DID THIS HAPPEN?
YOU DESTROYED THE BALANCE OF THE REALMS AND, IN DOING SO, YOU RIPPED YOUR FATHER'S EMPIRE INTO A NIGHTMARE.
THIS IS NOT MY FAULT!
I DON'T EVEN KNOW WHAT THIS IS!

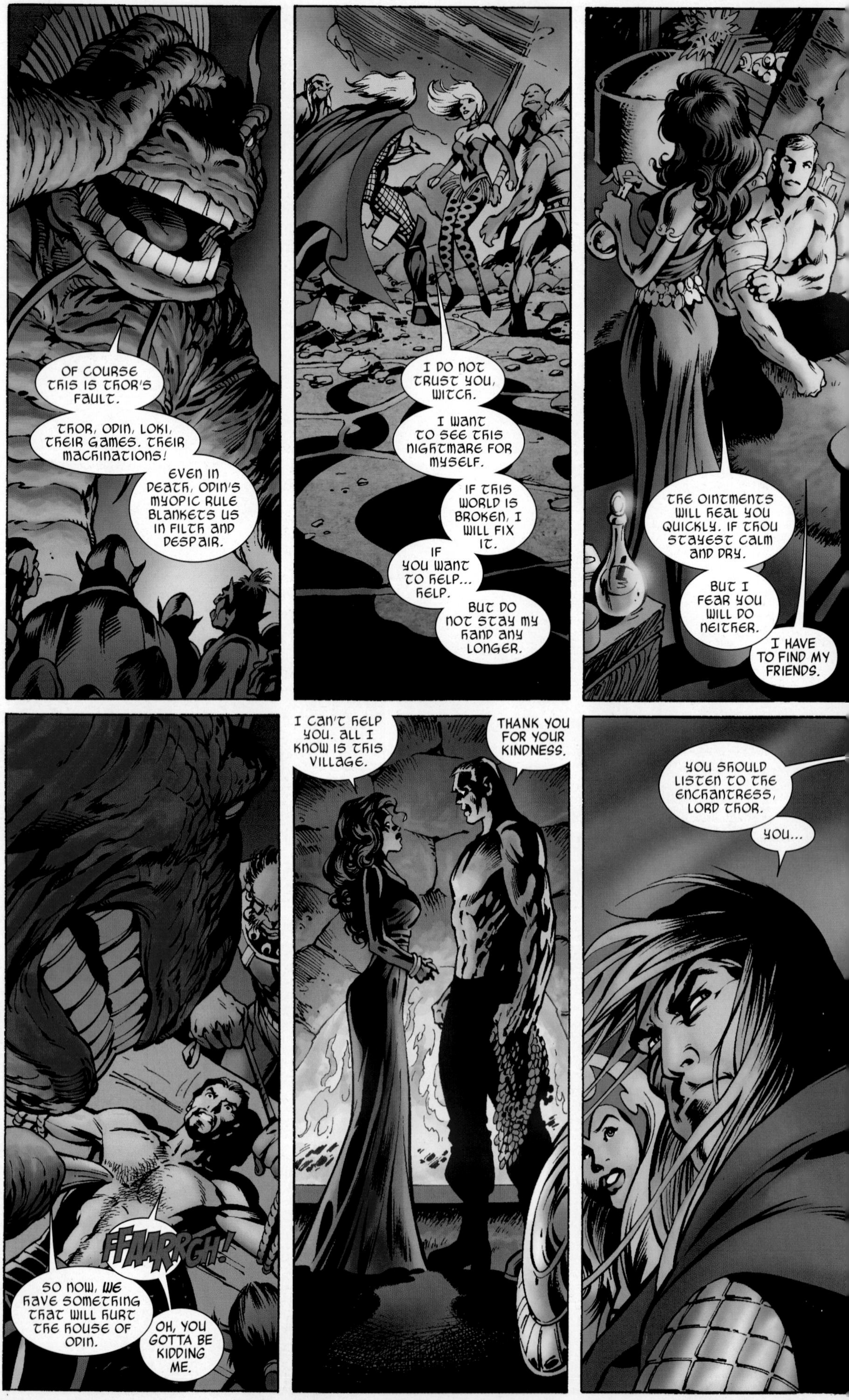
OF COURSE THIS IS THOR'S FAULT.
THOR, ODIN, LOKI, THEIR GAMES. THEIR MACHINATIONS!
EVEN IN DEATH, ODIN'S MYOPIC RULE BLANKETS US IN FILTH AND DESPAIR.
I DO NOT TRUST YOU, WITCH.
I WANT TO SEE THIS NIGHTMARE FOR MYSELF.
IF THIS WORLD IS BROKEN, I WILL FIX IT.
IF YOU WANT TO HELP... HELP.
BUT DO NOT STAY MY HAND ANY LONGER.
THE OINTMENTS WILL HEAL YOU QUICKLY. IF THOU STAYEST CALM AND DRY.
BUT I FEAR YOU WILL DO NEITHER.
I HAVE TO FIND MY FRIENDS.
FFAARRGH!
SO NOW, WE HAVE SOMETHING THAT WILL HURT THE HOUSE OF ODIN.
OH, YOU GOTTA BE KIDDING ME.
I CAN'T HELP YOU. ALL I KNOW IS THIS VILLAGE.
THANK YOU FOR YOUR KINDNESS.
YOU SHOULD LISTEN TO THE ENCHANTRESS, LORD THOR.
YOU...

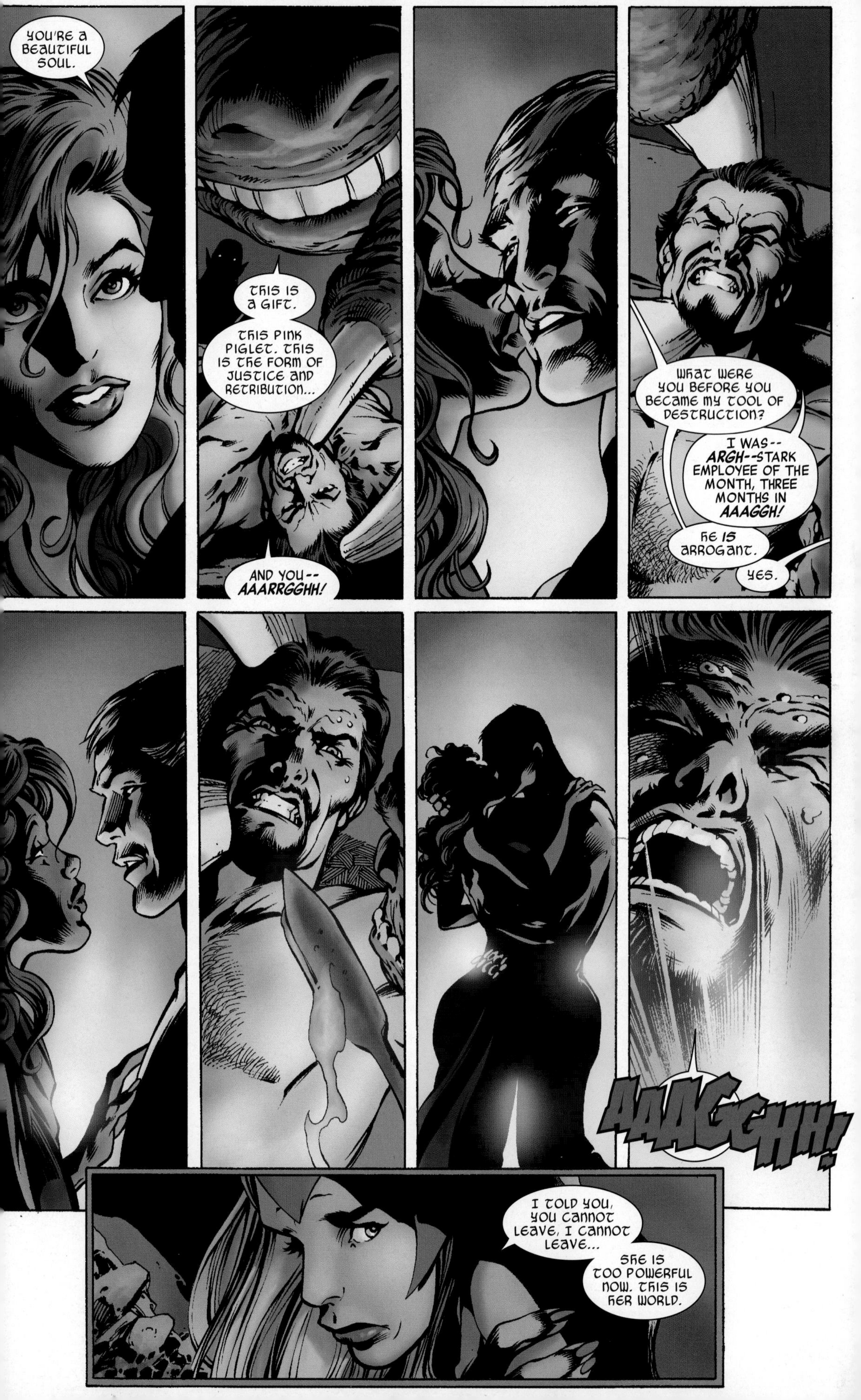
YOU'RE A BEAUTIFUL SOUL.
THIS IS A GIFT.
THIS PINK PIGLET. THIS IS THE FORM OF JUSTICE AND RETRIBUTION...
AND YOU-- AAARRGGHH!
WHAT WERE YOU BEFORE YOU BECAME MY TOOL OF DESTRUCTION?
I WAS-- ARGH--STARK EMPLOYEE OF THE MONTH, THREE MONTHS IN AAAGGH!
HE IS ARROGANT.
YES.
AAAGGHH!
I TOLD YOU, YOU CANNOT LEAVE, I CANNOT LEAVE...
SHE IS TOO POWERFUL NOW. THIS IS HER WORLD.

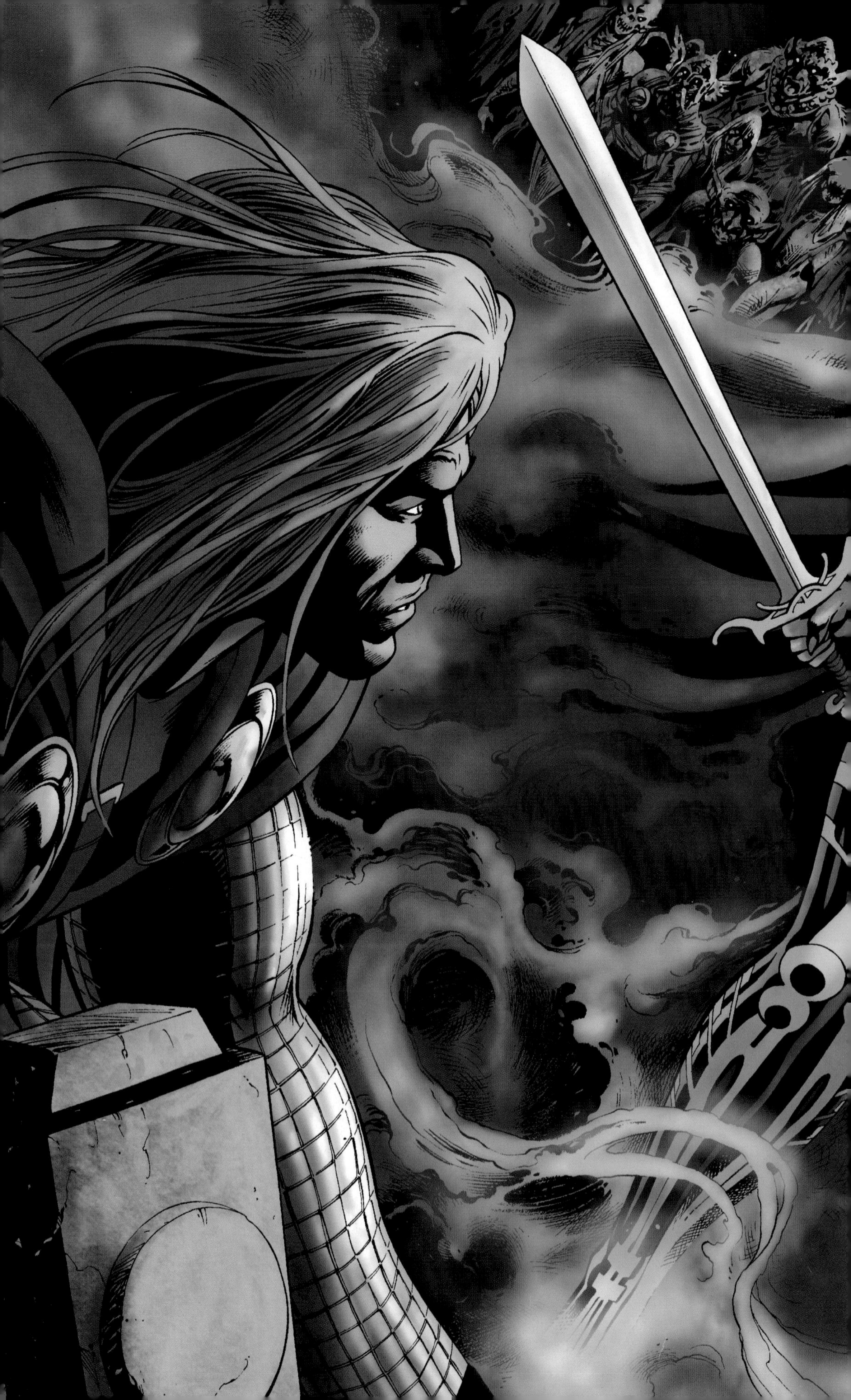

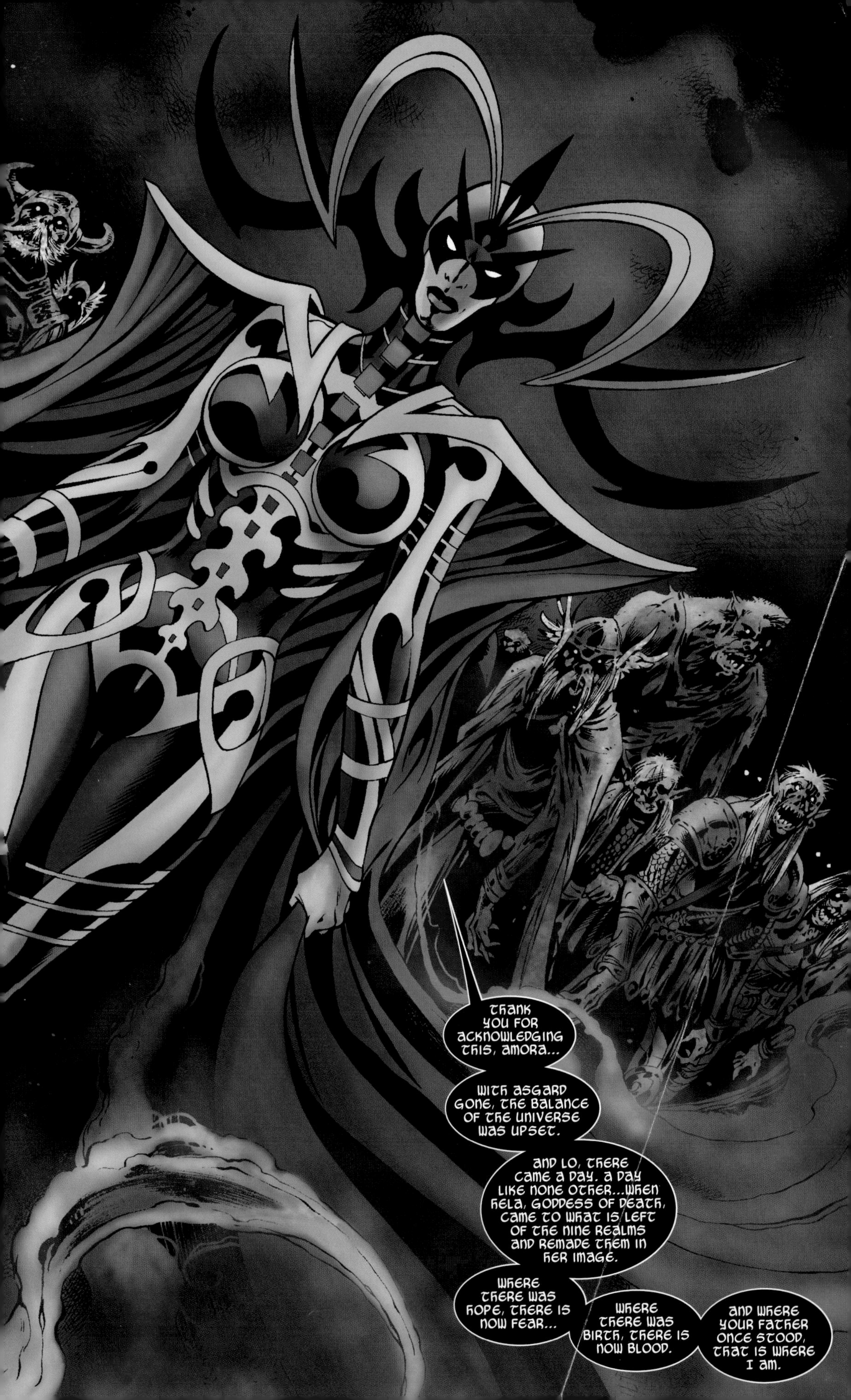

THANK YOU FOR ACKNOWLEDGING THIS, AMORA...
WITH ASGARD GONE, THE BALANCE OF THE UNIVERSE WAS UPSET.
AND LO, THERE CAME A DAY. A DAY LIKE NONE OTHER...WHEN HELA, GODDESS OF DEATH, CAME TO WHAT IS LEFT OF THE NINE REALMS AND REMADE THEM IN HER IMAGE.
WHERE THERE WAS HOPE, THERE IS NOW FEAR...
WHERE THERE WAS BIRTH, THERE IS NOW BLOOD.
AND WHERE YOUR FATHER ONCE STOOD, THAT IS WHERE I AM.

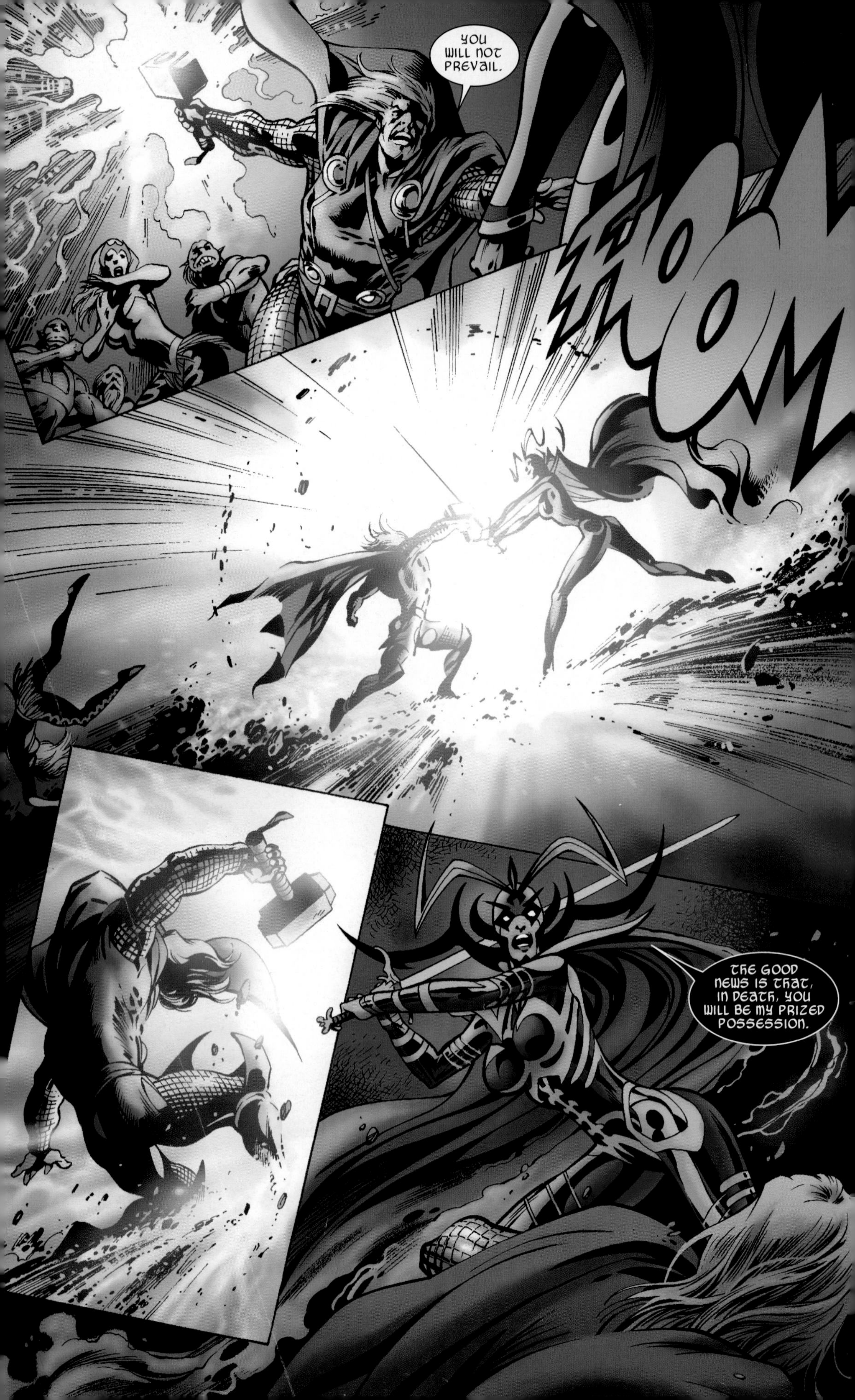
YOU WILL NOT PREVAIL.
THOOM
THE GOOD NEWS IS THAT, IN DEATH, YOU WILL BE MY PRIZED POSSESSION.

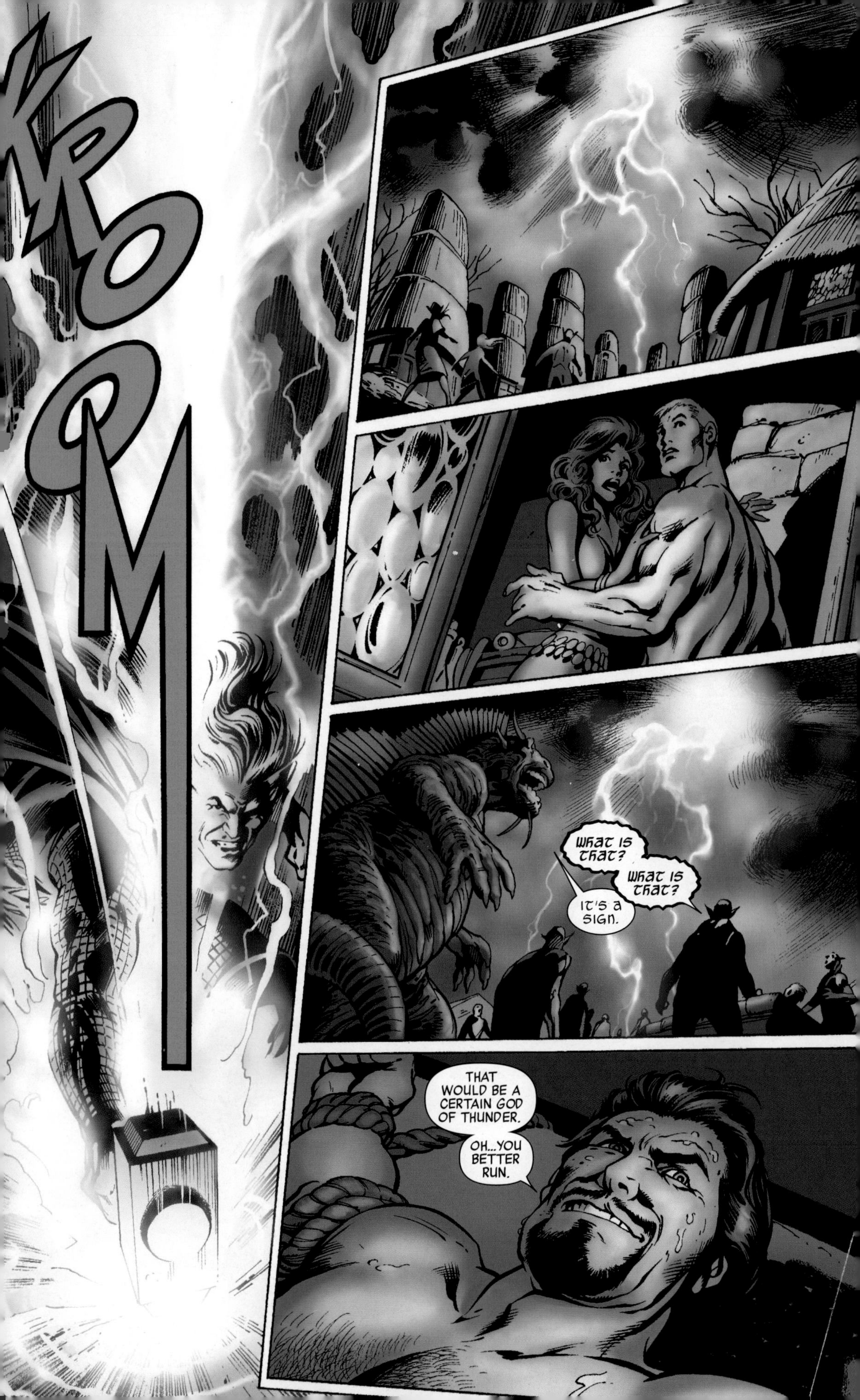
KROOM
WHAT IS THAT?
IT'S A SIGN.
WHAT IS THAT?
THAT WOULD BE A CERTAIN GOD OF THUNDER.
OH...YOU BETTER RUN.

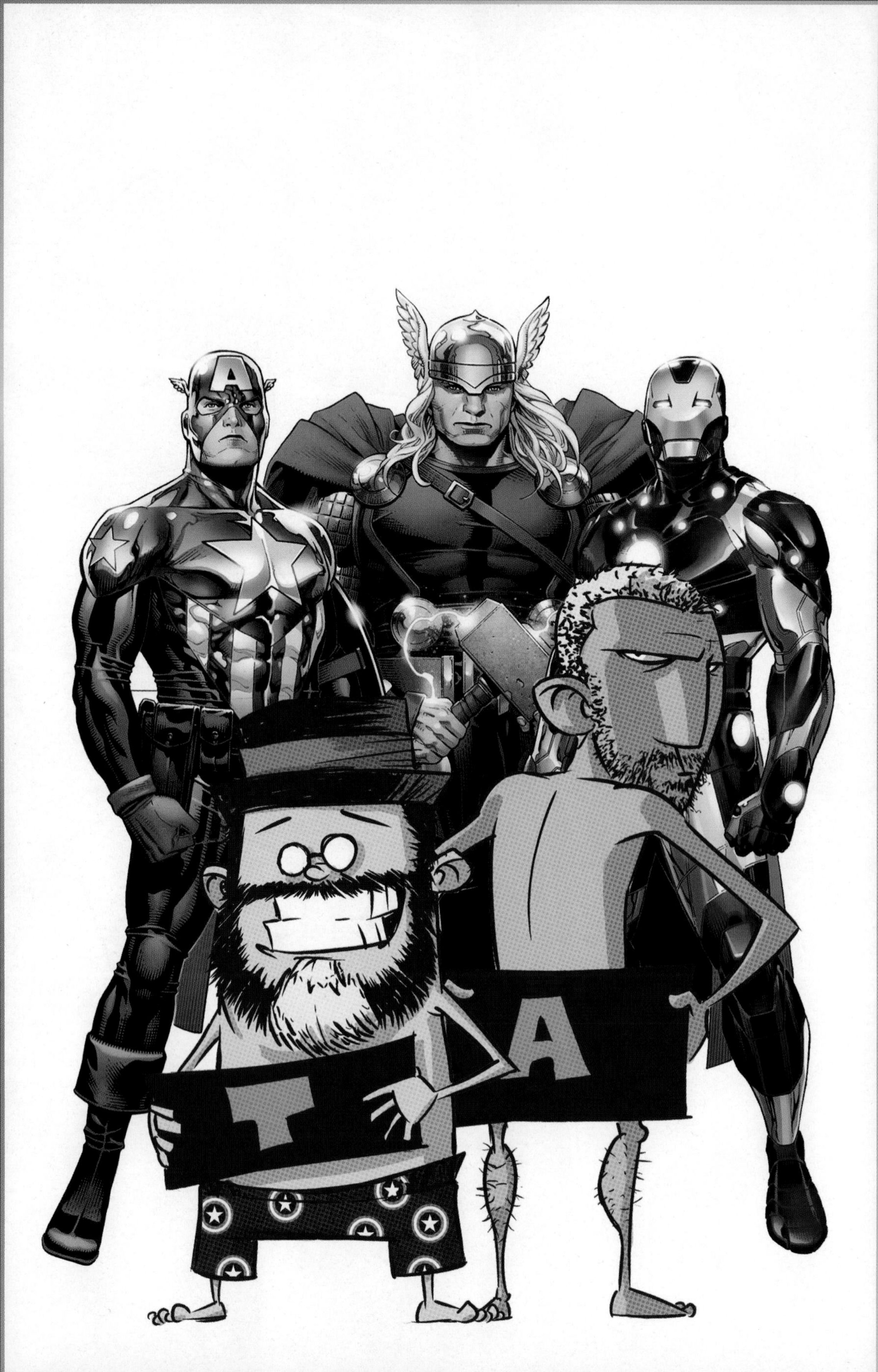

#3 NYCC VARIANT BY JIM CHEUNG & SKOTTIE YOUNG

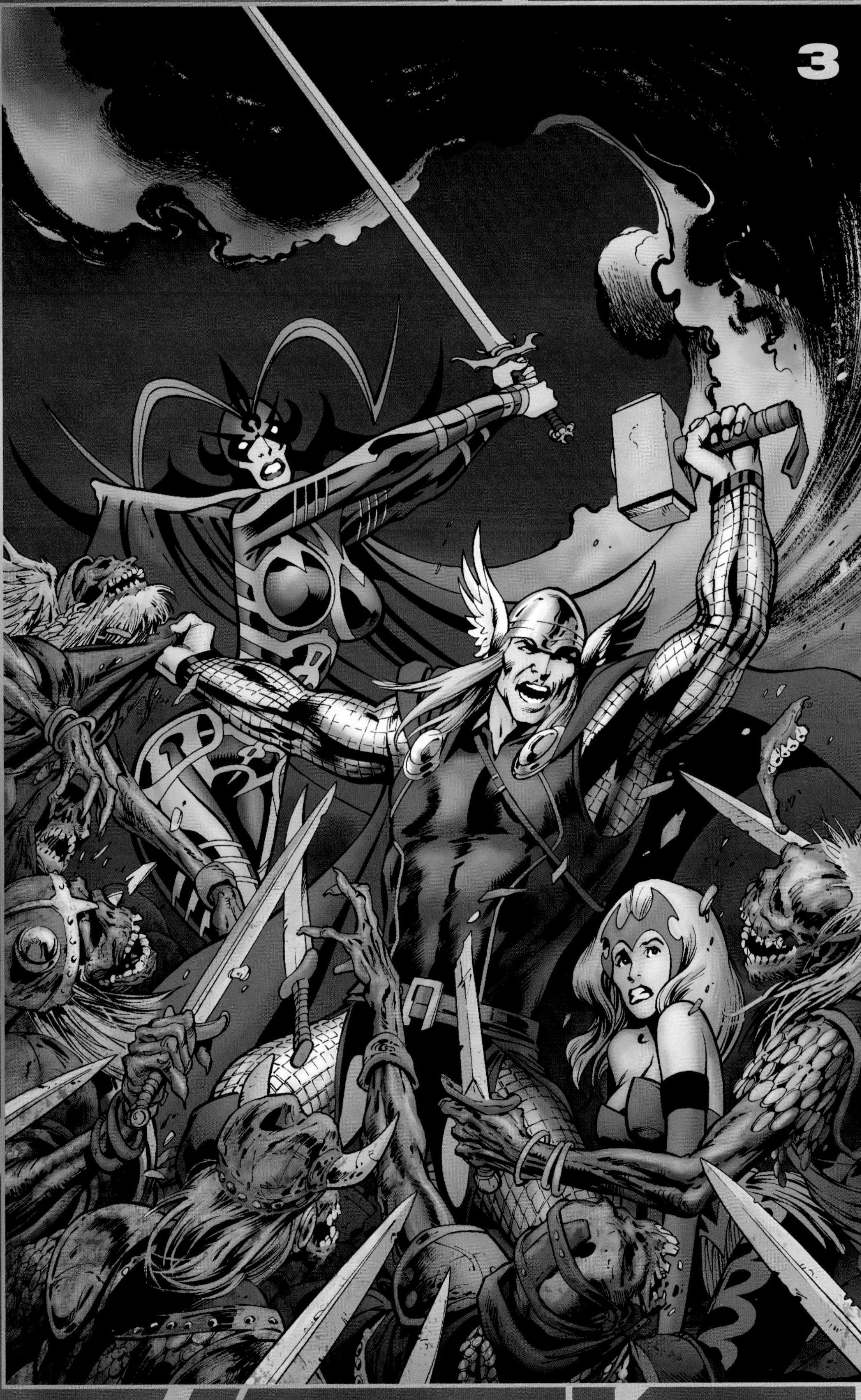
3

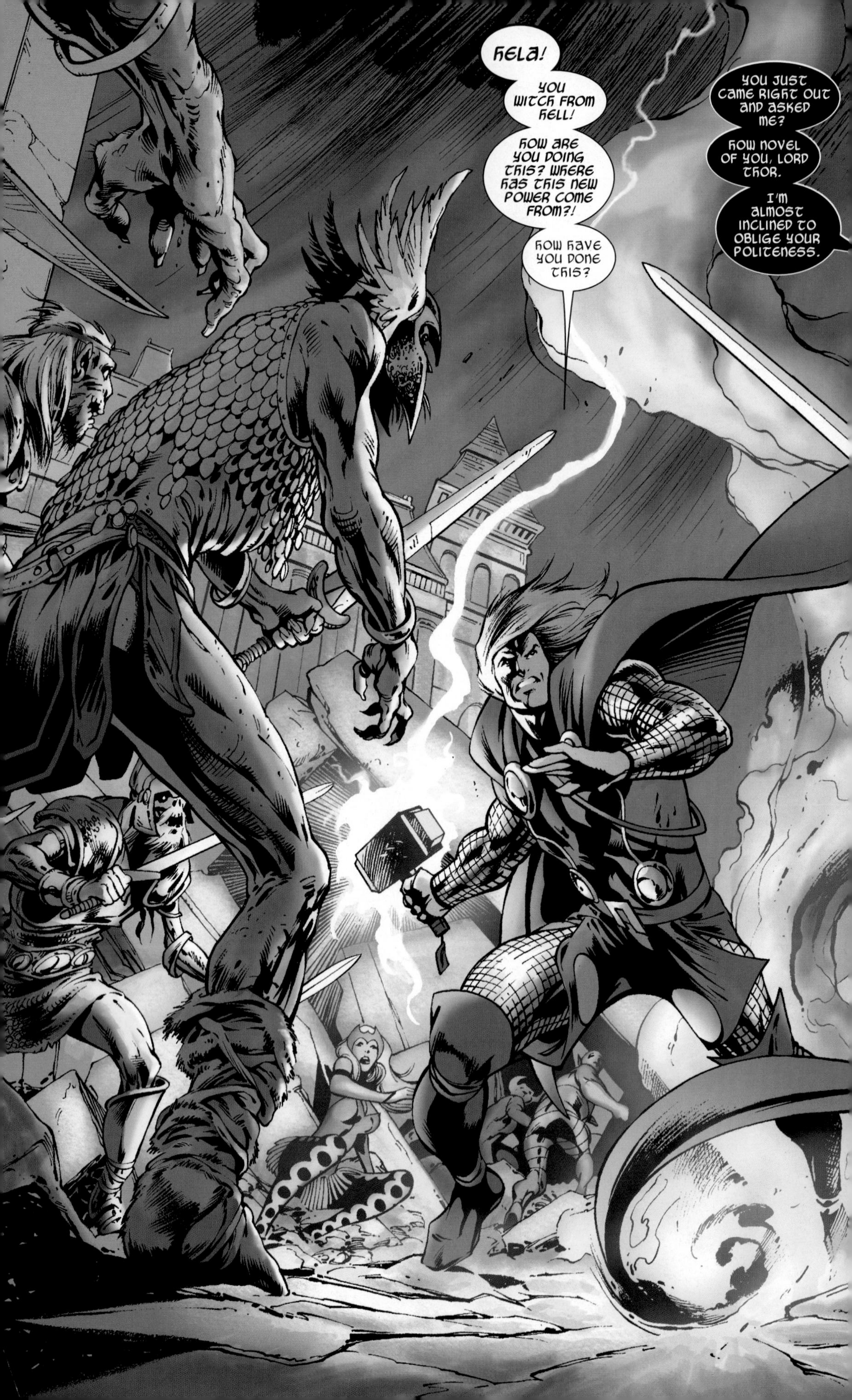
HELA!
YOU WITCH FROM HELL!
HOW ARE YOU DOING THIS? WHERE HAS THIS NEW POWER COME FROM?!
HOW HAVE YOU DONE THIS?
YOU JUST CAME RIGHT OUT AND ASKED ME?
HOW NOVEL OF YOU, LORD THOR.
I'M ALMOST INCLINED TO OBLIGE YOUR POLITENESS.

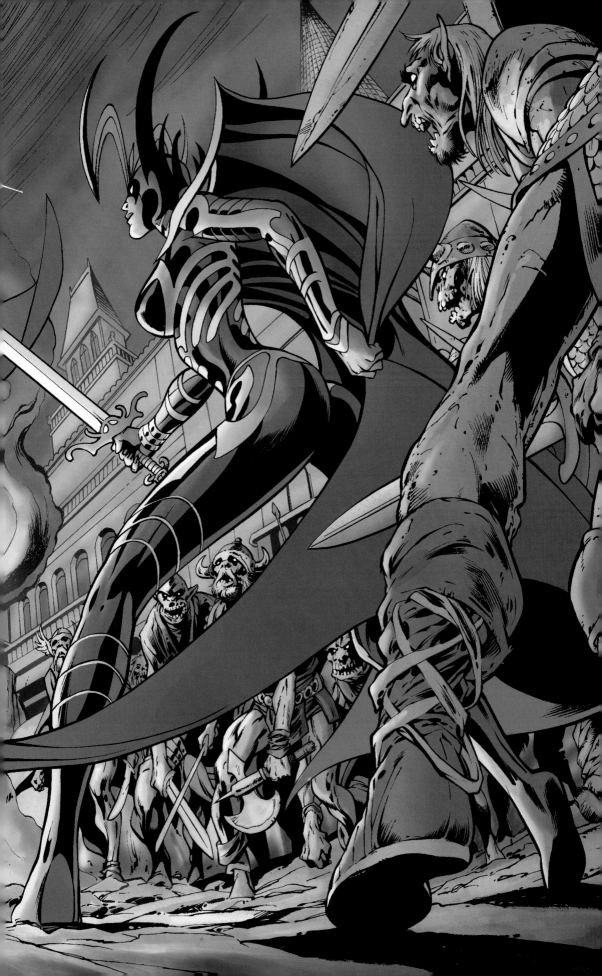

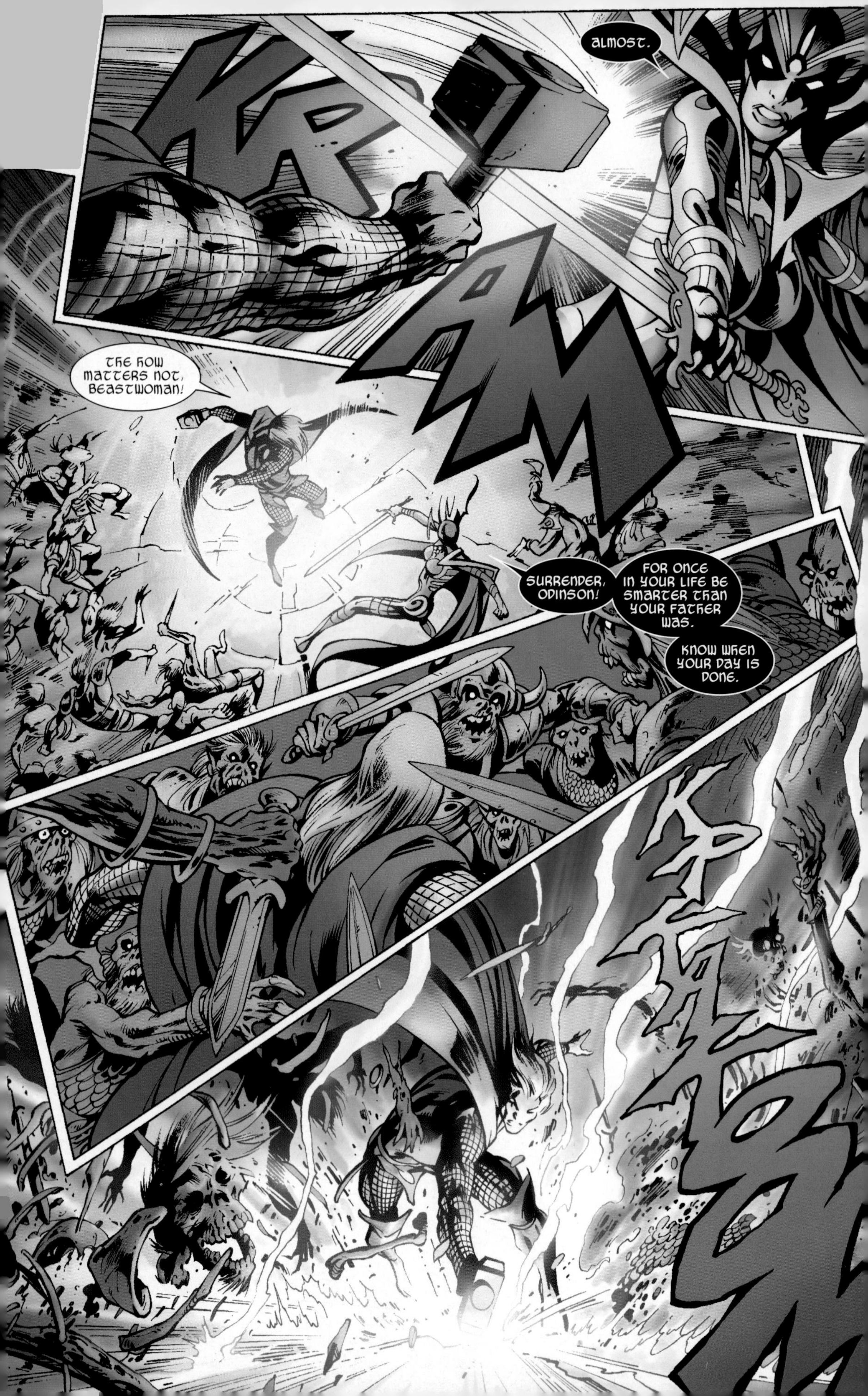

ALMOST.
KRAM
THE HOW MATTERS NOT, BEASTWOMAN!
SURRENDER, ODINSON!
FOR ONCE IN YOUR LIFE BE SMARTER THAN YOUR FATHER WAS.
KNOW WHEN YOUR DAY IS DONE.

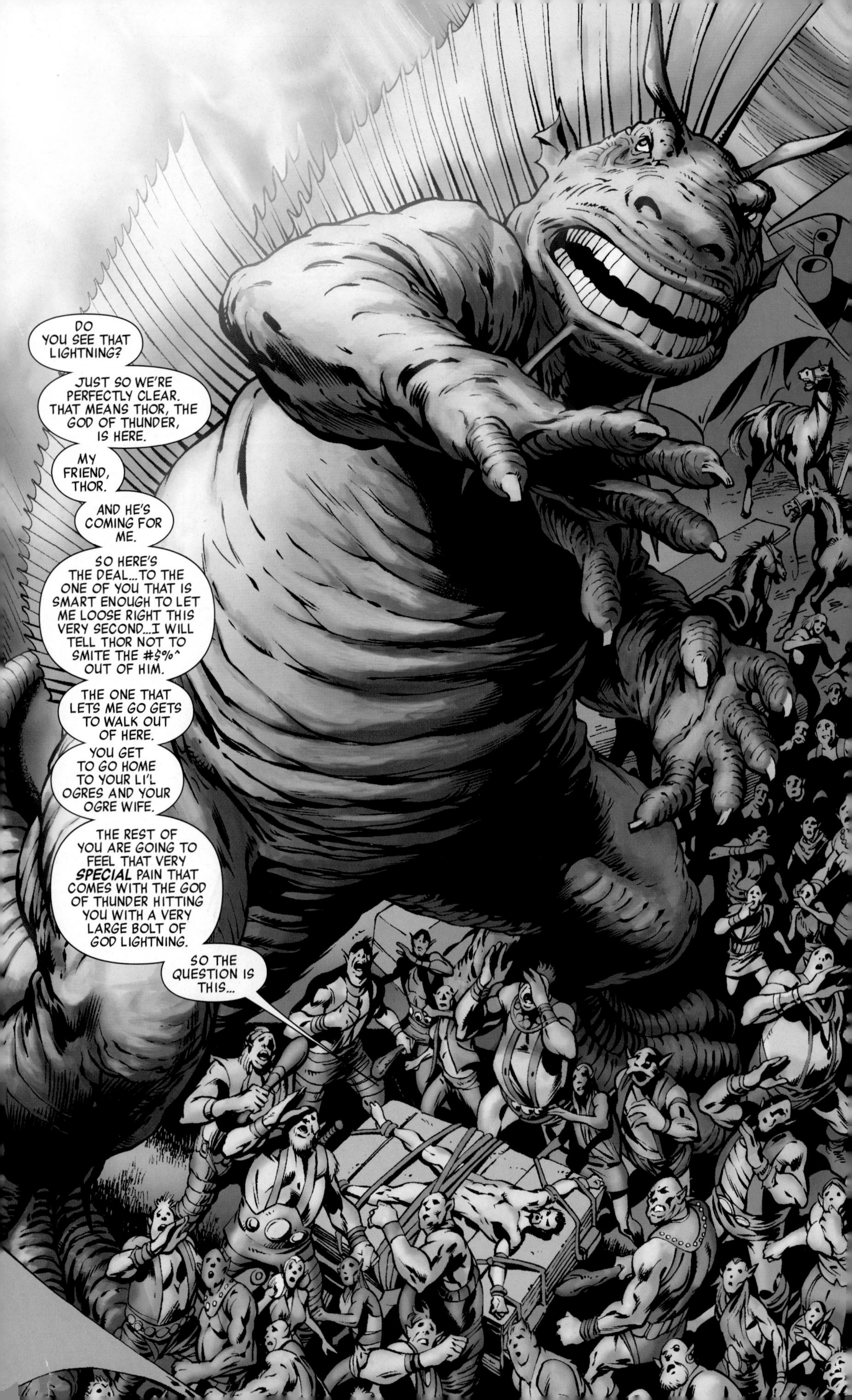
DO YOU SEE THAT LIGHTNING?
JUST SO WE'RE PERFECTLY CLEAR. THAT MEANS THOR, THE GOD OF THUNDER, IS HERE.
MY FRIEND, THOR.
AND HE'S COMING FOR ME.
SO HERE'S THE DEAL...TO THE ONE OF YOU THAT IS SMART ENOUGH TO LET ME LOOSE RIGHT THIS VERY SECOND...I WILL TELL THOR NOT TO SMITE THE #$%^ OUT OF HIM.
THE ONE THAT LETS ME GO GETS TO WALK OUT OF HERE.
YOU GET TO GO HOME TO YOUR LI'L OGRES AND YOUR OGRE WIFE.
THE REST OF YOU ARE GOING TO FEEL THAT VERY **SPECIAL** PAIN THAT COMES WITH THE GOD OF THUNDER HITTING YOU WITH A VERY LARGE BOLT OF GOD LIGHTNING.
SO THE QUESTION IS THIS...

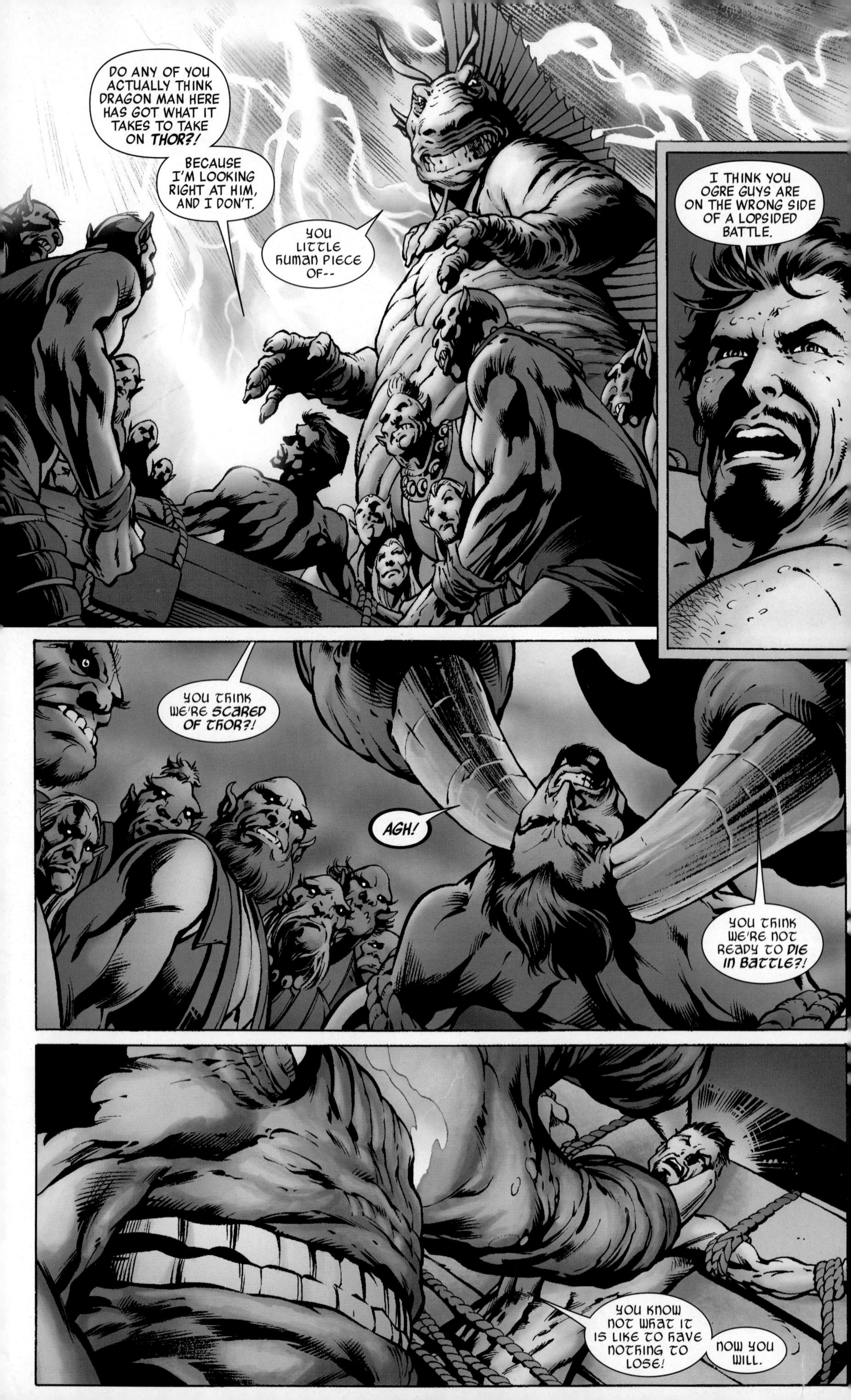
DO ANY OF YOU ACTUALLY THINK DRAGON MAN HERE HAS GOT WHAT IT TAKES TO TAKE ON THOR?!
BECAUSE I'M LOOKING RIGHT AT HIM, AND I DON'T.
YOU LITTLE HUMAN PIECE OF--
I THINK YOU OGRE GUYS ARE ON THE WRONG SIDE OF A LOPSIDED BATTLE.
YOU THINK WE'RE SCARED OF THOR?!
AGH!
YOU THINK WE'RE NOT READY TO DIE IN BATTLE?!
YOU KNOW NOT WHAT IT IS LIKE TO HAVE NOTHING TO LOSE!
NOW YOU WILL.

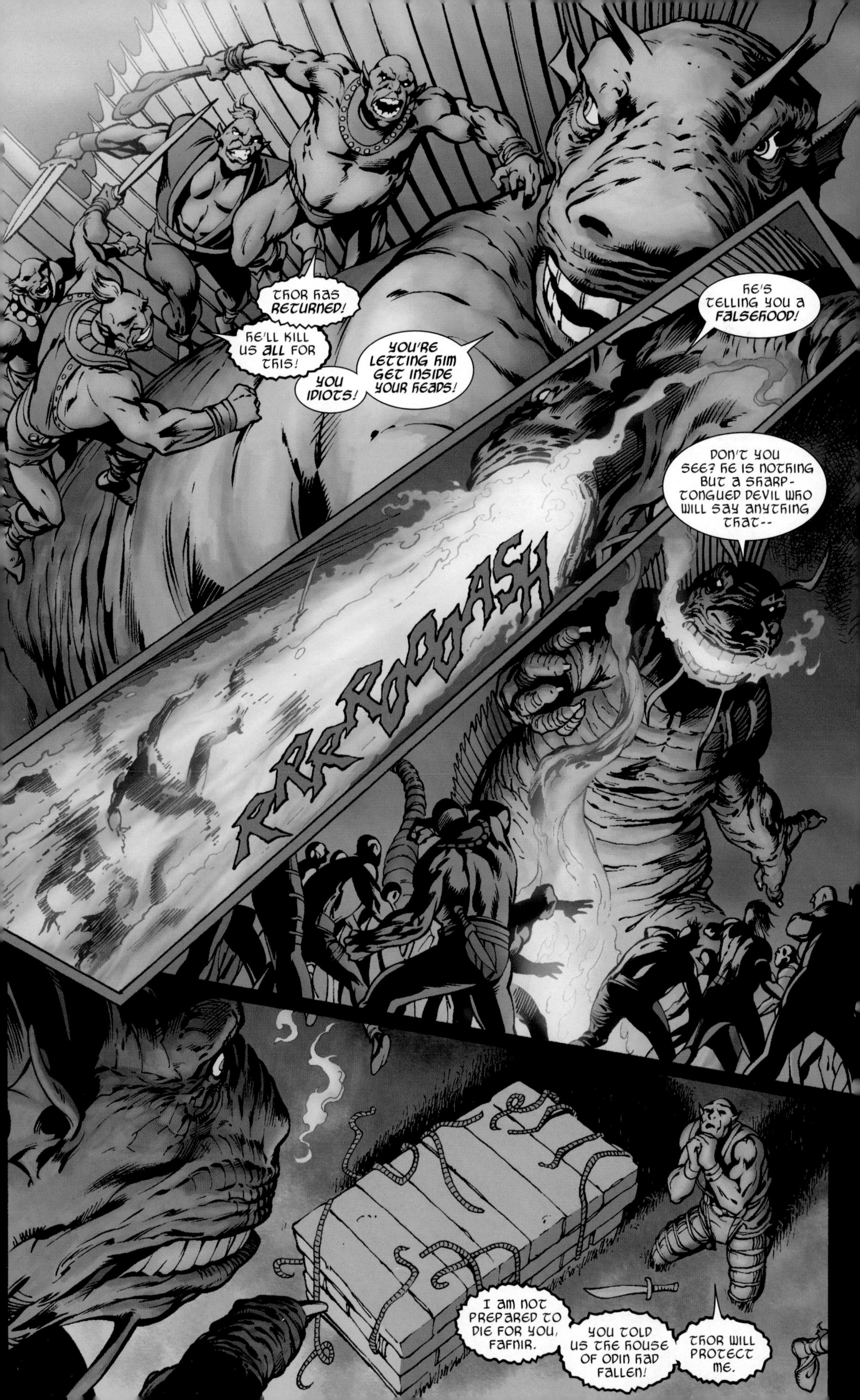
THOR HAS RETURNED!
HE'LL KILL US ALL FOR THIS!
YOU IDIOTS!
YOU'RE LETTING HIM GET INSIDE YOUR HEADS!
HE'S TELLING YOU A FALSEHOOD!
DON'T YOU SEE? HE IS NOTHING BUT A SHARP-TONGUED DEVIL WHO WILL SAY ANYTHING THAT--
RRRROOOOASH
I AM NOT PREPARED TO DIE FOR YOU, FAFNIR.
YOU TOLD US THE HOUSE OF ODIN HAD FALLEN!
THOR WILL PROTECT ME.

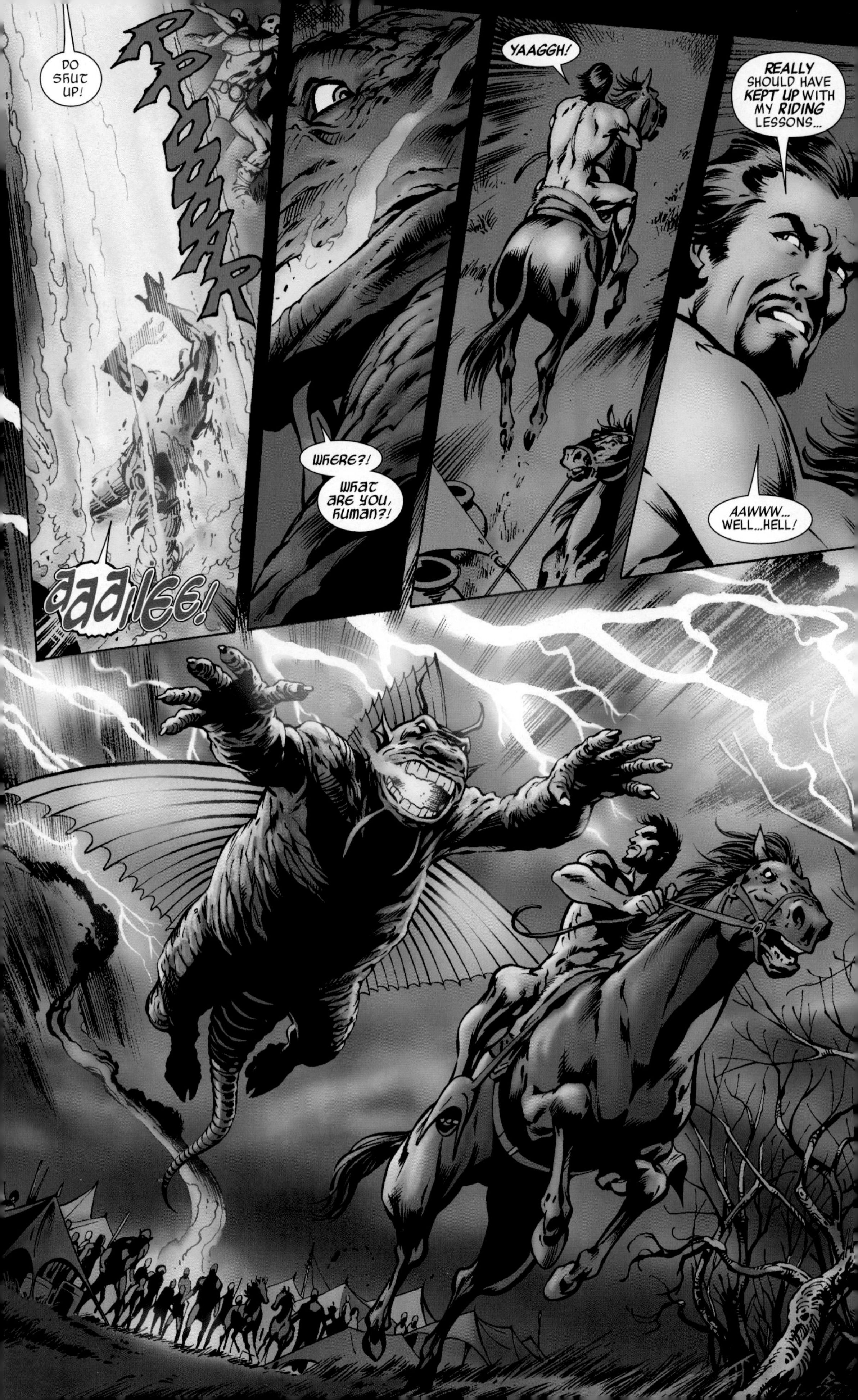
DO SHUT UP!
RRROOOAR
AAAIIEEE!
WHERE?!
WHAT ARE YOU, HUMAN?!
YAAGGH!
REALLY SHOULD HAVE KEPT UP WITH MY RIDING LESSONS...
AAWWW... WELL...HELL!

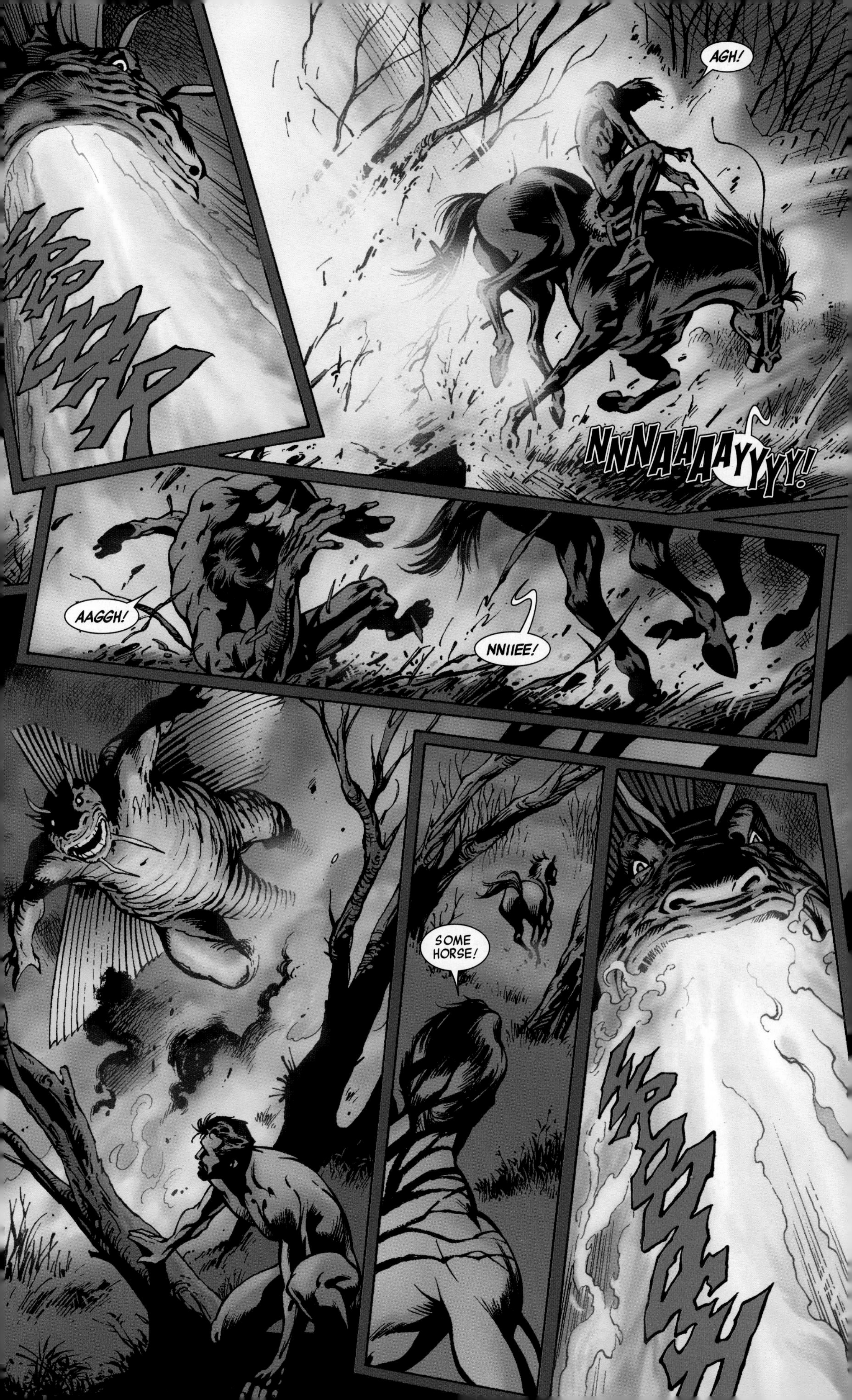
AGH!
NNNAAAAYYYY!
AAGGH!
NNIIEE!
SOME HORSE!

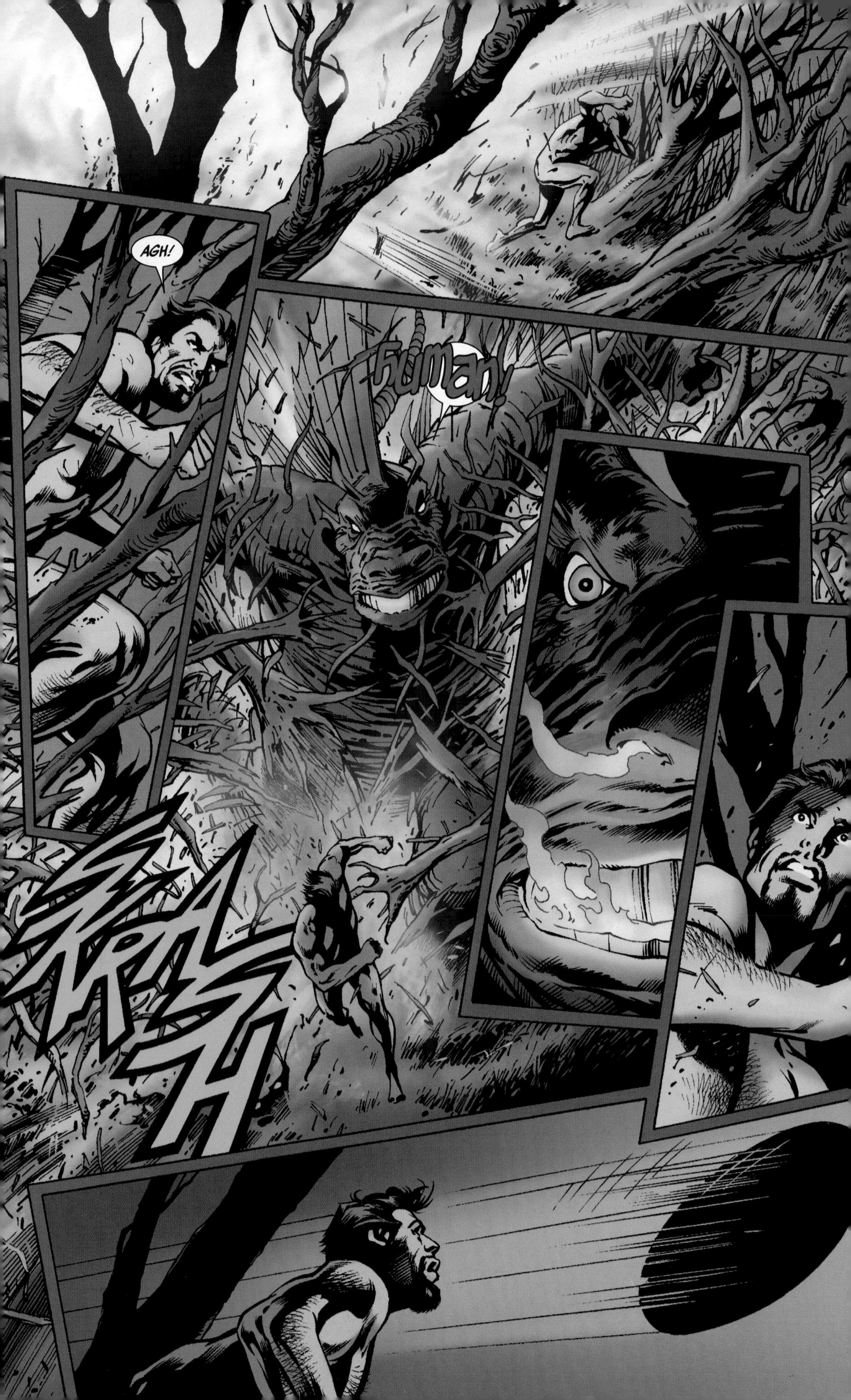
AGH!
Human!

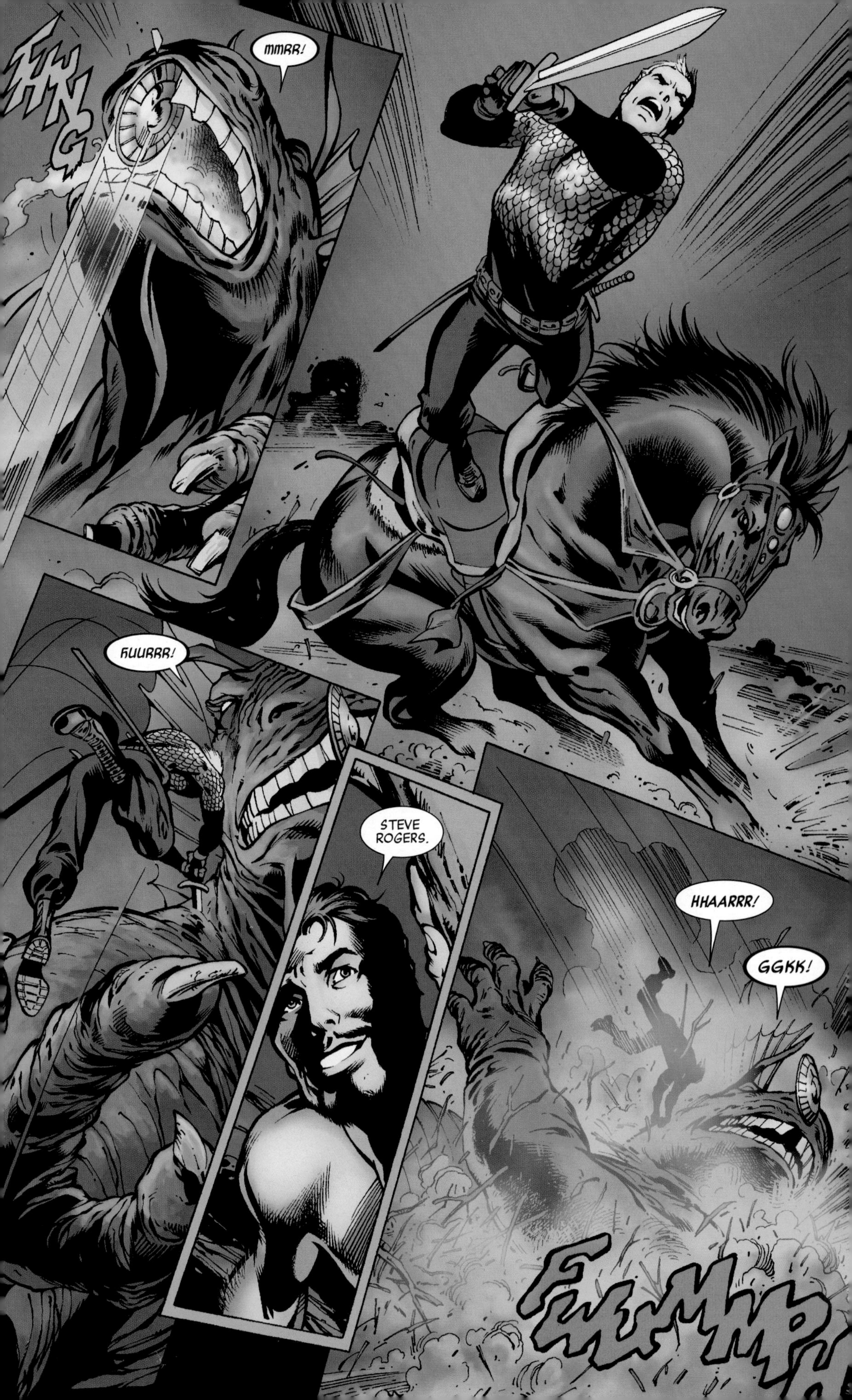
FWNG
MMRR!
HUURRR!
STEVE ROGERS.
HHAARRR!
GGKK!
FWUMP!

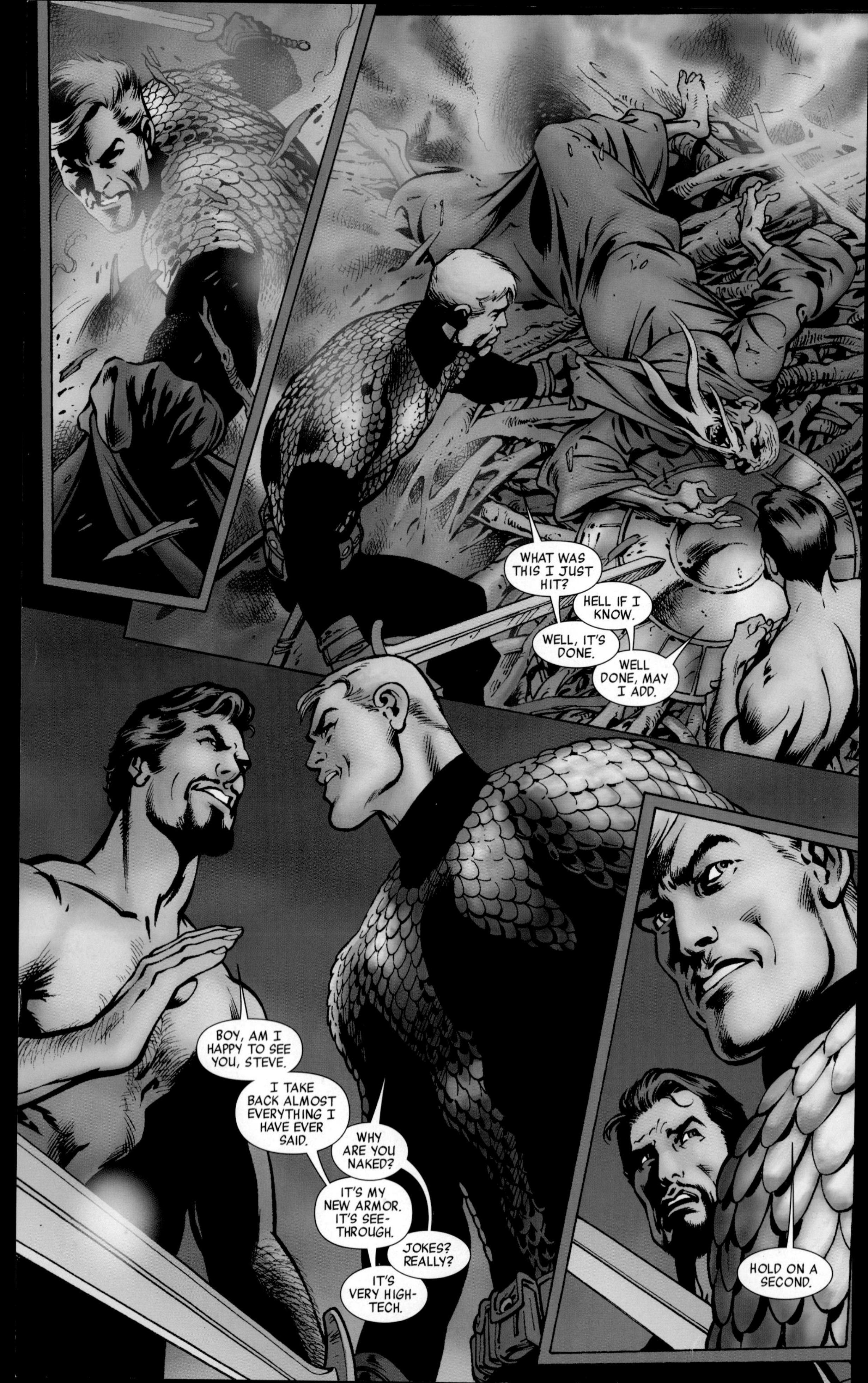
WHAT WAS THIS I JUST HIT?
HELL IF I KNOW.
WELL, IT'S DONE.
WELL DONE, MAY I ADD.
BOY, AM I HAPPY TO SEE YOU, STEVE.
I TAKE BACK ALMOST EVERYTHING I HAVE EVER SAID.
WHY ARE YOU NAKED?
IT'S MY NEW ARMOR. IT'S SEE-THROUGH.
JOKES? REALLY?
IT'S VERY HIGH-TECH.
HOLD ON A SECOND.

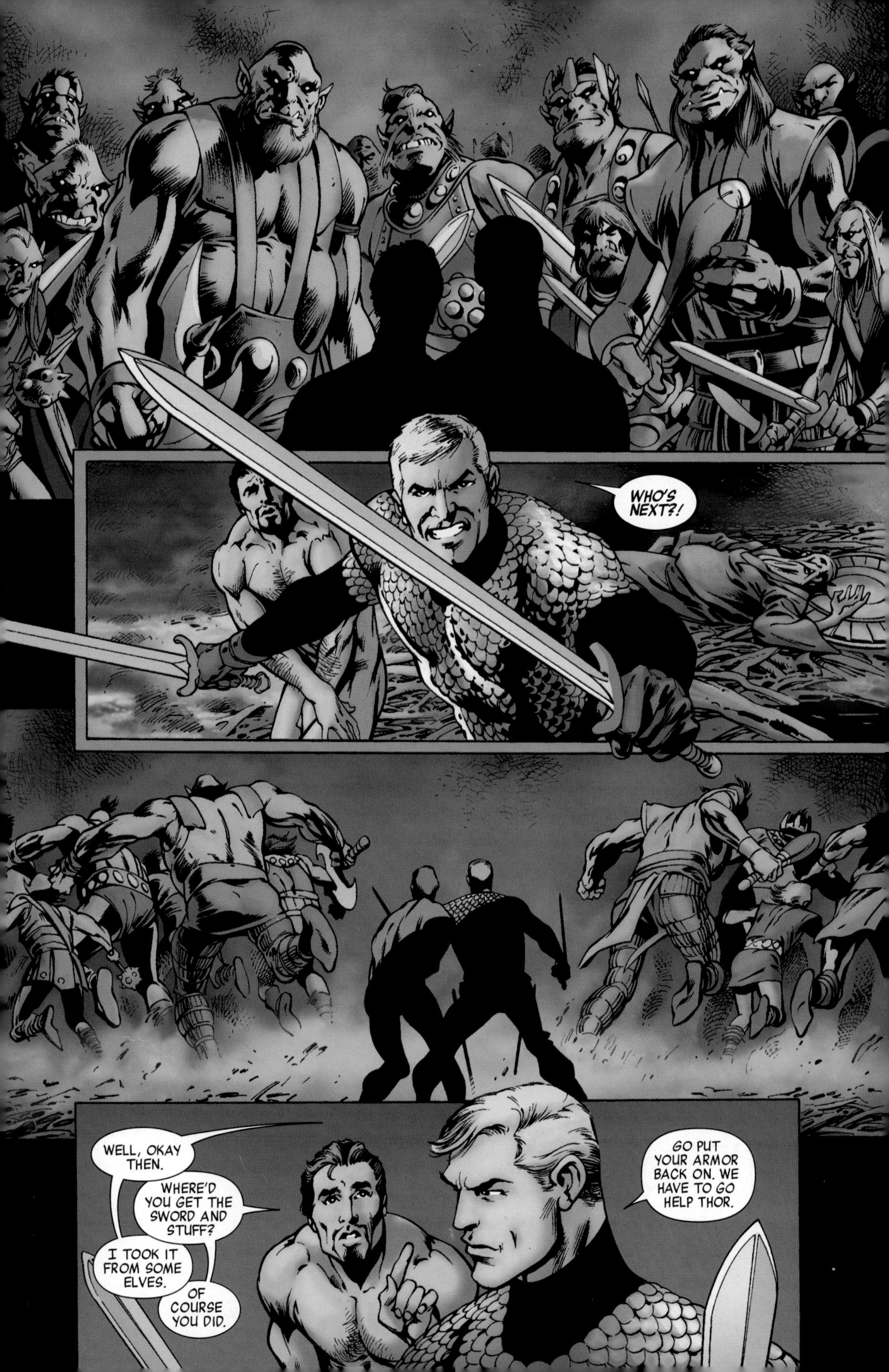
WHO'S NEXT?!
WELL, OKAY THEN.
WHERE'D YOU GET THE SWORD AND STUFF?
I TOOK IT FROM SOME ELVES.
OF COURSE YOU DID.
GO PUT YOUR ARMOR BACK ON. WE HAVE TO GO HELP THOR.

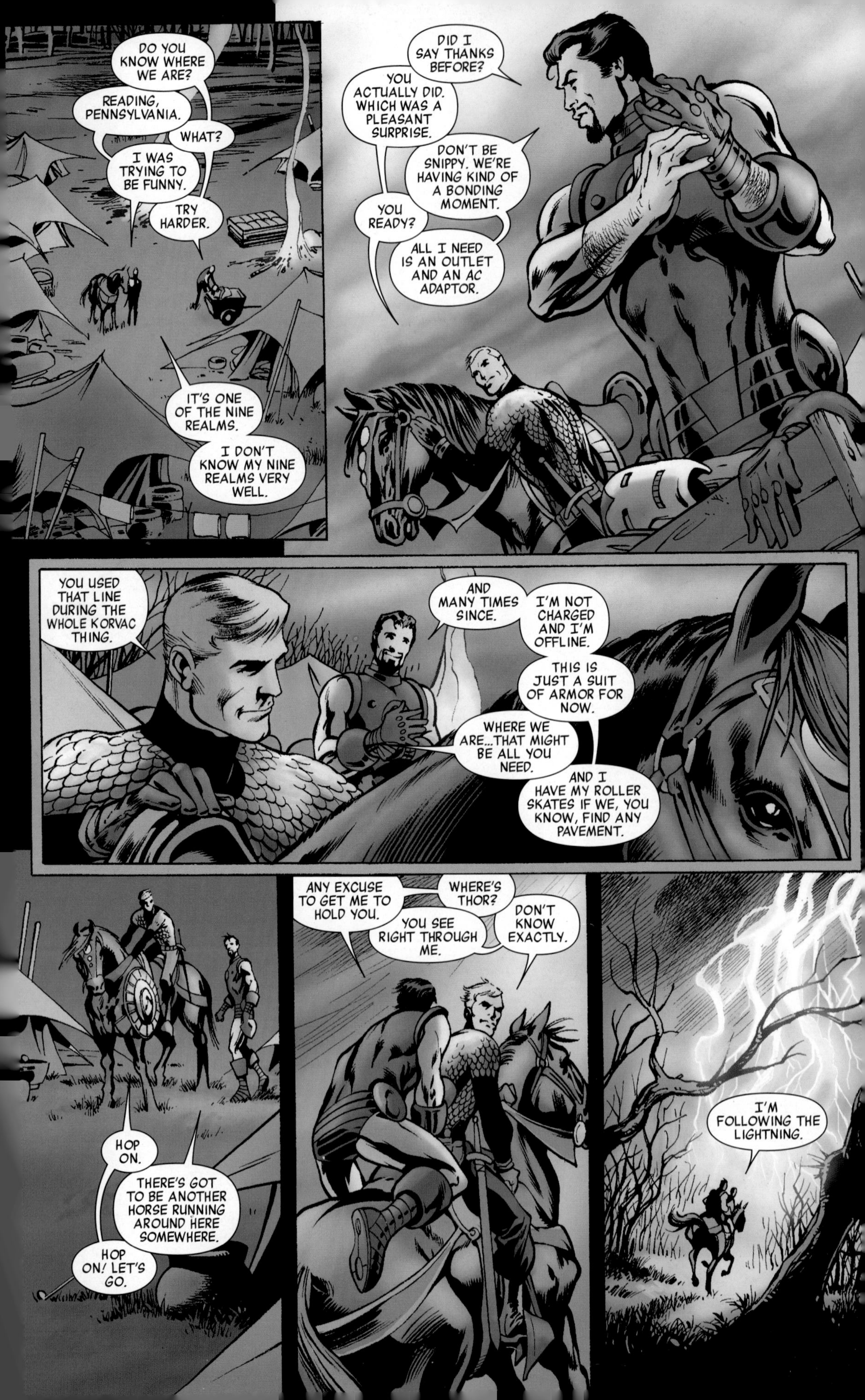
DO YOU KNOW WHERE WE ARE?
READING, PENNSYLVANIA.
WHAT?
I WAS TRYING TO BE FUNNY.
TRY HARDER.
IT'S ONE OF THE NINE REALMS.
I DON'T KNOW MY NINE REALMS VERY WELL.
DID I SAY THANKS BEFORE?
YOU ACTUALLY DID. WHICH WAS A PLEASANT SURPRISE.
DON'T BE SNIPPY. WE'RE HAVING KIND OF A BONDING MOMENT.
YOU READY?
ALL I NEED IS AN OUTLET AND AN AC ADAPTOR.
YOU USED THAT LINE DURING THE WHOLE KORVAC THING.
AND MANY TIMES SINCE.
I'M NOT CHARGED AND I'M OFFLINE.
THIS IS JUST A SUIT OF ARMOR FOR NOW.
WHERE WE ARE...THAT MIGHT BE ALL YOU NEED.
AND I HAVE MY ROLLER SKATES IF WE, YOU KNOW, FIND ANY PAVEMENT.
HOP ON.
THERE'S GOT TO BE ANOTHER HORSE RUNNING AROUND HERE SOMEWHERE.
HOP ON! LET'S GO.
ANY EXCUSE TO GET ME TO HOLD YOU.
YOU SEE RIGHT THROUGH ME.
WHERE'S THOR?
DON'T KNOW EXACTLY.
I'M FOLLOWING THE LIGHTNING.

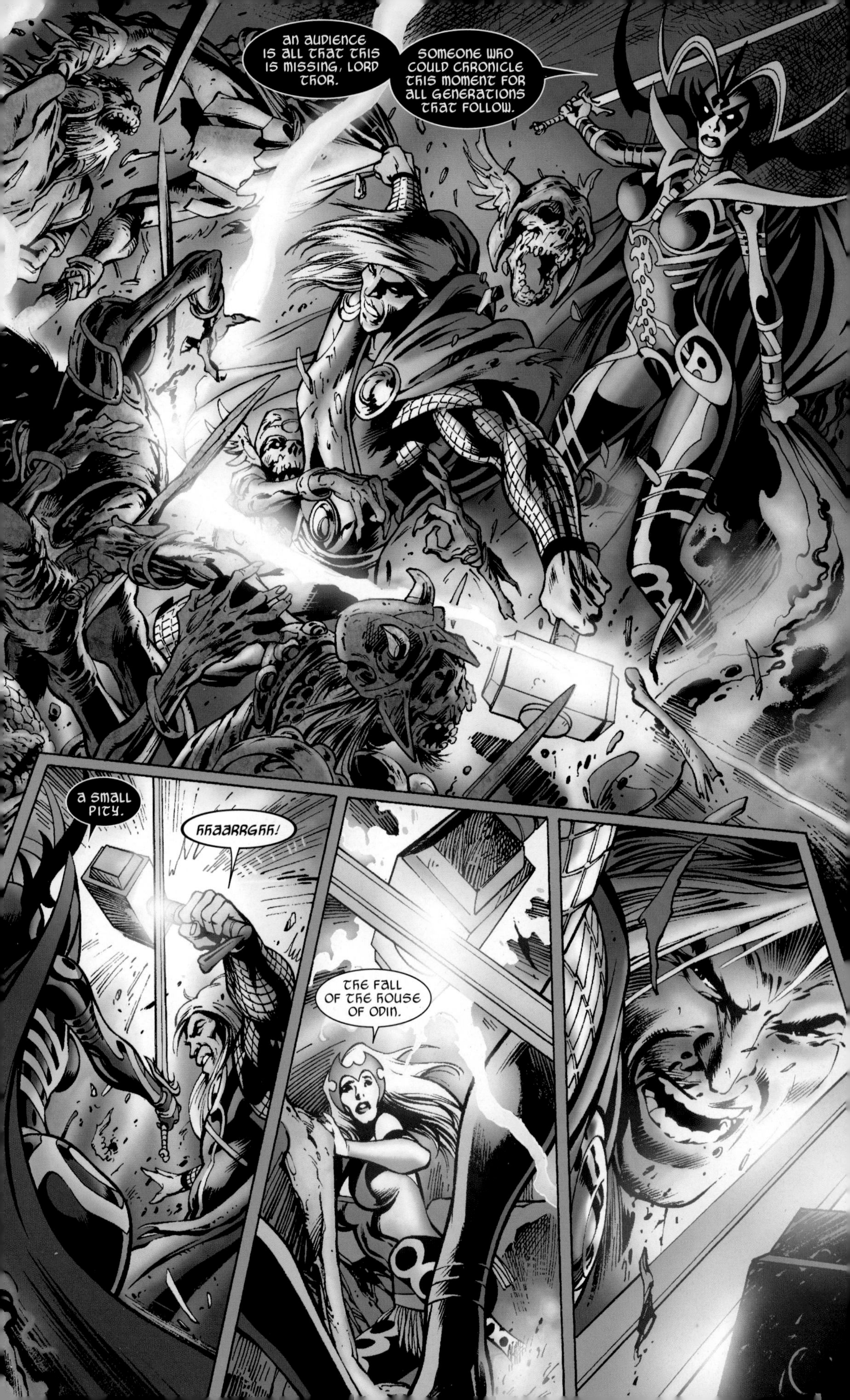
AN AUDIENCE IS ALL THAT THIS IS MISSING, LORD THOR.
SOMEONE WHO COULD CHRONICLE THIS MOMENT FOR ALL GENERATIONS THAT FOLLOW.
A SMALL PITY.
HHAARRGHH!
THE FALL OF THE HOUSE OF ODIN.

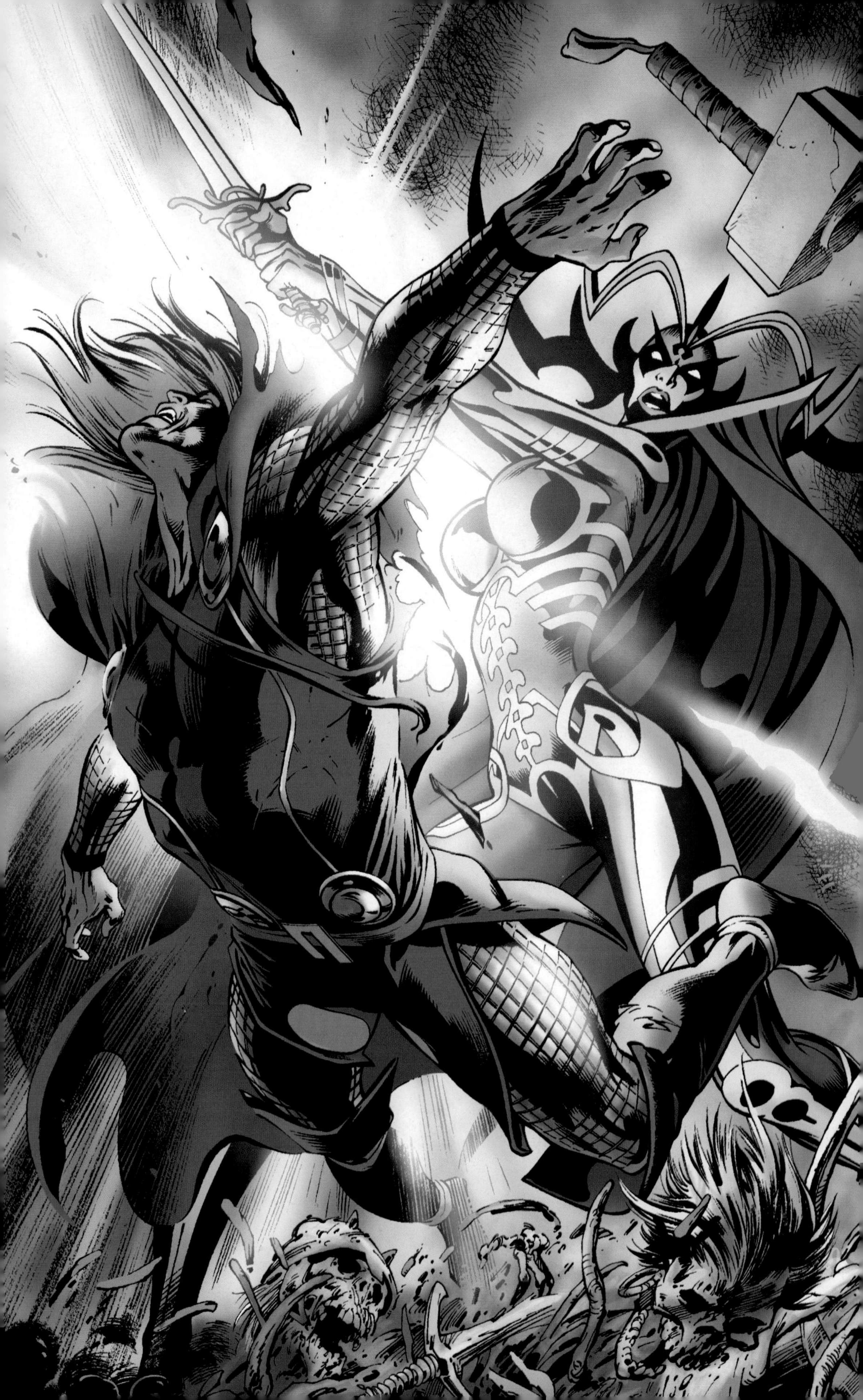

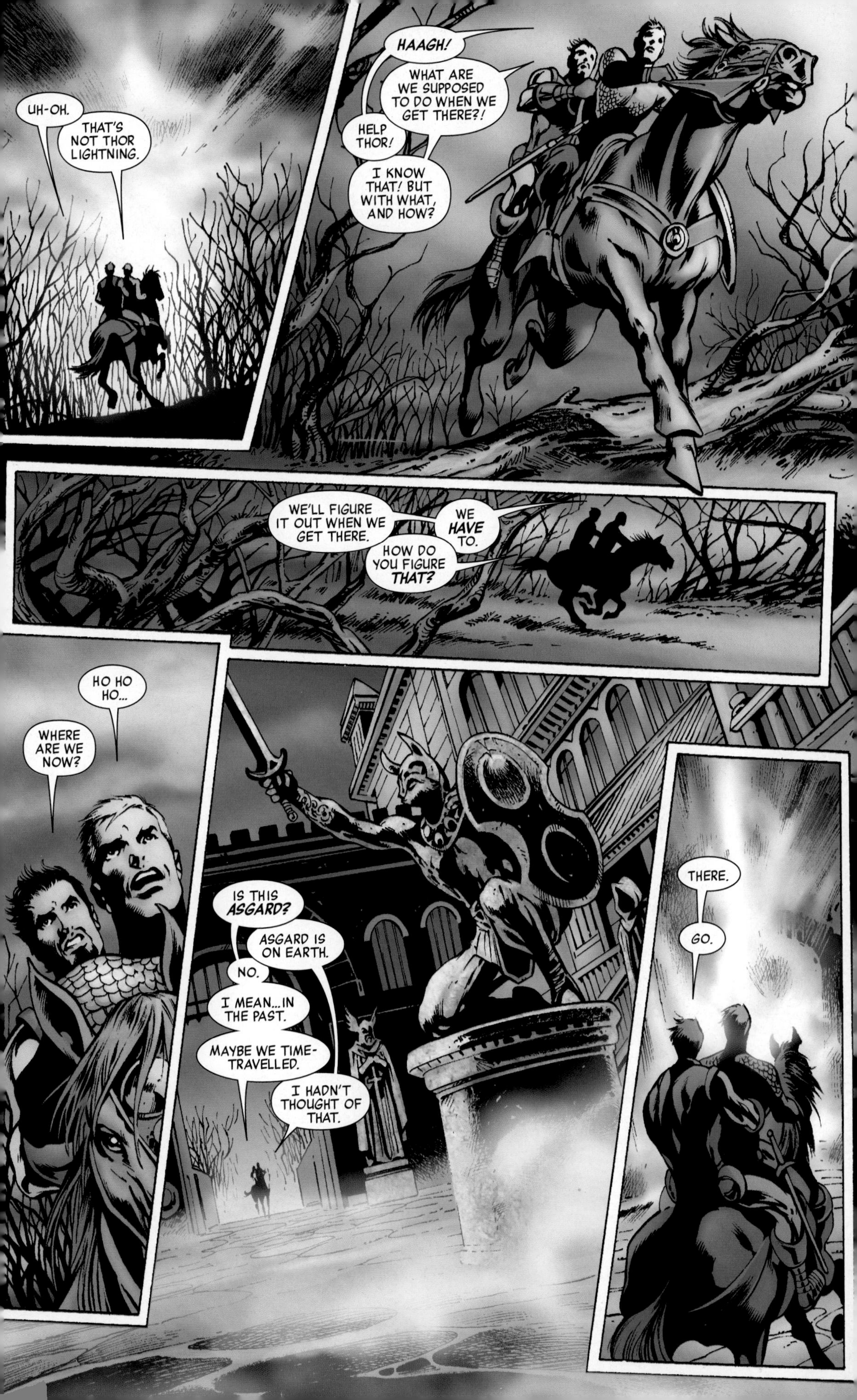
UH-OH.
THAT'S NOT THOR LIGHTNING.
HAAGH!
WHAT ARE WE SUPPOSED TO DO WHEN WE GET THERE?!
HELP THOR!
I KNOW THAT! BUT WITH WHAT, AND HOW?
WE'LL FIGURE IT OUT WHEN WE GET THERE.
WE HAVE TO.
HOW DO YOU FIGURE THAT?
HO HO HO...
WHERE ARE WE NOW?
IS THIS ASGARD?
ASGARD IS ON EARTH.
NO.
I MEAN...IN THE PAST.
MAYBE WE TIME-TRAVELLED.
I HADN'T THOUGHT OF THAT.
THERE.
GO.

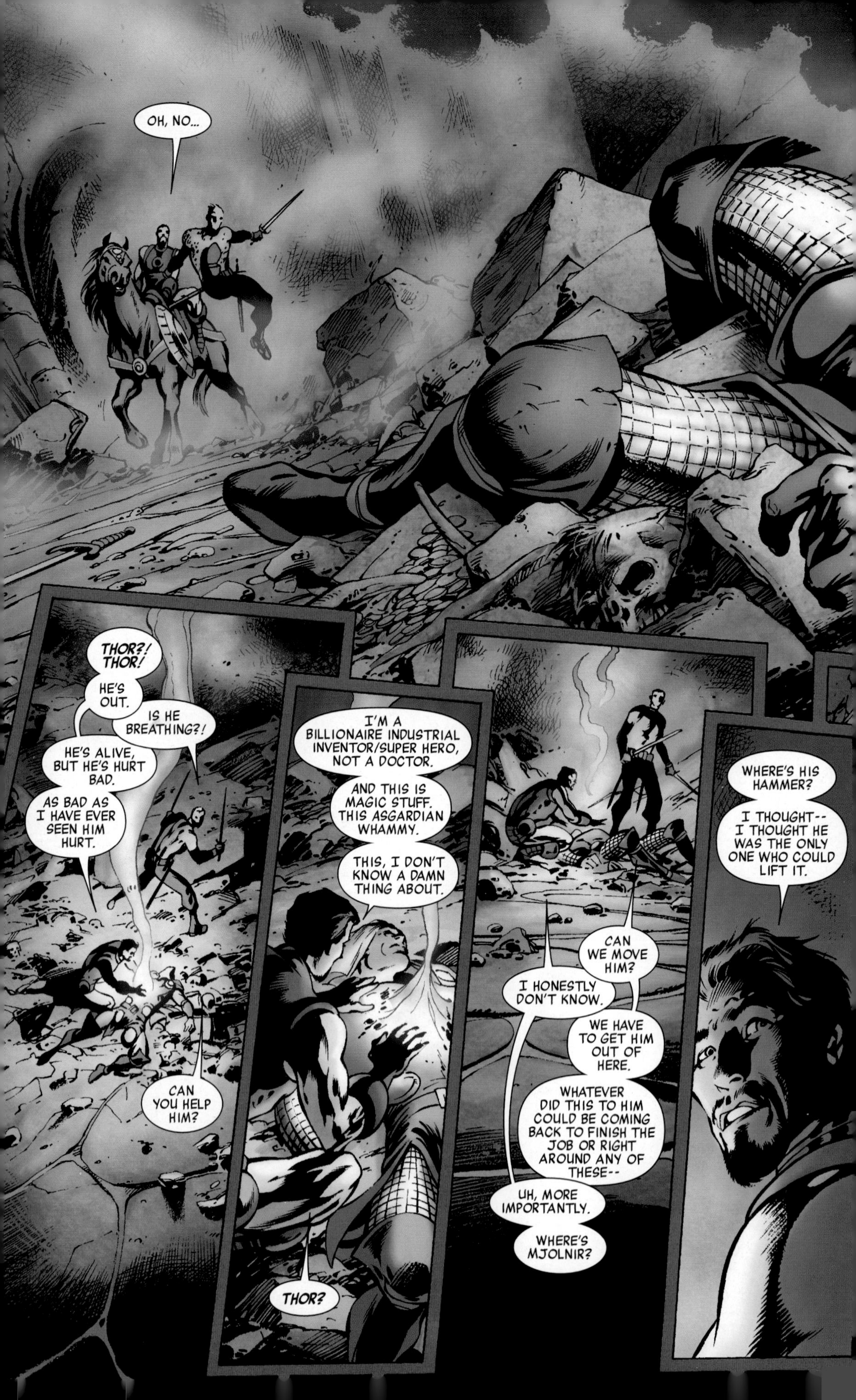
OH, NO...
THOR?! THOR!
HE'S OUT.
IS HE BREATHING?!
HE'S ALIVE, BUT HE'S HURT BAD.
AS BAD AS I HAVE EVER SEEN HIM HURT.
CAN YOU HELP HIM?
I'M A BILLIONAIRE INDUSTRIAL INVENTOR/SUPER HERO, NOT A DOCTOR.
AND THIS IS MAGIC STUFF. THIS ASGARDIAN WHAMMY.
THIS, I DON'T KNOW A DAMN THING ABOUT.
THOR?
CAN WE MOVE HIM?
I HONESTLY DON'T KNOW.
WE HAVE TO GET HIM OUT OF HERE.
WHATEVER DID THIS TO HIM COULD BE COMING BACK TO FINISH THE JOB OR RIGHT AROUND ANY OF THESE--
UH, MORE IMPORTANTLY.
WHERE'S MJOLNIR?
WHERE'S HIS HAMMER?
I THOUGHT-- I THOUGHT HE WAS THE ONLY ONE WHO COULD LIFT IT.

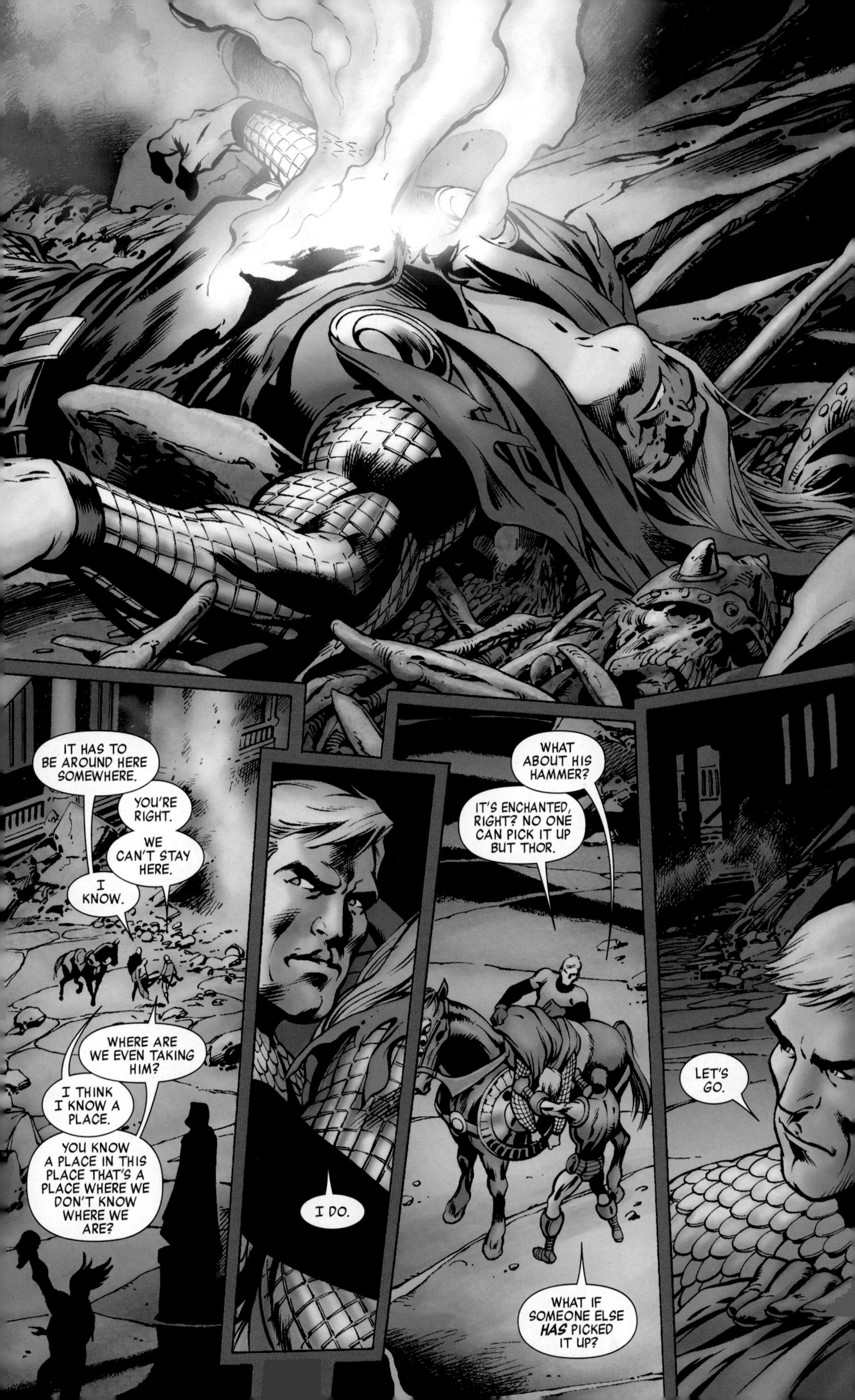
IT HAS TO BE AROUND HERE SOMEWHERE.
YOU'RE RIGHT.
WE CAN'T STAY HERE.
I KNOW.
WHERE ARE WE EVEN TAKING HIM?
I THINK I KNOW A PLACE.
YOU KNOW A PLACE IN THIS PLACE THAT'S A PLACE WHERE WE DON'T KNOW WHERE WE ARE?
I DO.
WHAT ABOUT HIS HAMMER?
IT'S ENCHANTED, RIGHT? NO ONE CAN PICK IT UP BUT THOR.
WHAT IF SOMEONE ELSE HAS PICKED IT UP?
LET'S GO.

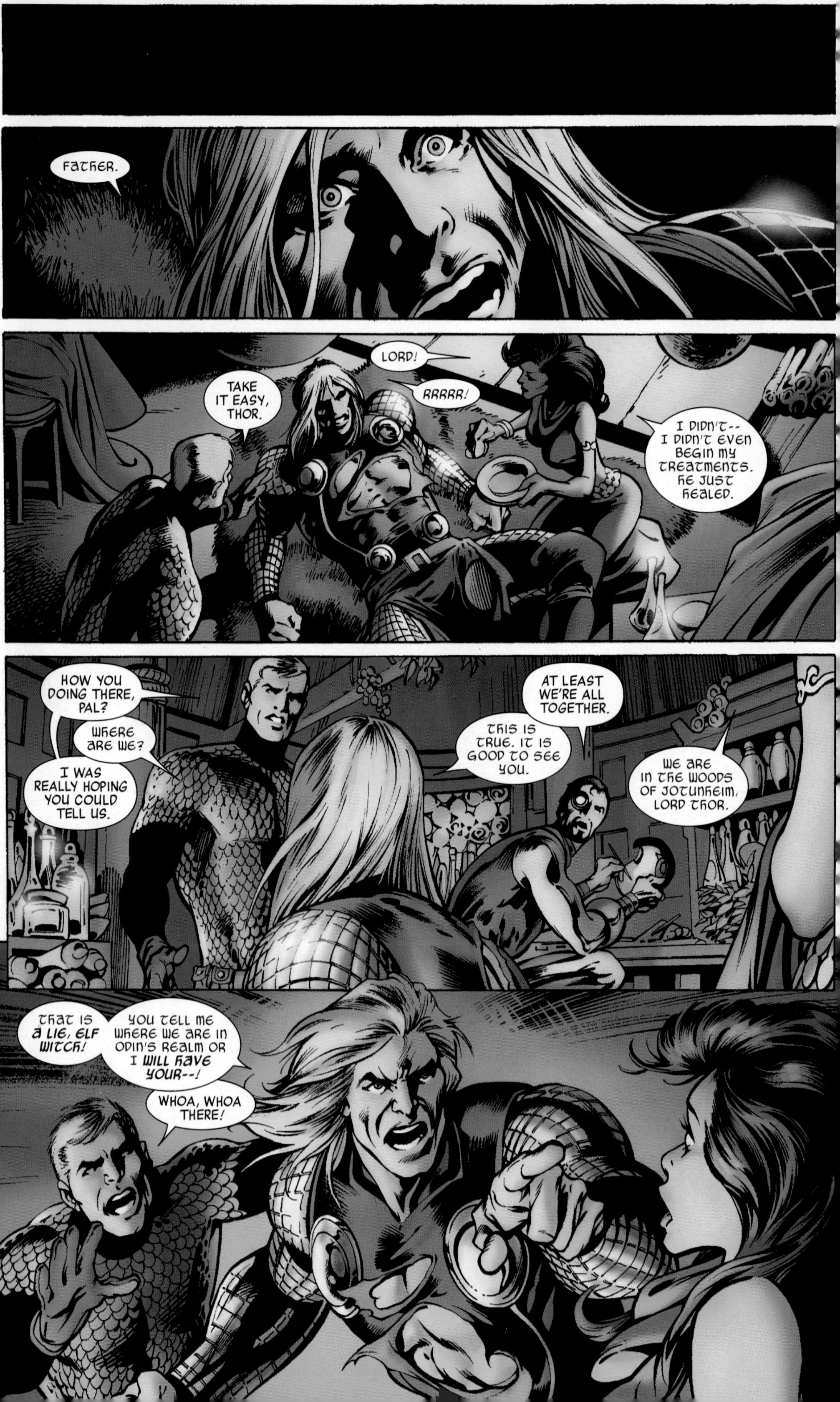
FATHER.
LORD!
TAKE IT EASY, THOR.
RRRRR!
I DIDN'T-- I DIDN'T EVEN BEGIN MY TREATMENTS. HE JUST HEALED.
HOW YOU DOING THERE, PAL?
WHERE ARE WE?
I WAS REALLY HOPING YOU COULD TELL US.
AT LEAST WE'RE ALL TOGETHER.
THIS IS TRUE. IT IS GOOD TO SEE YOU.
WE ARE IN THE WOODS OF JOTUNHEIM, LORD THOR.
THAT IS A LIE, ELF WITCH!
YOU TELL ME WHERE WE ARE IN ODIN'S REALM OR I WILL HAVE YOUR--!
WHOA, WHOA THERE!

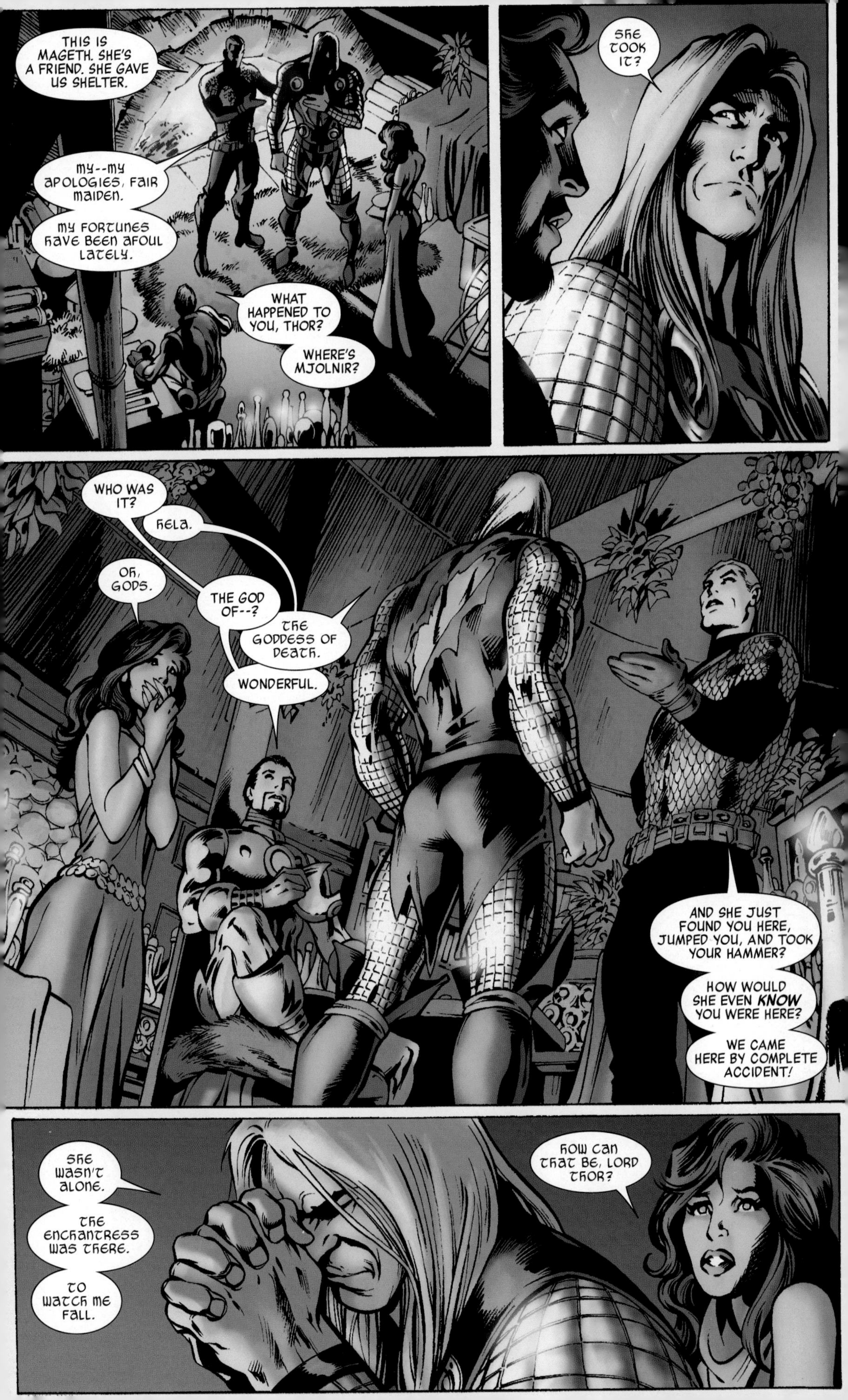
THIS IS MAGETH. SHE'S A FRIEND. SHE GAVE US SHELTER.
MY--MY APOLOGIES, FAIR MAIDEN.
MY FORTUNES HAVE BEEN AFOUL LATELY.
WHAT HAPPENED TO YOU, THOR?
WHERE'S MJOLNIR?
SHE TOOK IT?
WHO WAS IT?
HELA.
OH, GODS.
THE GOD OF--?
THE GODDESS OF DEATH.
WONDERFUL.
AND SHE JUST FOUND YOU HERE, JUMPED YOU, AND TOOK YOUR HAMMER?
HOW WOULD SHE EVEN KNOW YOU WERE HERE?
WE CAME HERE BY COMPLETE ACCIDENT!
SHE WASN'T ALONE.
THE ENCHANTRESS WAS THERE.
TO WATCH ME FALL.
HOW CAN THAT BE, LORD THOR?

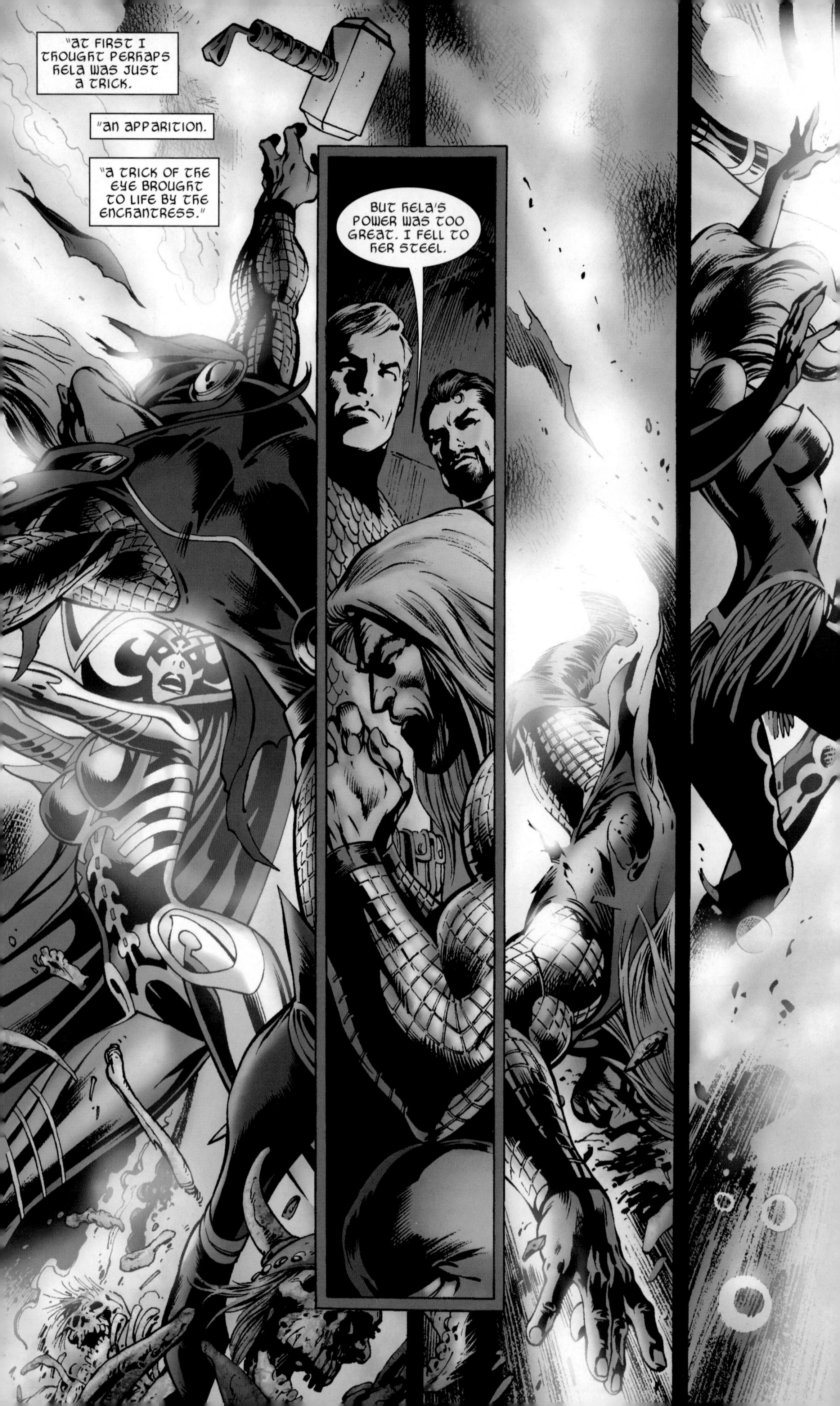
"AT FIRST I THOUGHT PERHAPS HELA WAS JUST A TRICK.
"AN APPARITION.
"A TRICK OF THE EYE BROUGHT TO LIFE BY THE ENCHANTRESS."
BUT HELA'S POWER WAS TOO GREAT. I FELL TO HER STEEL.

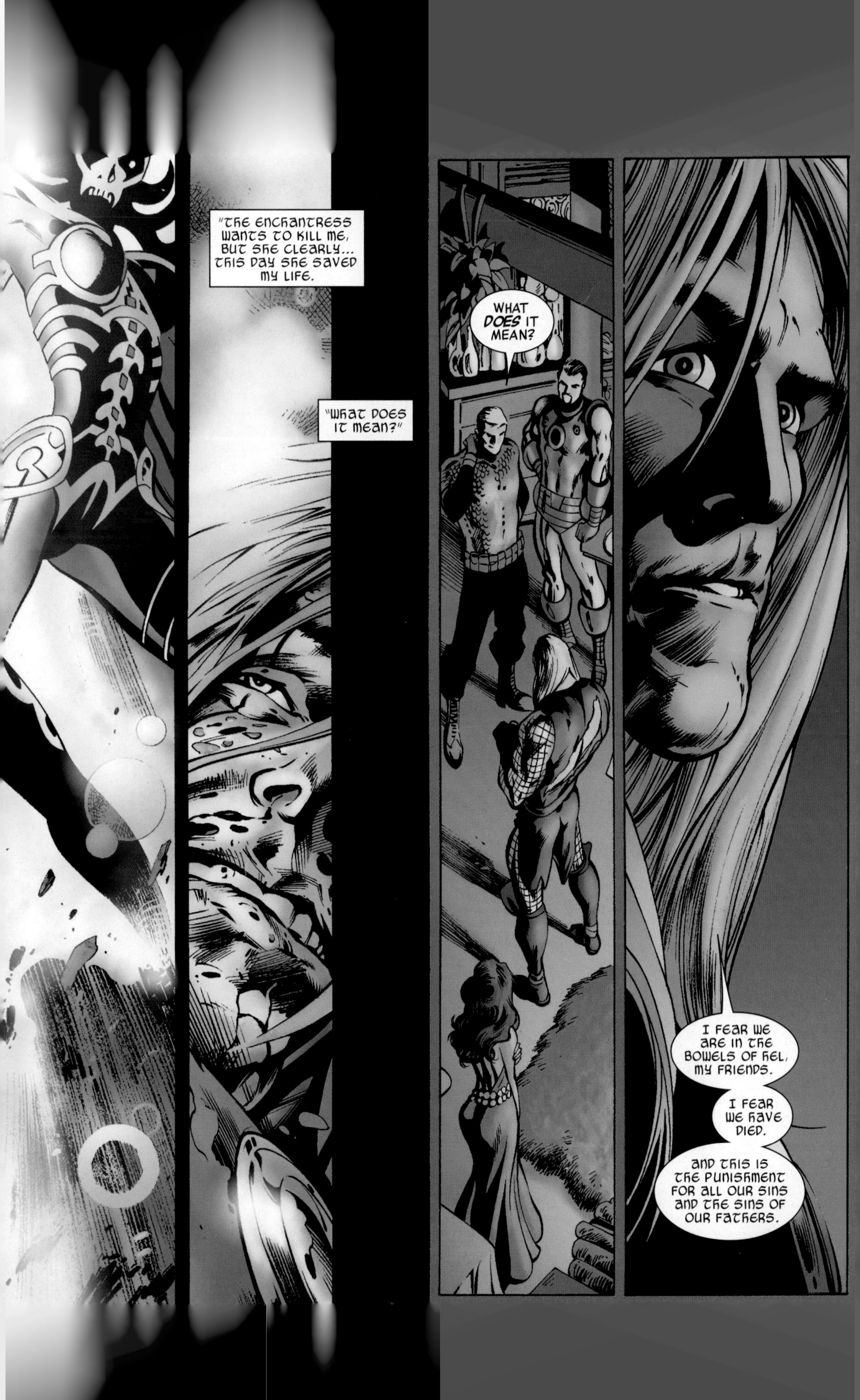
"THE ENCHANTRESS WANTS TO KILL ME, BUT SHE CLEARLY... THIS DAY SHE SAVED MY LIFE.
"WHAT DOES IT MEAN?"
WHAT DOES IT MEAN?
I FEAR WE ARE IN THE BOWELS OF HEL, MY FRIENDS.
I FEAR WE HAVE DIED.
AND THIS IS THE PUNISHMENT FOR ALL OUR SINS AND THE SINS OF OUR FATHERS.

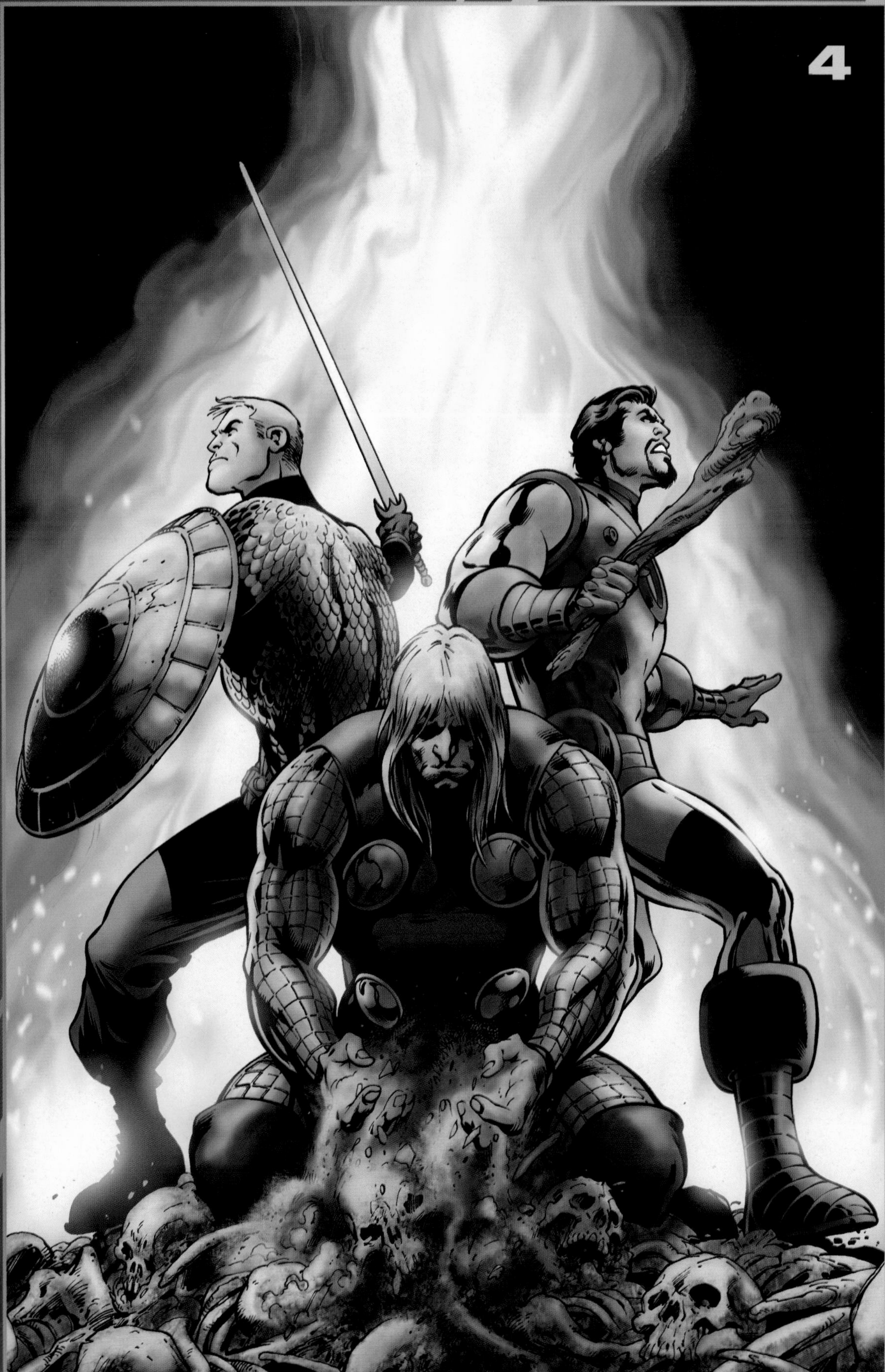
4

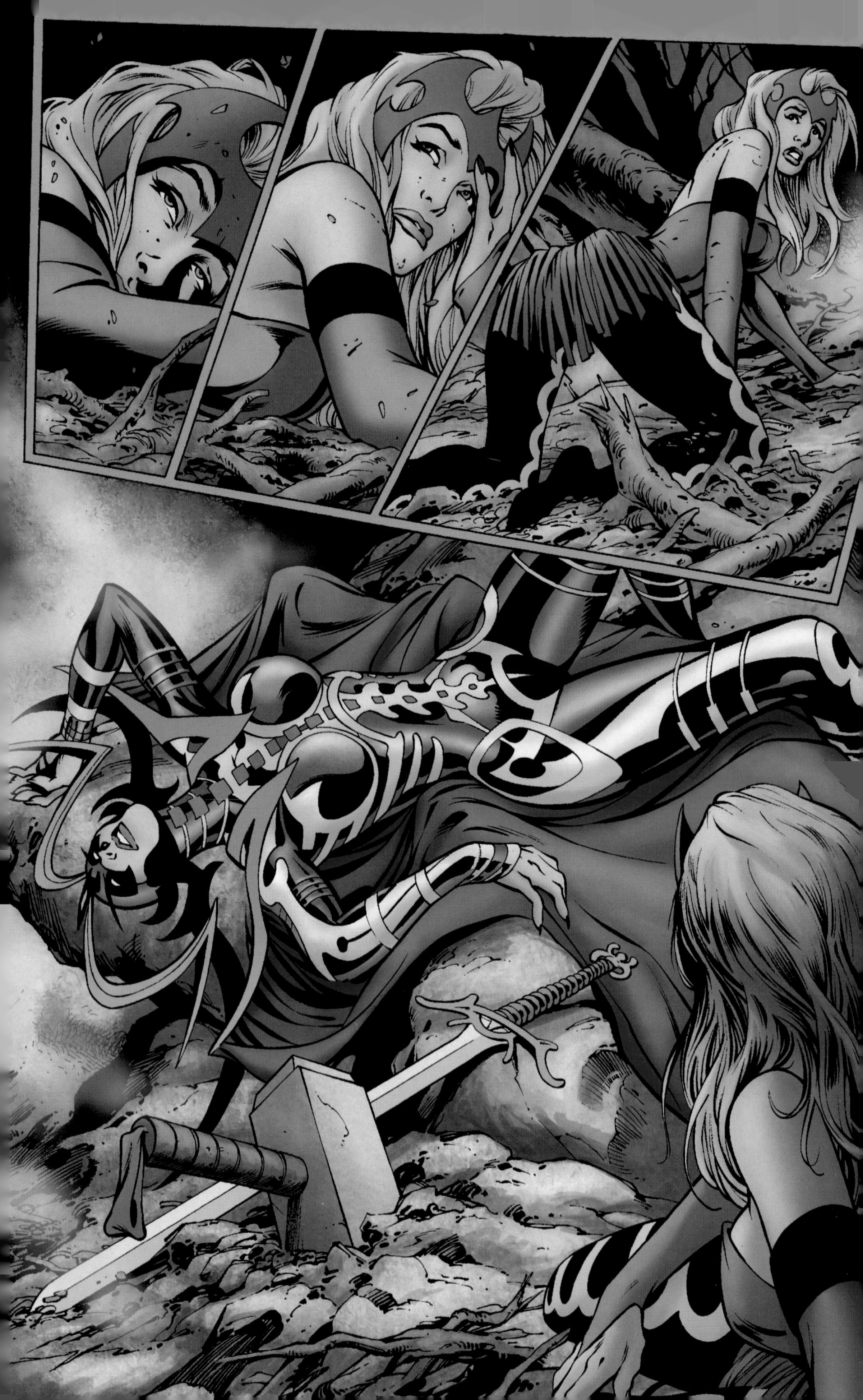

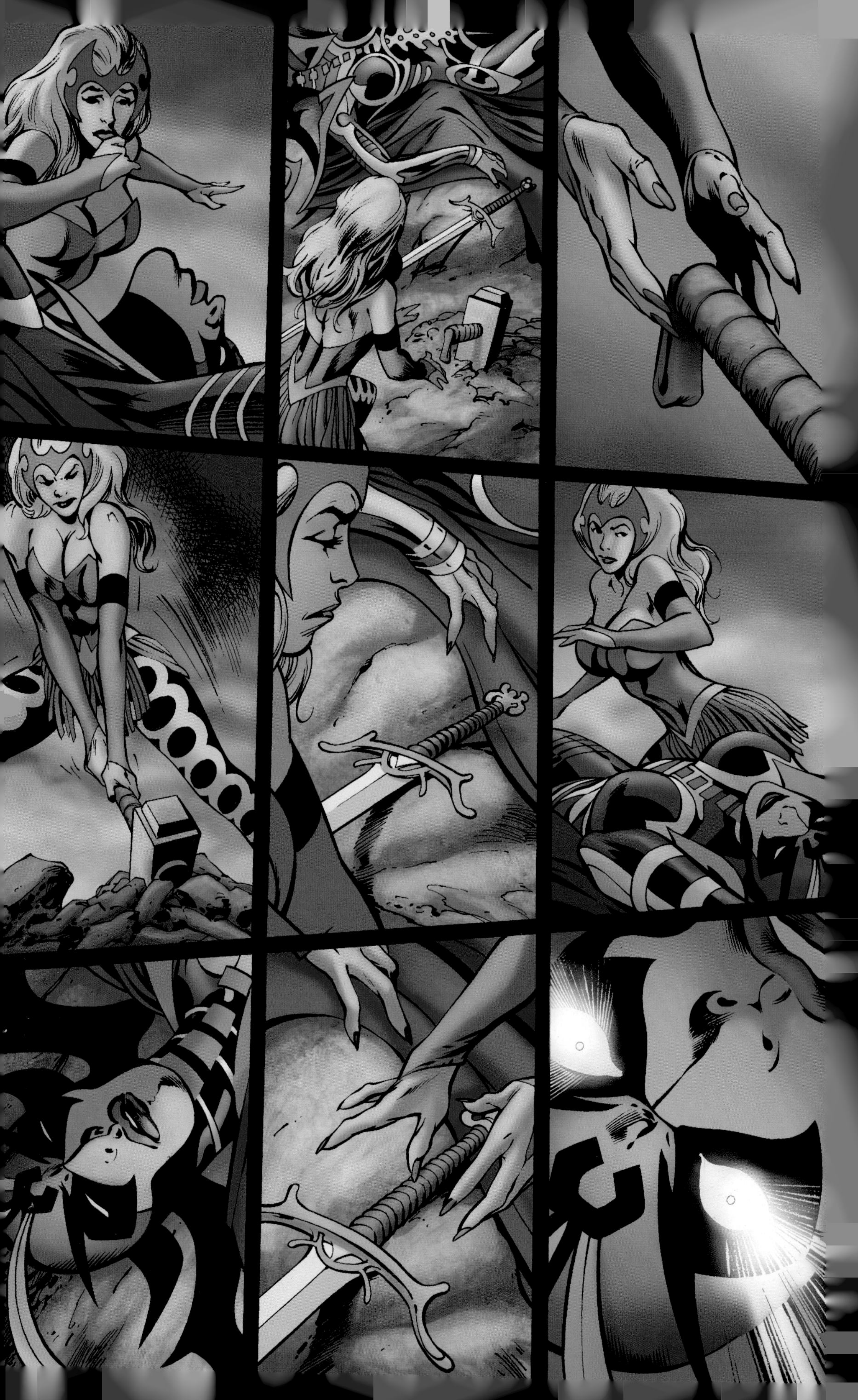

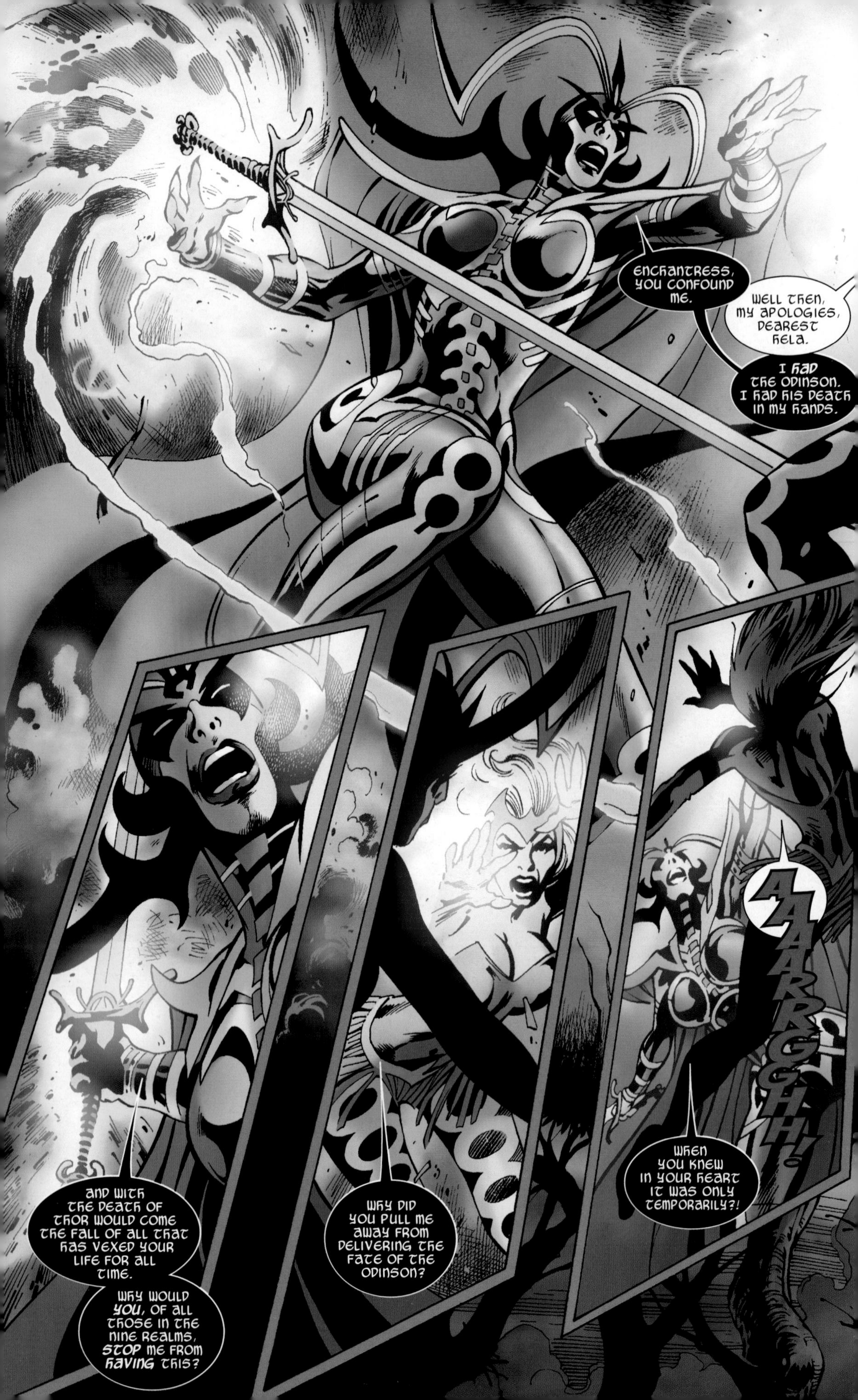
ENCHANTRESS, YOU CONFOUND ME.
WELL THEN, MY APOLOGIES, DEAREST HELA.
I HAD THE ODINSON. I HAD HIS DEATH IN MY HANDS.
AND WITH THE DEATH OF THOR WOULD COME THE FALL OF ALL THAT HAS VEXED YOUR LIFE FOR ALL TIME.
WHY WOULD YOU, OF ALL THOSE IN THE NINE REALMS, STOP ME FROM HAVING THIS?
WHY DID YOU PULL ME AWAY FROM DELIVERING THE FATE OF THE ODINSON?
WHEN YOU KNEW IN YOUR HEART IT WAS ONLY TEMPORARILY?!
AAARRGGHH!

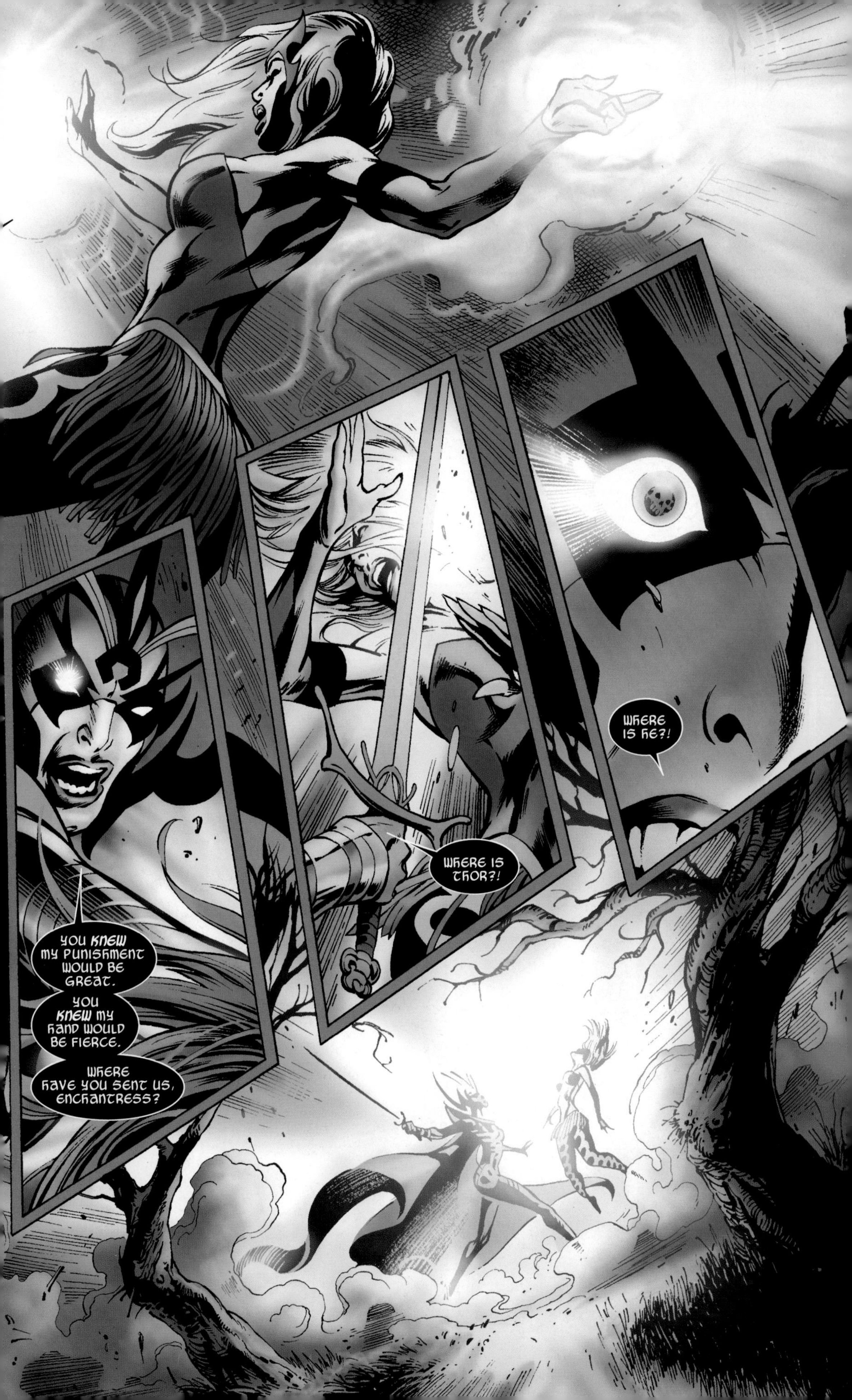

WHERE IS HE?!
WHERE IS THOR?!
YOU KNEW MY PUNISHMENT WOULD BE GREAT.
YOU KNEW MY HAND WOULD BE FIERCE.
WHERE HAVE YOU SENT US, ENCHANTRESS?

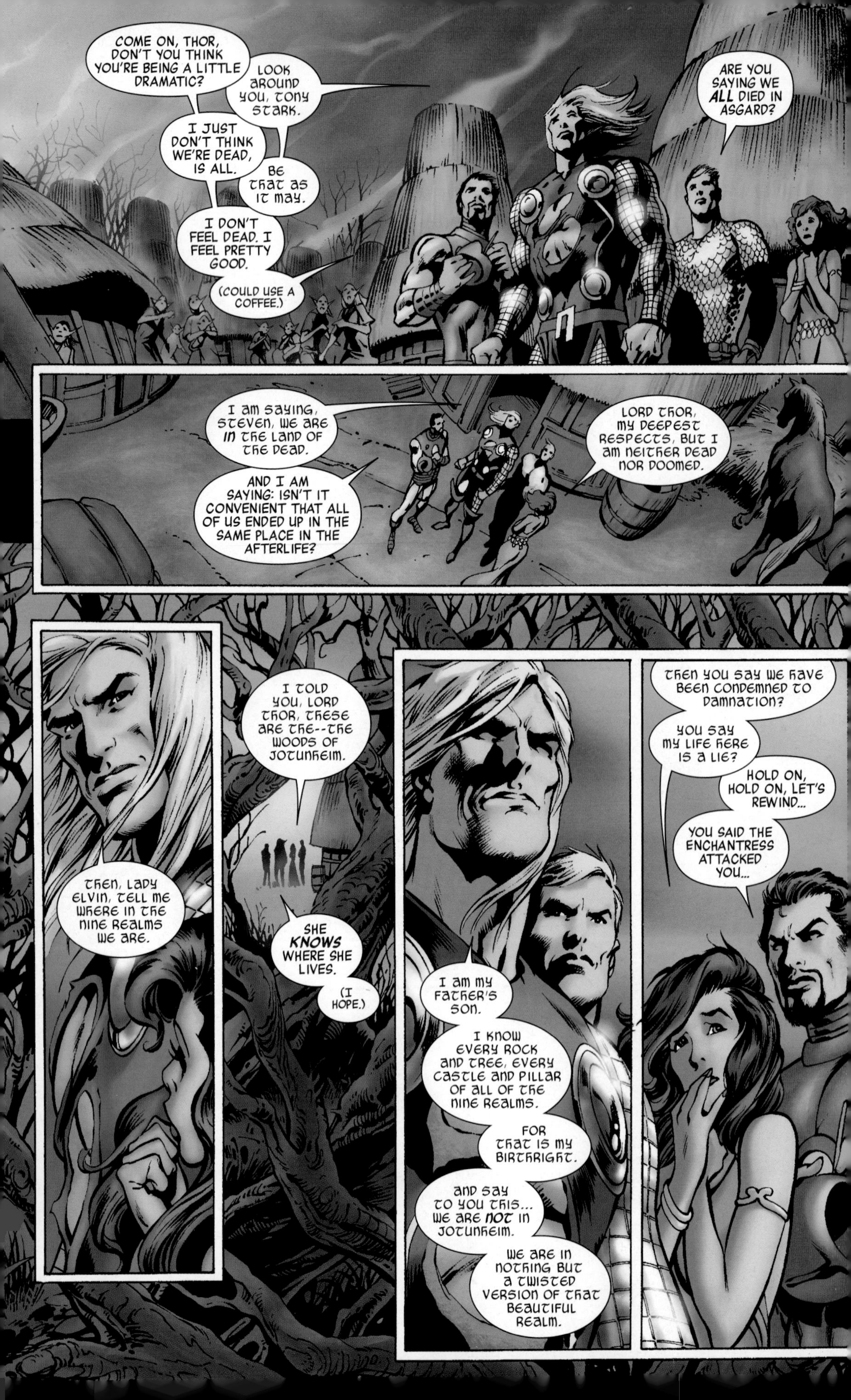
COME ON, THOR, DON'T YOU THINK YOU'RE BEING A LITTLE DRAMATIC?
LOOK AROUND YOU, TONY STARK.
I JUST DON'T THINK WE'RE DEAD, IS ALL.
BE THAT AS IT MAY.
I DON'T FEEL DEAD. I FEEL PRETTY GOOD.
(COULD USE A COFFEE.)
ARE YOU SAYING WE ALL DIED IN ASGARD?
I AM SAYING, STEVEN, WE ARE IN THE LAND OF THE DEAD.
AND I AM SAYING: ISN'T IT CONVENIENT THAT ALL OF US ENDED UP IN THE SAME PLACE IN THE AFTERLIFE?
LORD THOR, MY DEEPEST RESPECTS, BUT I AM NEITHER DEAD NOR DOOMED.
THEN, LADY ELVIN, TELL ME WHERE IN THE NINE REALMS WE ARE.
I TOLD YOU, LORD THOR, THESE ARE THE--THE WOODS OF JOTUNHEIM.
SHE KNOWS WHERE SHE LIVES.
(I HOPE.)
I AM MY FATHER'S SON.
I KNOW EVERY ROCK AND TREE, EVERY CASTLE AND PILLAR OF ALL OF THE NINE REALMS.
FOR THAT IS MY BIRTHRIGHT.
AND SAY TO YOU THIS... WE ARE NOT IN JOTUNHEIM.
WE ARE IN NOTHING BUT A TWISTED VERSION OF THAT BEAUTIFUL REALM.
THEN YOU SAY WE HAVE BEEN CONDEMNED TO DAMNATION?
YOU SAY MY LIFE HERE IS A LIE?
HOLD ON, HOLD ON, LET'S REWIND...
YOU SAID THE ENCHANTRESS ATTACKED YOU...

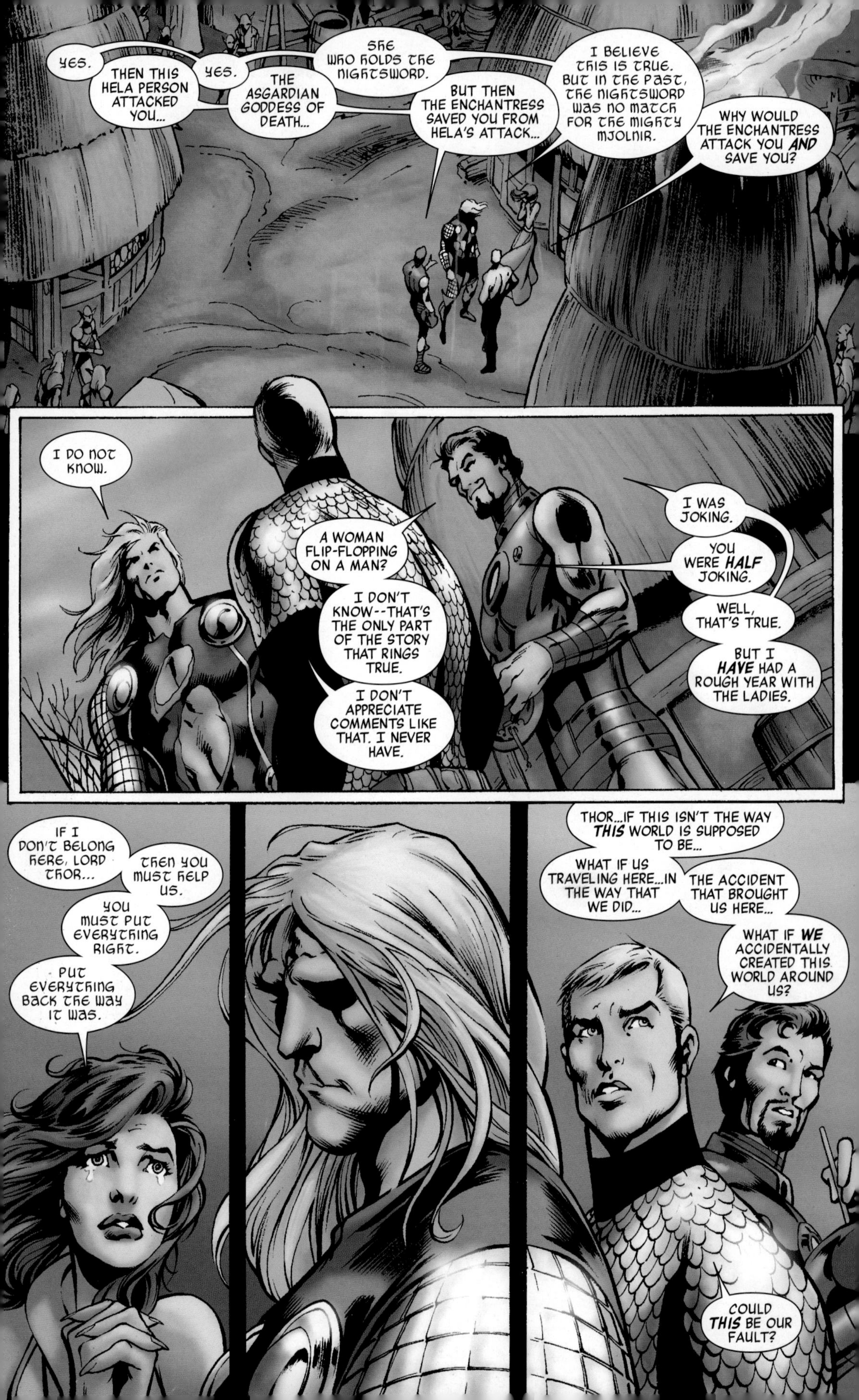

YES.
THEN THIS HELA PERSON ATTACKED YOU...
YES.
THE ASGARDIAN GODDESS OF DEATH...
SHE WHO HOLDS THE NIGHTSWORD.
BUT THEN THE ENCHANTRESS SAVED YOU FROM HELA'S ATTACK...
I BELIEVE THIS IS TRUE. BUT IN THE PAST, THE NIGHTSWORD WAS NO MATCH FOR THE MIGHTY MJOLNIR.
WHY WOULD THE ENCHANTRESS ATTACK YOU AND SAVE YOU?
I DO NOT KNOW.
A WOMAN FLIP-FLOPPING ON A MAN?
I DON'T KNOW--THAT'S THE ONLY PART OF THE STORY THAT RINGS TRUE.
I DON'T APPRECIATE COMMENTS LIKE THAT. I NEVER HAVE.
I WAS JOKING.
YOU WERE HALF JOKING.
WELL, THAT'S TRUE.
BUT I HAVE HAD A ROUGH YEAR WITH THE LADIES.
IF I DON'T BELONG HERE, LORD THOR...
THEN YOU MUST HELP US.
YOU MUST PUT EVERYTHING RIGHT.
PUT EVERYTHING BACK THE WAY IT WAS.
THOR...IF THIS ISN'T THE WAY THIS WORLD IS SUPPOSED TO BE...
WHAT IF US TRAVELING HERE...IN THE WAY THAT WE DID...
THE ACCIDENT THAT BROUGHT US HERE...
WHAT IF WE ACCIDENTALLY CREATED THIS WORLD AROUND US?
COULD THIS BE OUR FAULT?

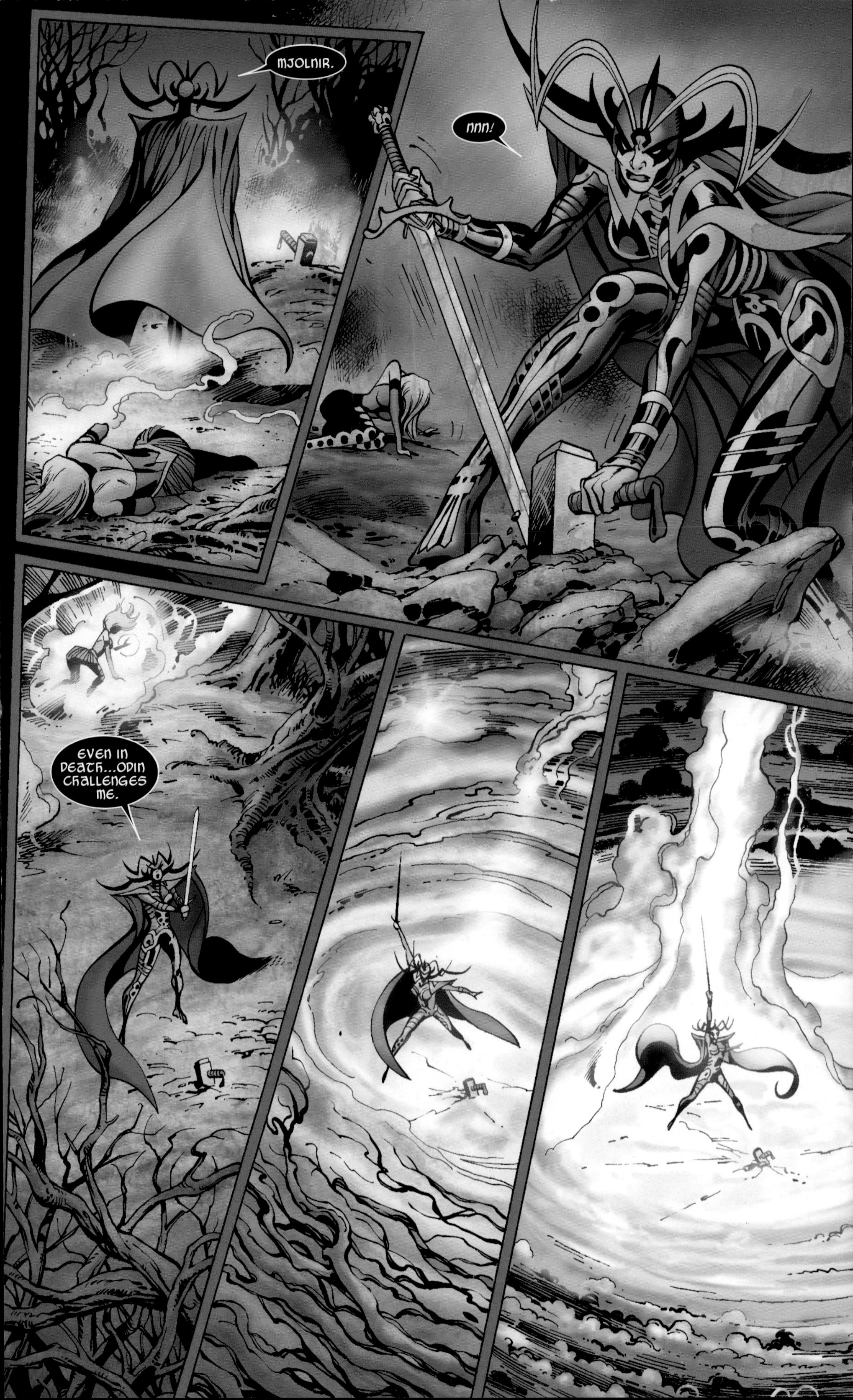
MJOLNIR.
NNN!
EVEN IN DEATH...ODIN CHALLENGES ME.

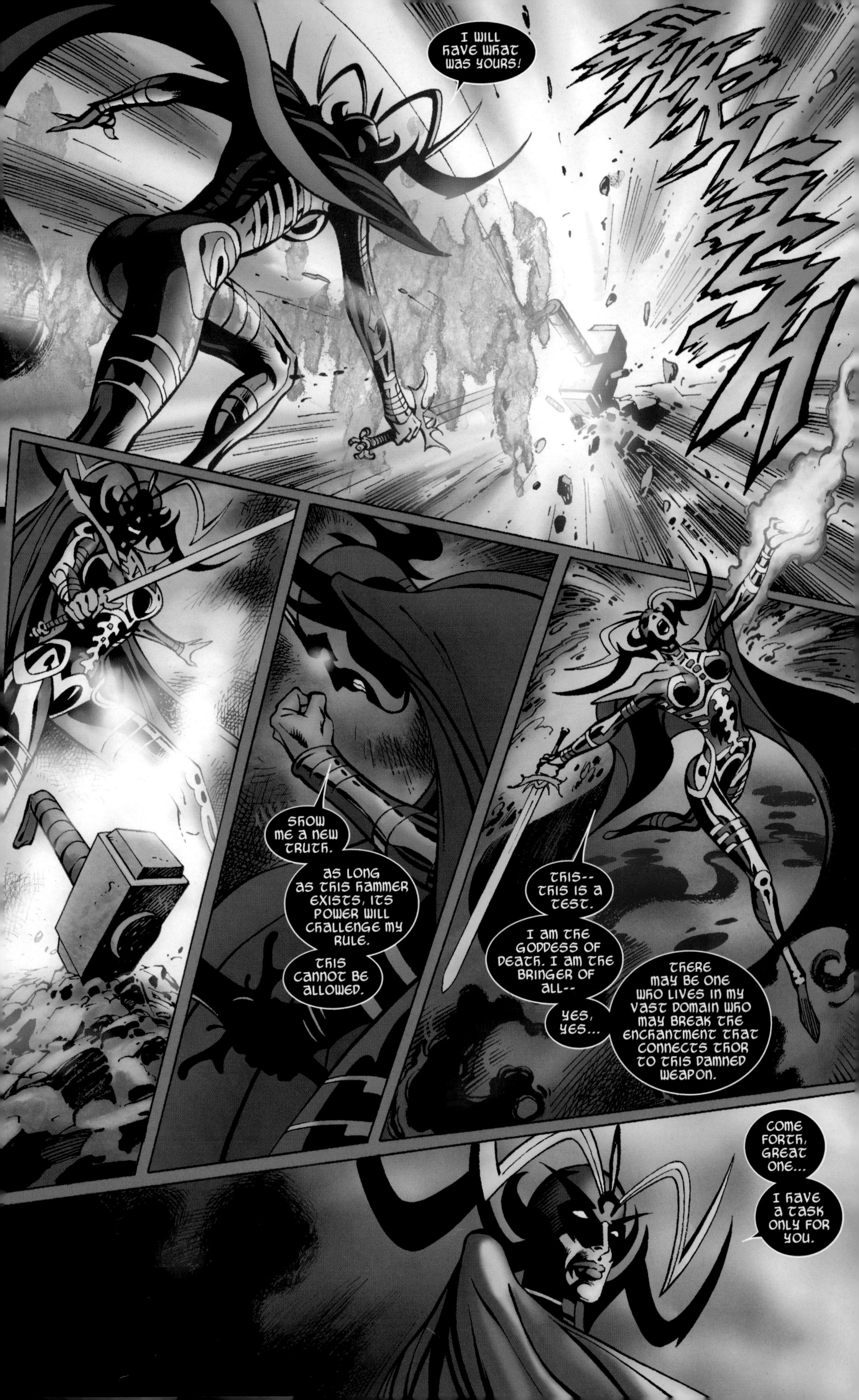
I WILL HAVE WHAT WAS YOURS!
SHOW ME A NEW TRUTH.
AS LONG AS THIS HAMMER EXISTS, ITS POWER WILL CHALLENGE MY RULE.
THIS CANNOT BE ALLOWED.
THIS-- THIS IS A TEST.
I AM THE GODDESS OF DEATH. I AM THE BRINGER OF ALL--
YES, YES...
THERE MAY BE ONE WHO LIVES IN MY VAST DOMAIN WHO MAY BREAK THE ENCHANTMENT THAT CONNECTS THOR TO THIS DAMNED WEAPON.
COME FORTH, GREAT ONE...
I HAVE A TASK ONLY FOR YOU.

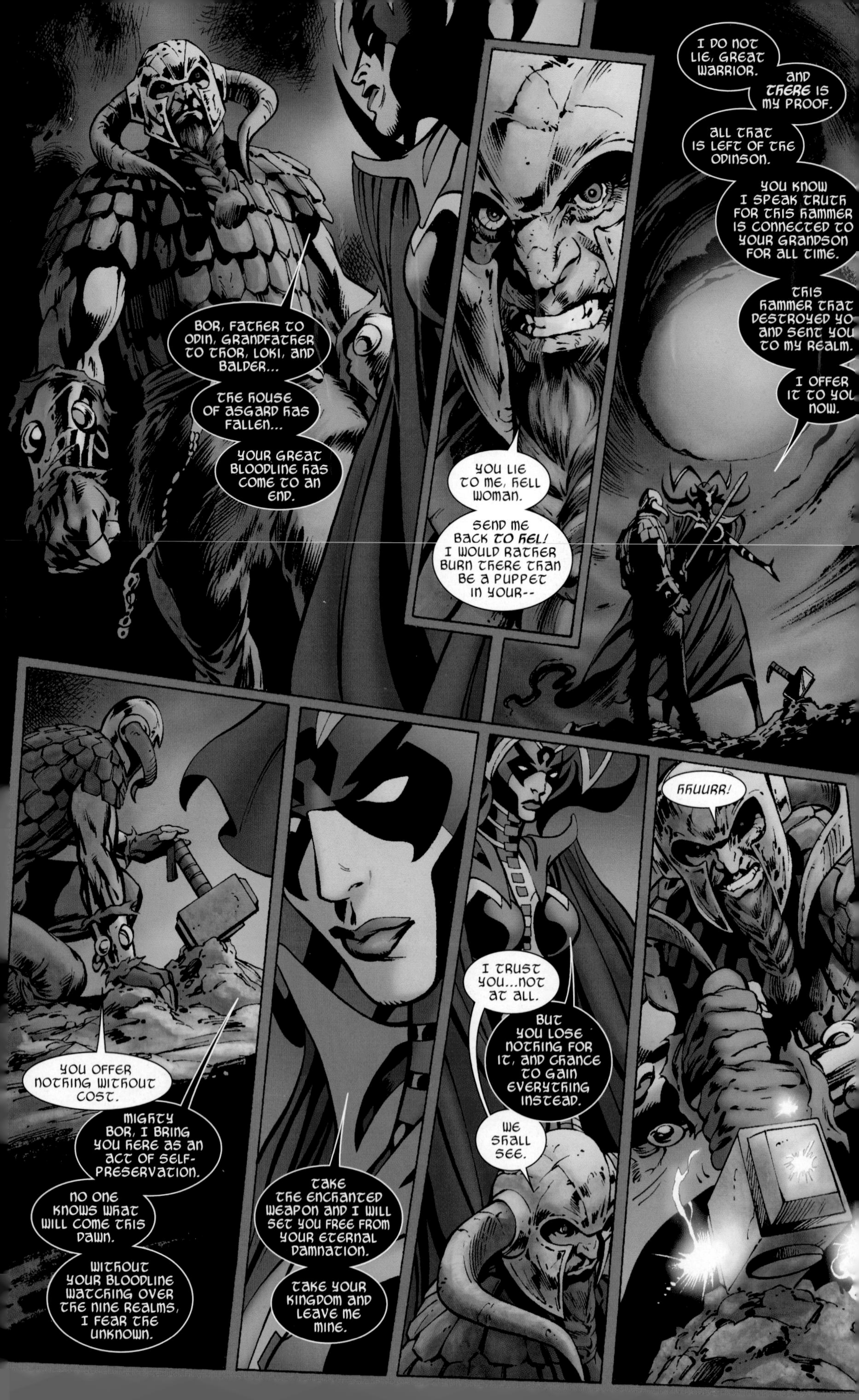
BOR, FATHER TO ODIN, GRANDFATHER TO THOR, LOKI, AND BALDER...
THE HOUSE OF ASGARD HAS FALLEN...
YOUR GREAT BLOODLINE HAS COME TO AN END.
YOU LIE TO ME, HELL WOMAN.
SEND ME BACK TO HEL! I WOULD RATHER BURN THERE THAN BE A PUPPET IN YOUR--
I DO NOT LIE, GREAT WARRIOR.
AND THERE IS MY PROOF.
ALL THAT IS LEFT OF THE ODINSON.
YOU KNOW I SPEAK TRUTH FOR THIS HAMMER IS CONNECTED TO YOUR GRANDSON FOR ALL TIME.
I OFFER IT TO YOU NOW.
YOU OFFER NOTHING WITHOUT COST.
MIGHTY BOR, I BRING YOU HERE AS AN ACT OF SELF-PRESERVATION.
NO ONE KNOWS WHAT WILL COME THIS DAWN.
WITHOUT YOUR BLOODLINE WATCHING OVER THE NINE REALMS, I FEAR THE UNKNOWN.
TAKE THE ENCHANTED WEAPON AND I WILL SET YOU FREE FROM YOUR ETERNAL DAMNATION.
TAKE YOUR KINGDOM AND LEAVE ME MINE.
I TRUST YOU...NOT AT ALL.
BUT YOU LOSE NOTHING FOR IT, AND CHANCE TO GAIN EVERYTHING INSTEAD.
WE SHALL SEE.
HHUURR!

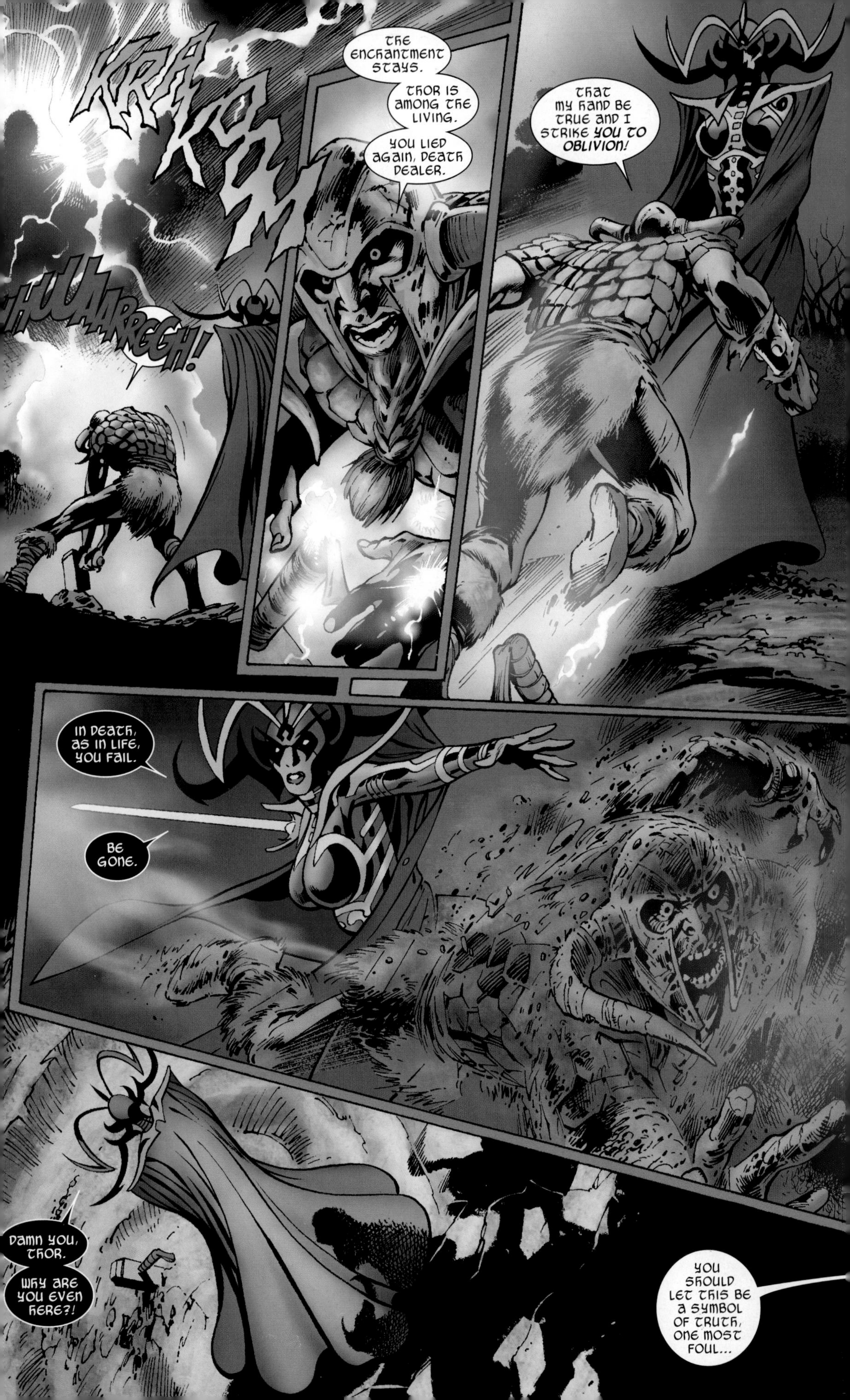
KRA KOOM
THE ENCHANTMENT STAYS.
THOR IS AMONG THE LIVING.
YOU LIED AGAIN, DEATH DEALER.
THAT MY HAND BE TRUE AND I STRIKE YOU TO OBLIVION!
HUUAARRGGH!
IN DEATH, AS IN LIFE, YOU FAIL.
BE GONE.
DAMN YOU, THOR.
WHY ARE YOU EVEN HERE?!
YOU SHOULD LET THIS BE A SYMBOL OF TRUTH, ONE MOST FOUL...

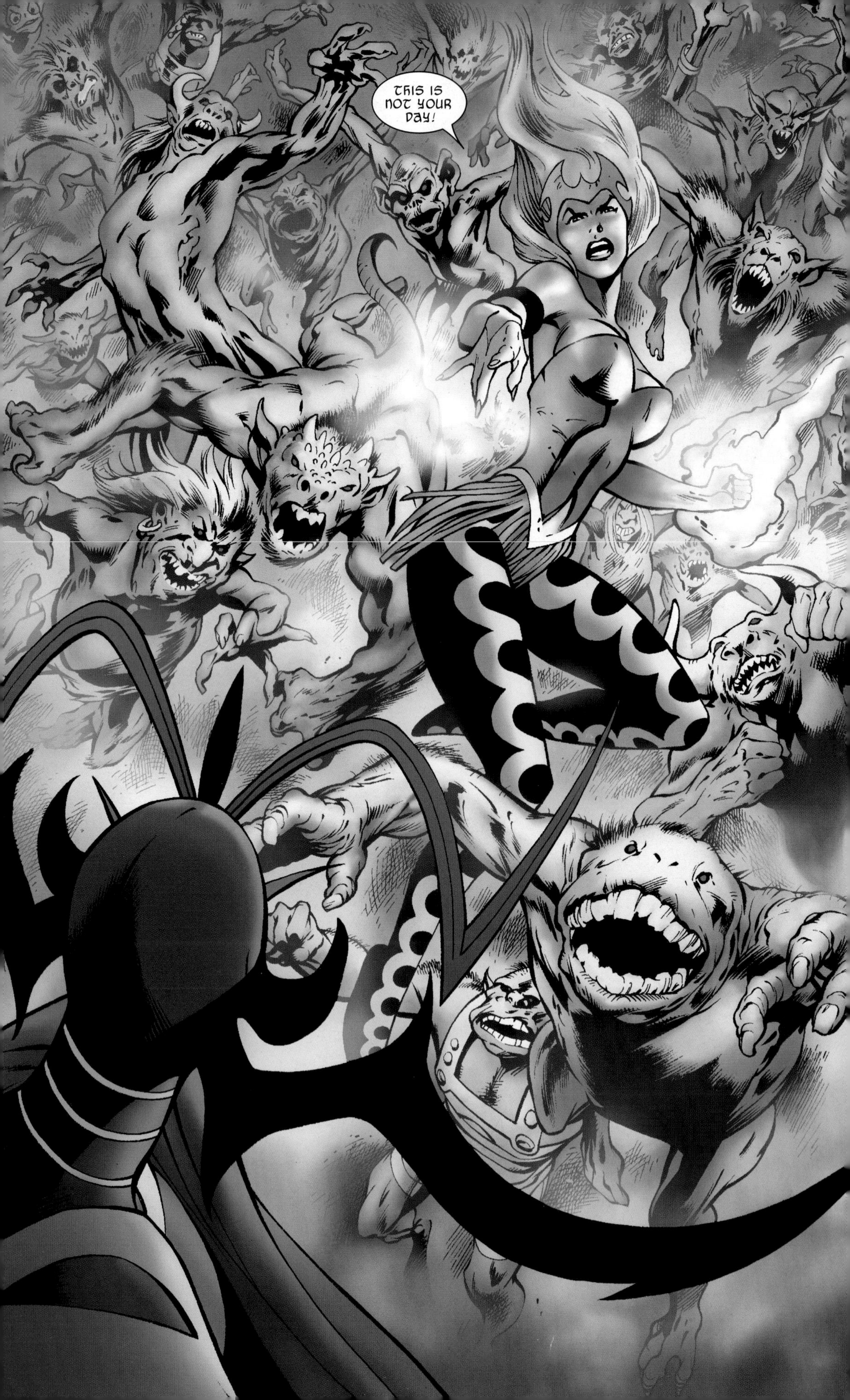
THIS IS NOT YOUR DAY!

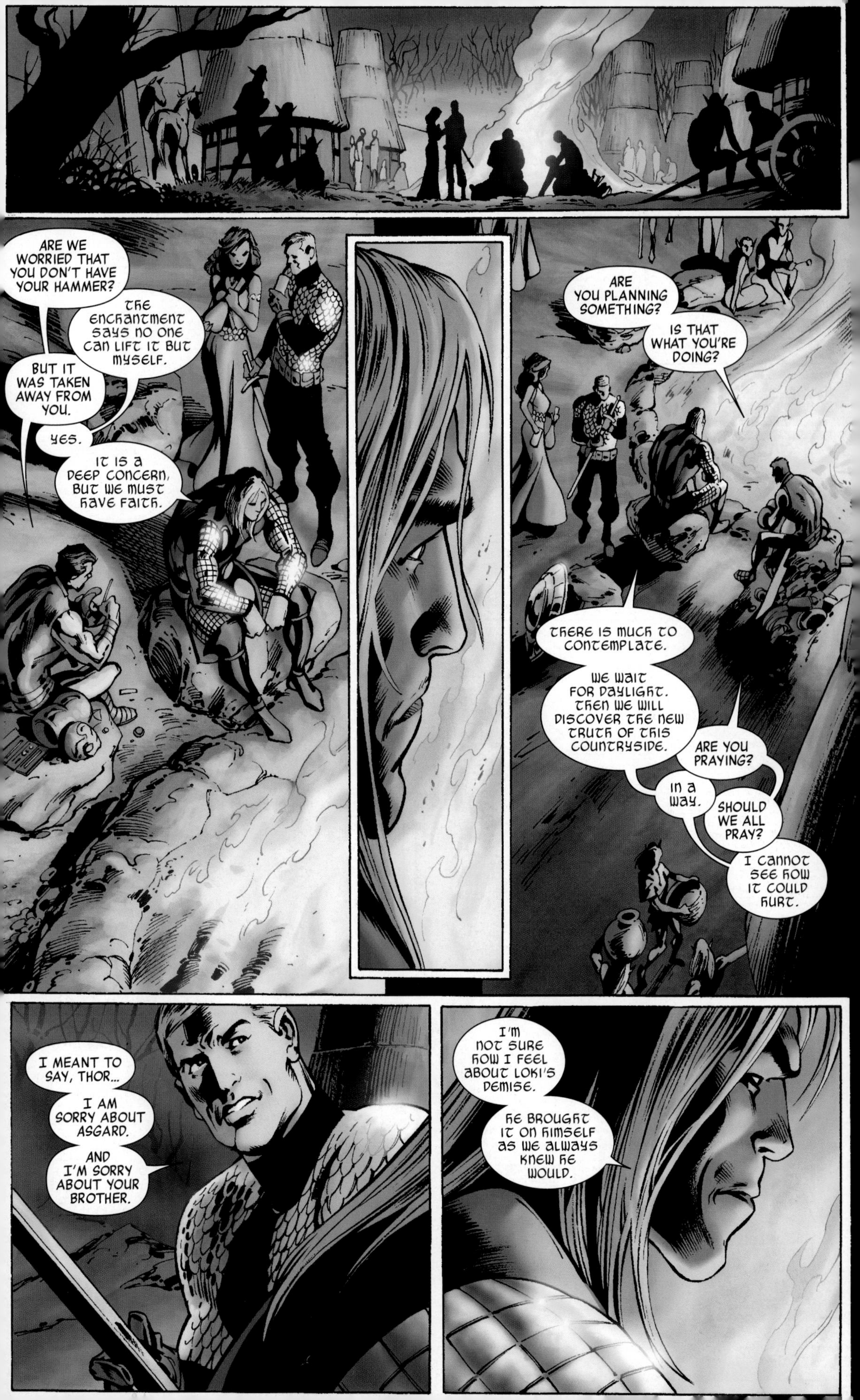
ARE WE WORRIED THAT YOU DON'T HAVE YOUR HAMMER?
THE ENCHANTMENT SAYS NO ONE CAN LIFT IT BUT MYSELF.
BUT IT WAS TAKEN AWAY FROM YOU.
YES.
IT IS A DEEP CONCERN, BUT WE MUST HAVE FAITH.
ARE YOU PLANNING SOMETHING?
IS THAT WHAT YOU'RE DOING?
THERE IS MUCH TO CONTEMPLATE.
WE WAIT FOR DAYLIGHT. THEN WE WILL DISCOVER THE NEW TRUTH OF THIS COUNTRYSIDE.
ARE YOU PRAYING?
IN A WAY.
SHOULD WE ALL PRAY?
I CANNOT SEE HOW IT COULD HURT.
I MEANT TO SAY, THOR...
I AM SORRY ABOUT ASGARD.
AND I'M SORRY ABOUT YOUR BROTHER.
I'M NOT SURE HOW I FEEL ABOUT LOKI'S DEMISE.
HE BROUGHT IT ON HIMSELF AS WE ALWAYS KNEW HE WOULD.

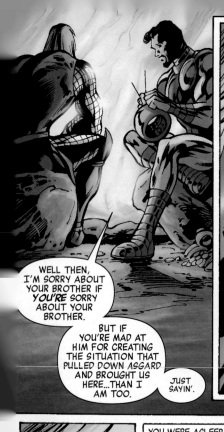

WELL THEN, I'M SORRY ABOUT YOUR BROTHER IF *YOU'RE* SORRY ABOUT YOUR BROTHER.

BUT IF YOU'RE MAD AT HIM FOR CREATING THE SITUATION THAT PULLED DOWN ASGARD AND BROUGHT US HERE...THAN I AM TOO.

JUST SAYIN'.

YOU KNOW...

IF NOT FOR THE FACT THAT WE MAY BE *DEAD,* AND WE DON'T KNOW WHERE WE *ARE,* AND THE *GOBLINS* AND THE *DRAGONS* AND THE *ELVES...*

OR THE FACT THAT THERE'S NO *BATHROOM...*

THIS IS ACTUALLY KIND OF *NICE.*

YOU WERE ASLEEP FROM WORLD WAR TWO UP UNTIL THE DAY BEFORE YESTERDAY.

WHAT DO *YOU* NEED A VACATION FOR?

THAT'S TRUE, TOO.

HEY, I'VE BEEN MEANING TO ASK YOU...

YES. PATSY WALKER. SHE WAS AN AVENGER FOR TEN MINUTES.

I REMEMBER.

YOU GUYS EVER HOOK UP?

IS THIS GOING TO START ANOTHER FIGHT?

REMEMBER HELLCAT?

I'VE NEVER BEEN ON A REAL VACATION.

I GUESS THIS IS AS CLOSE AS I'M LIKELY TO GET.

WHAT?

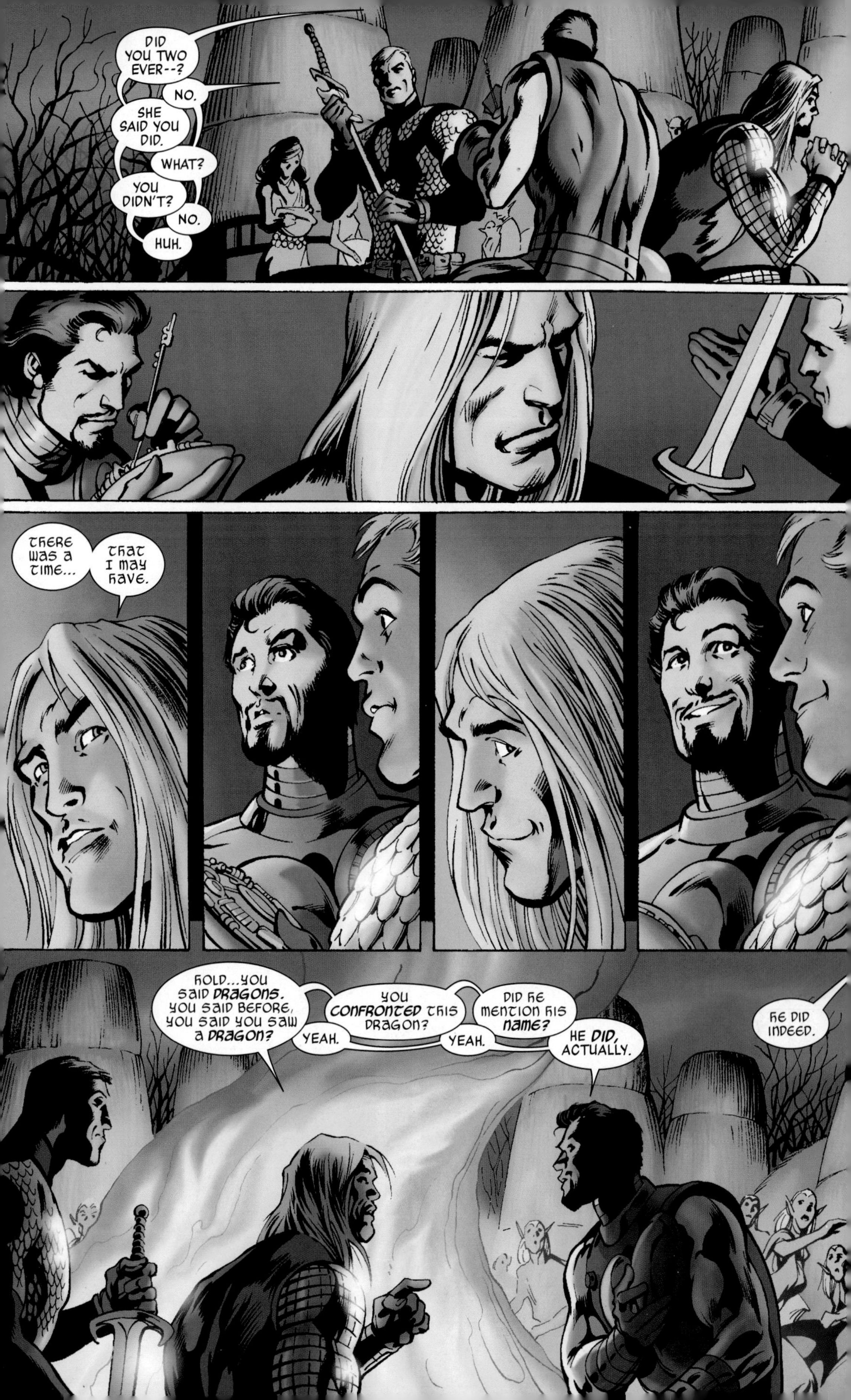
DID YOU TWO EVER--?
NO.
SHE SAID YOU DID.
WHAT?
YOU DIDN'T?
NO.
HUH.
THERE WAS A TIME...
THAT I MAY HAVE.
HOLD...YOU SAID DRAGONS. YOU SAID BEFORE, YOU SAID YOU SAW A DRAGON?
YEAH.
YOU CONFRONTED THIS DRAGON?
YEAH.
DID HE MENTION HIS NAME?
HE DID, ACTUALLY.
HE DID INDEED.

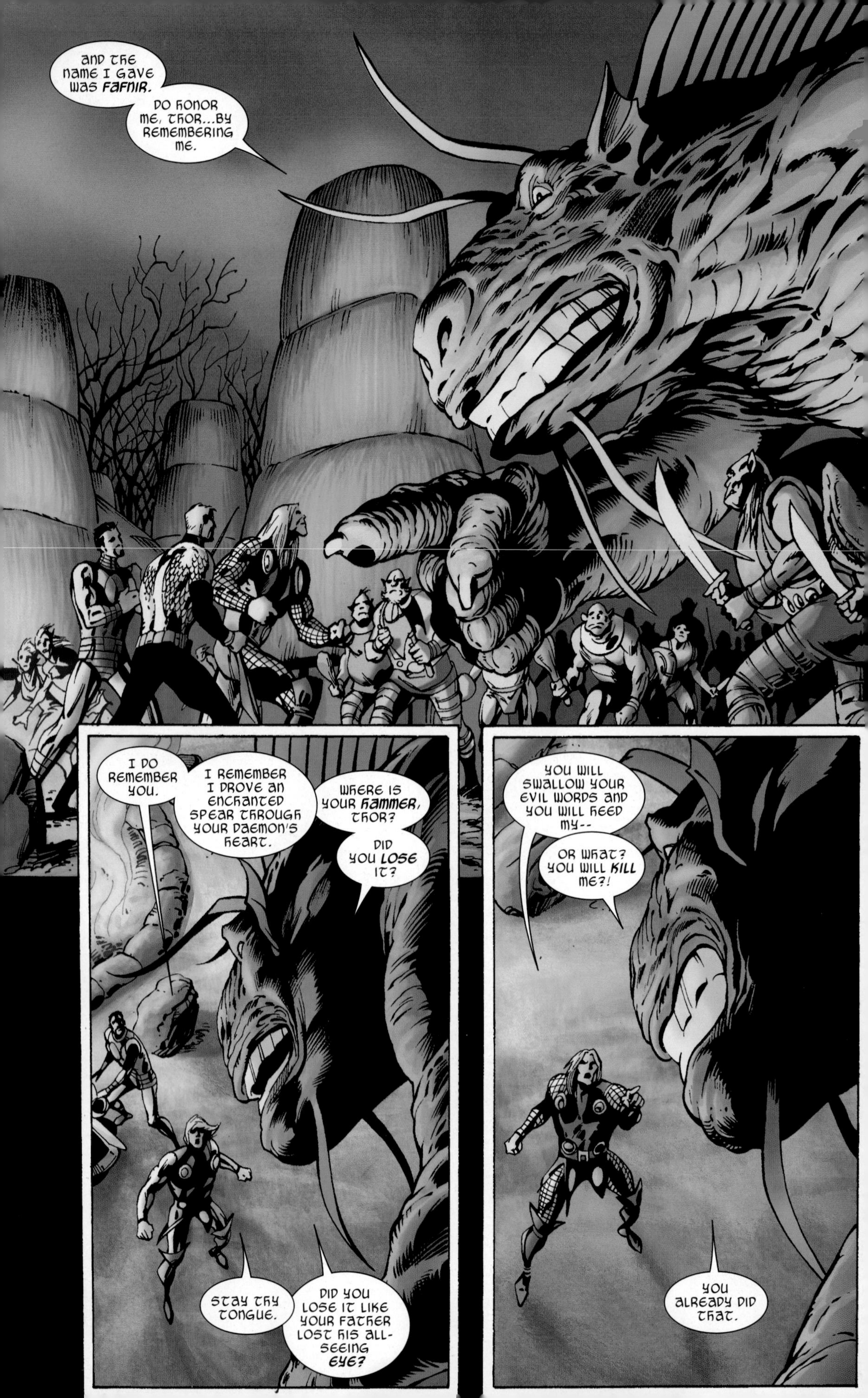
AND THE NAME I GAVE WAS FAFNIR.
DO HONOR ME, THOR...BY REMEMBERING ME.
I DO REMEMBER YOU.
I REMEMBER I DROVE AN ENCHANTED SPEAR THROUGH YOUR DAEMON'S HEART.
WHERE IS YOUR HAMMER, THOR?
DID YOU LOSE IT?
STAY THY TONGUE.
DID YOU LOSE IT LIKE YOUR FATHER LOST HIS ALL-SEEING EYE?
YOU WILL SWALLOW YOUR EVIL WORDS AND YOU WILL HEED MY--
OR WHAT? YOU WILL KILL ME?!
YOU ALREADY DID THAT.

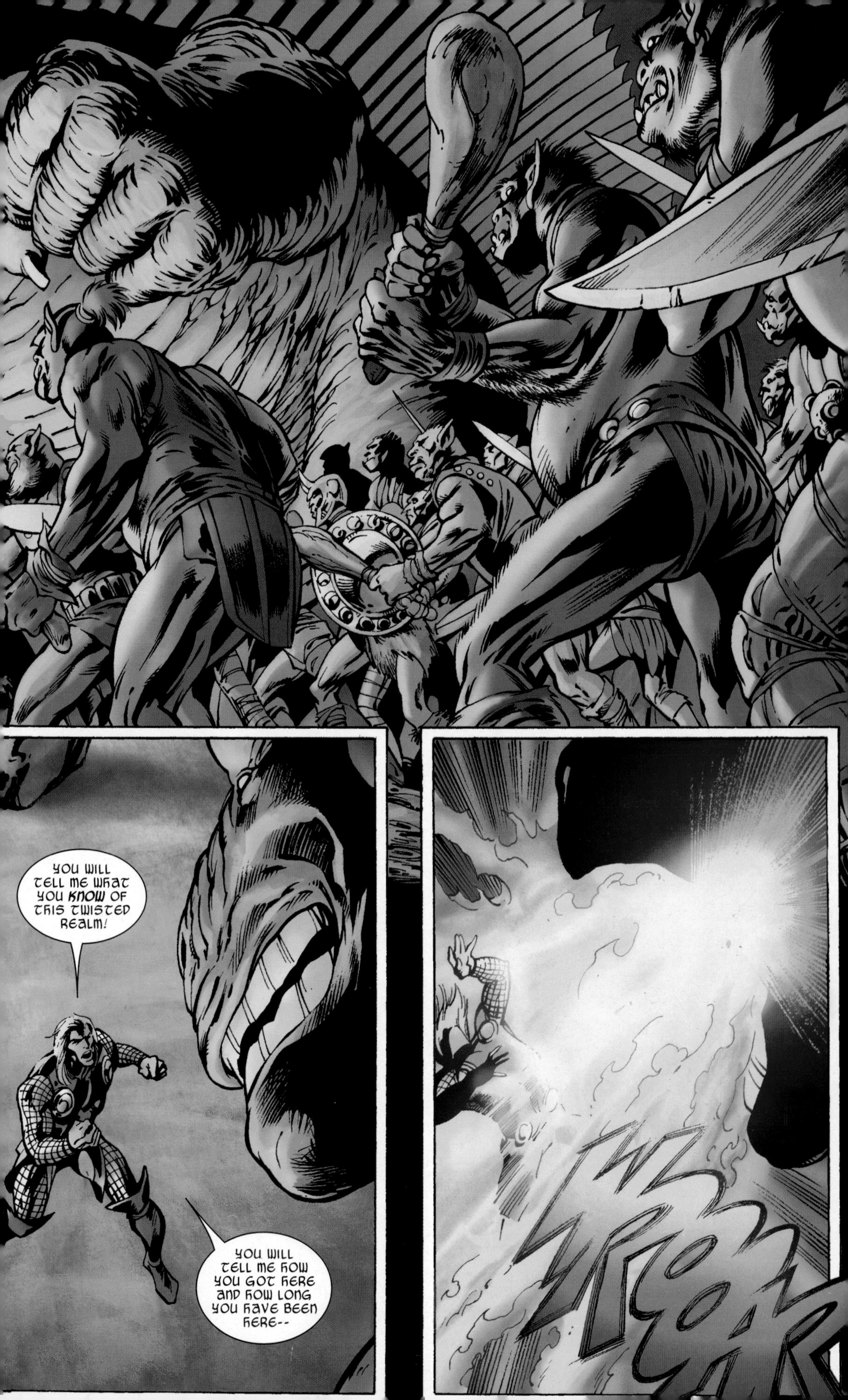
YOU WILL TELL ME WHAT YOU KNOW OF THIS TWISTED REALM!
YOU WILL TELL ME HOW YOU GOT HERE AND HOW LONG YOU HAVE BEEN HERE--

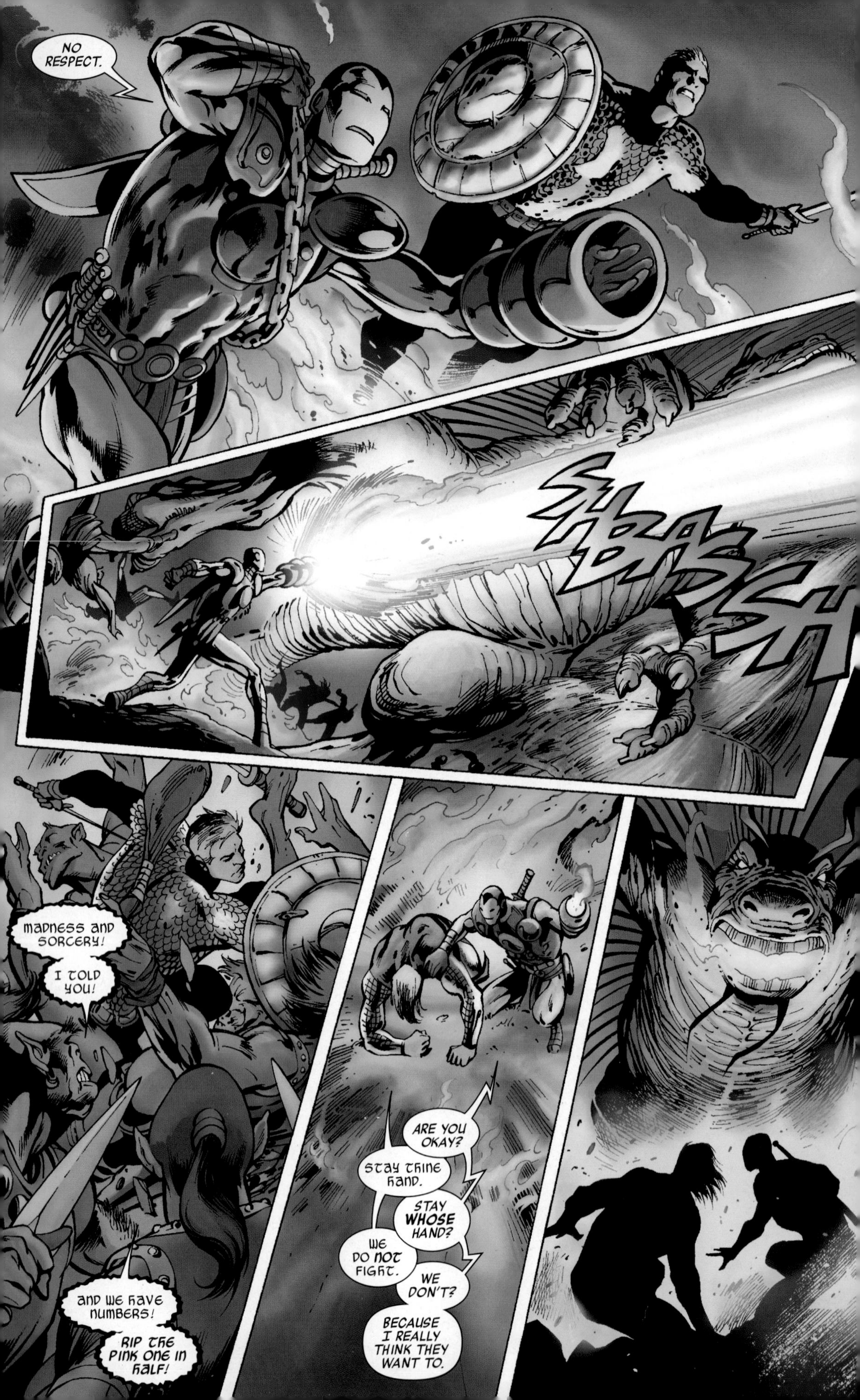
NO RESPECT.
SHRASSH
MADNESS AND SORCERY!
I TOLD YOU!
AND WE HAVE NUMBERS!
RIP THE PINK ONE IN HALF!
ARE YOU OKAY?
STAY THINE HAND.
STAY WHOSE HAND?
WE DO NOT FIGHT.
WE DON'T?
BECAUSE I REALLY THINK THEY WANT TO.

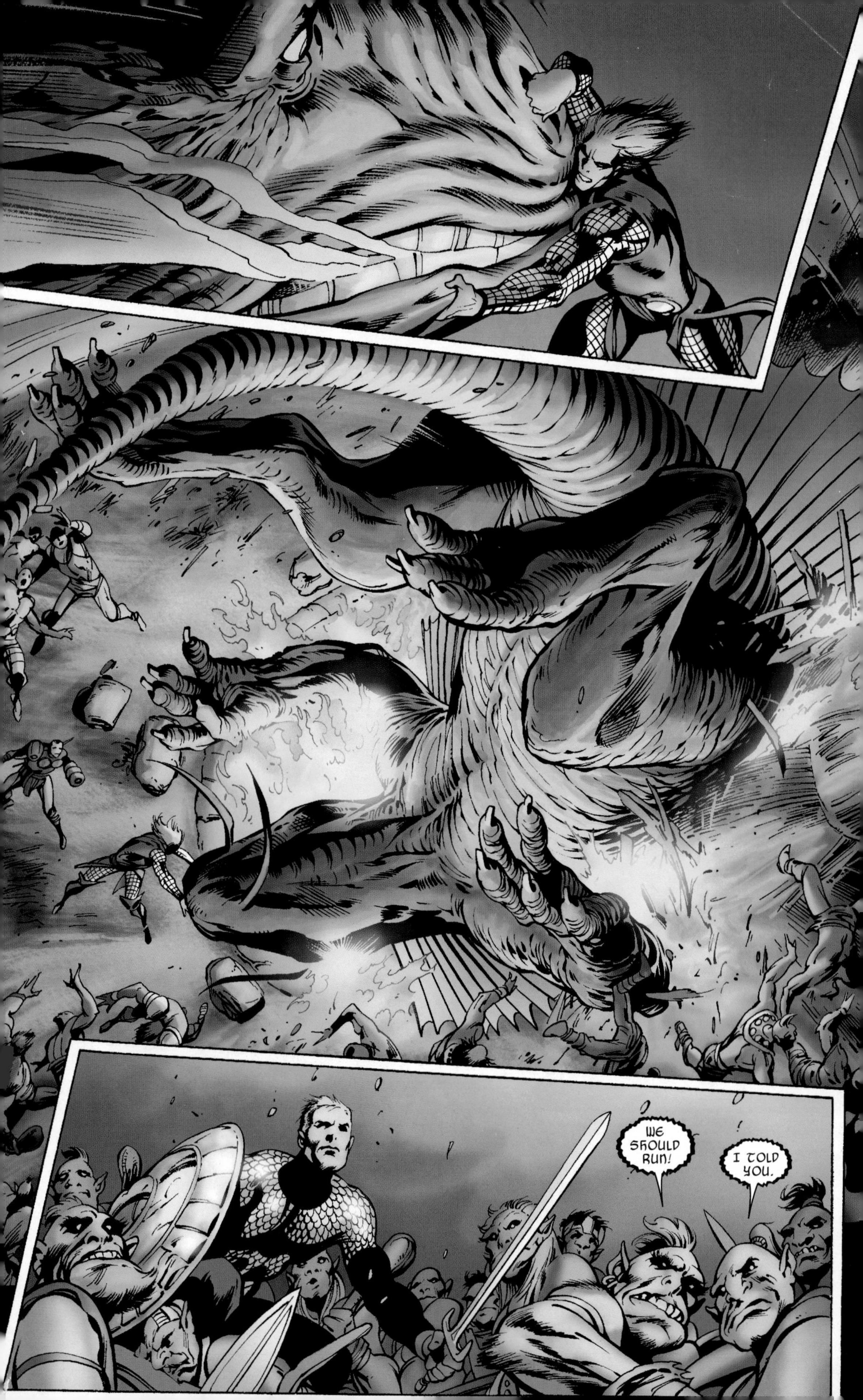
WE SHOULD RUN!
I TOLD YOU.

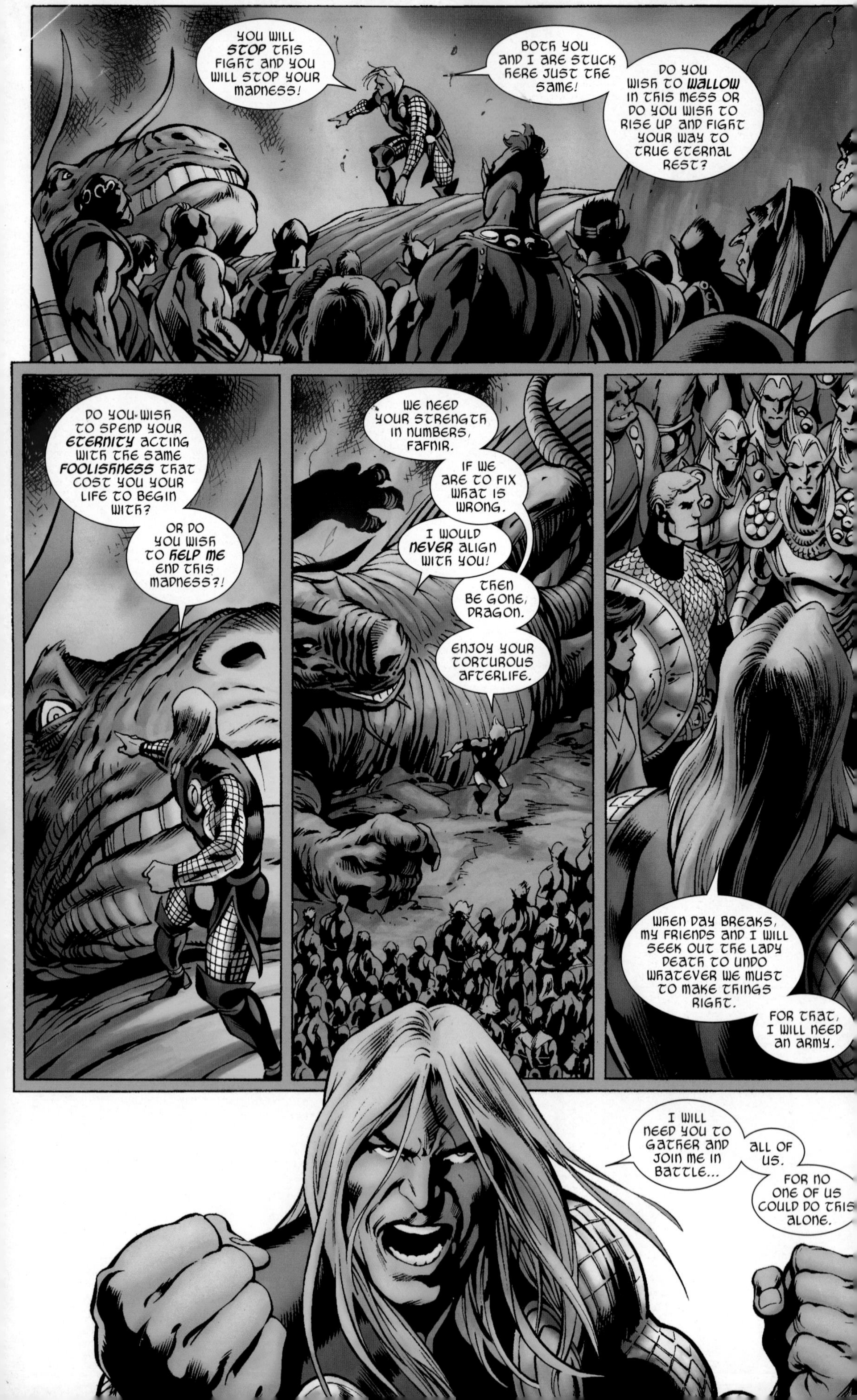
YOU WILL STOP THIS FIGHT AND YOU WILL STOP YOUR MADNESS!
BOTH YOU AND I ARE STUCK HERE JUST THE SAME!
DO YOU WISH TO WALLOW IN THIS MESS OR DO YOU WISH TO RISE UP AND FIGHT YOUR WAY TO TRUE ETERNAL REST?
DO YOU WISH TO SPEND YOUR ETERNITY ACTING WITH THE SAME FOOLISHNESS THAT COST YOU YOUR LIFE TO BEGIN WITH?
OR DO YOU WISH TO HELP ME END THIS MADNESS?!
WE NEED YOUR STRENGTH IN NUMBERS, FAFNIR.
IF WE ARE TO FIX WHAT IS WRONG.
I WOULD NEVER ALIGN WITH YOU!
THEN BE GONE, DRAGON.
ENJOY YOUR TORTUROUS AFTERLIFE.
WHEN DAY BREAKS, MY FRIENDS AND I WILL SEEK OUT THE LADY DEATH TO UNDO WHATEVER WE MUST TO MAKE THINGS RIGHT.
FOR THAT, I WILL NEED AN ARMY.
I WILL NEED YOU TO GATHER AND JOIN ME IN BATTLE...
ALL OF US.
FOR NO ONE OF US COULD DO THIS ALONE.

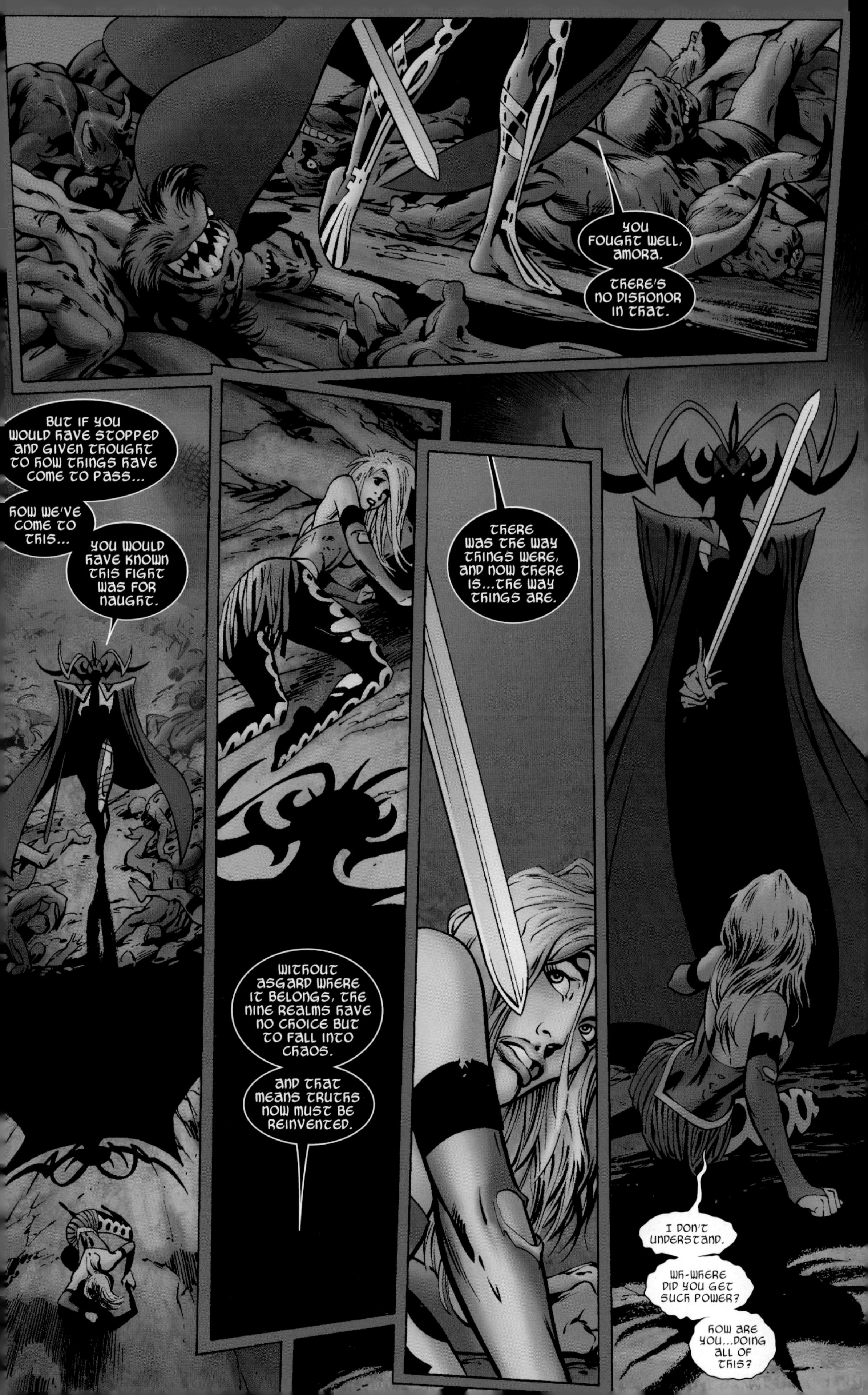
YOU FOUGHT WELL, AMORA.
THERE'S NO DISHONOR IN THAT.
BUT IF YOU WOULD HAVE STOPPED AND GIVEN THOUGHT TO HOW THINGS HAVE COME TO PASS...
HOW WE'VE COME TO THIS...
YOU WOULD HAVE KNOWN THIS FIGHT WAS FOR NAUGHT.
WITHOUT ASGARD WHERE IT BELONGS, THE NINE REALMS HAVE NO CHOICE BUT TO FALL INTO CHAOS.
AND THAT MEANS TRUTHS NOW MUST BE REINVENTED.
THERE WAS THE WAY THINGS WERE, AND NOW THERE IS...THE WAY THINGS ARE.
I DON'T UNDERSTAND.
WH-WHERE DID YOU GET SUCH POWER?
HOW ARE YOU...DOING ALL OF THIS?

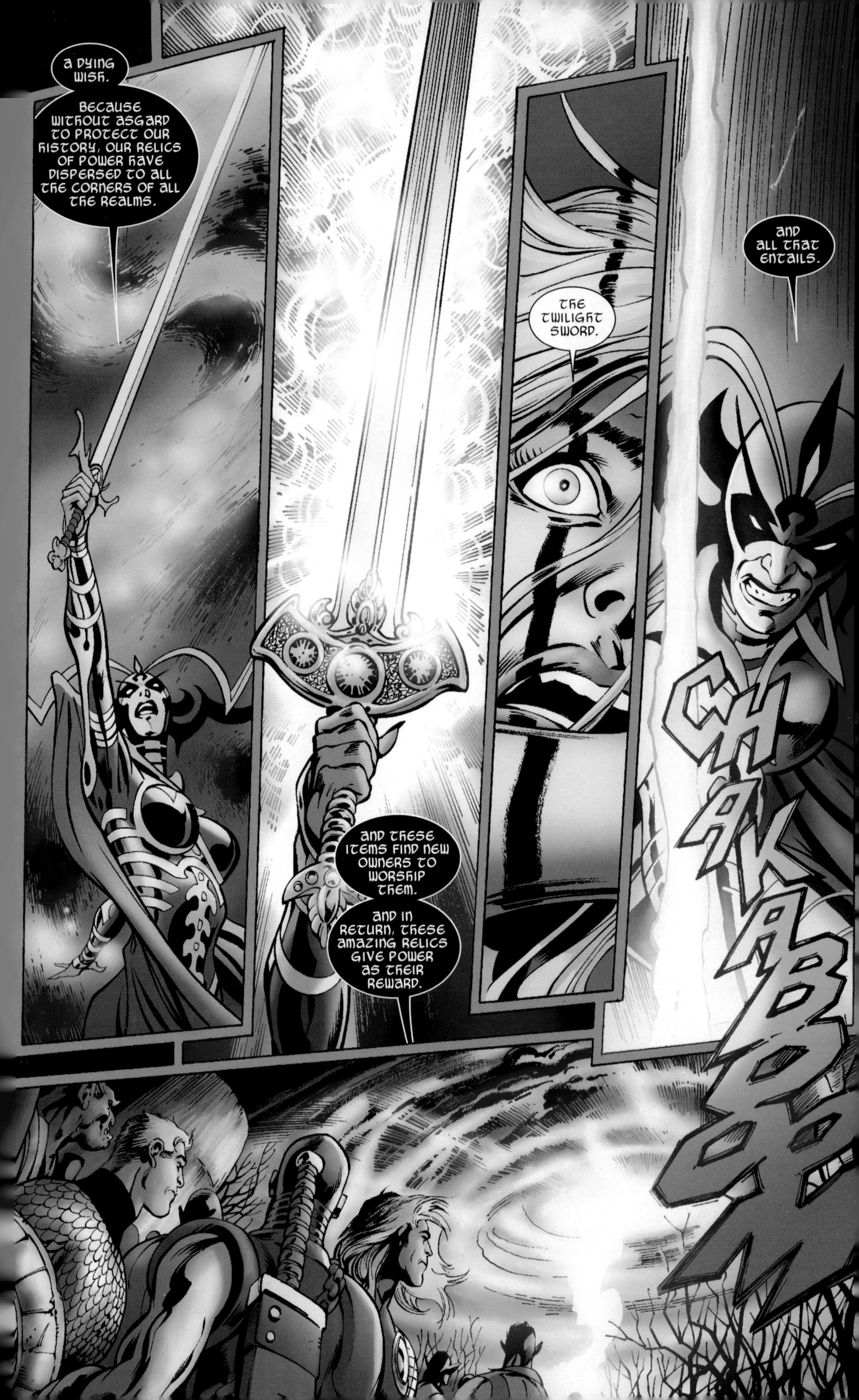
A DYING WISH.
BECAUSE WITHOUT ASGARD TO PROTECT OUR HISTORY, OUR RELICS OF POWER HAVE DISPERSED TO ALL THE CORNERS OF ALL THE REALMS.
AND THESE ITEMS FIND NEW OWNERS TO WORSHIP THEM.
AND IN RETURN, THESE AMAZING RELICS GIVE POWER AS THEIR REWARD.
THE TWILIGHT SWORD.
AND ALL THAT ENTAILS.
CHAKABOOM

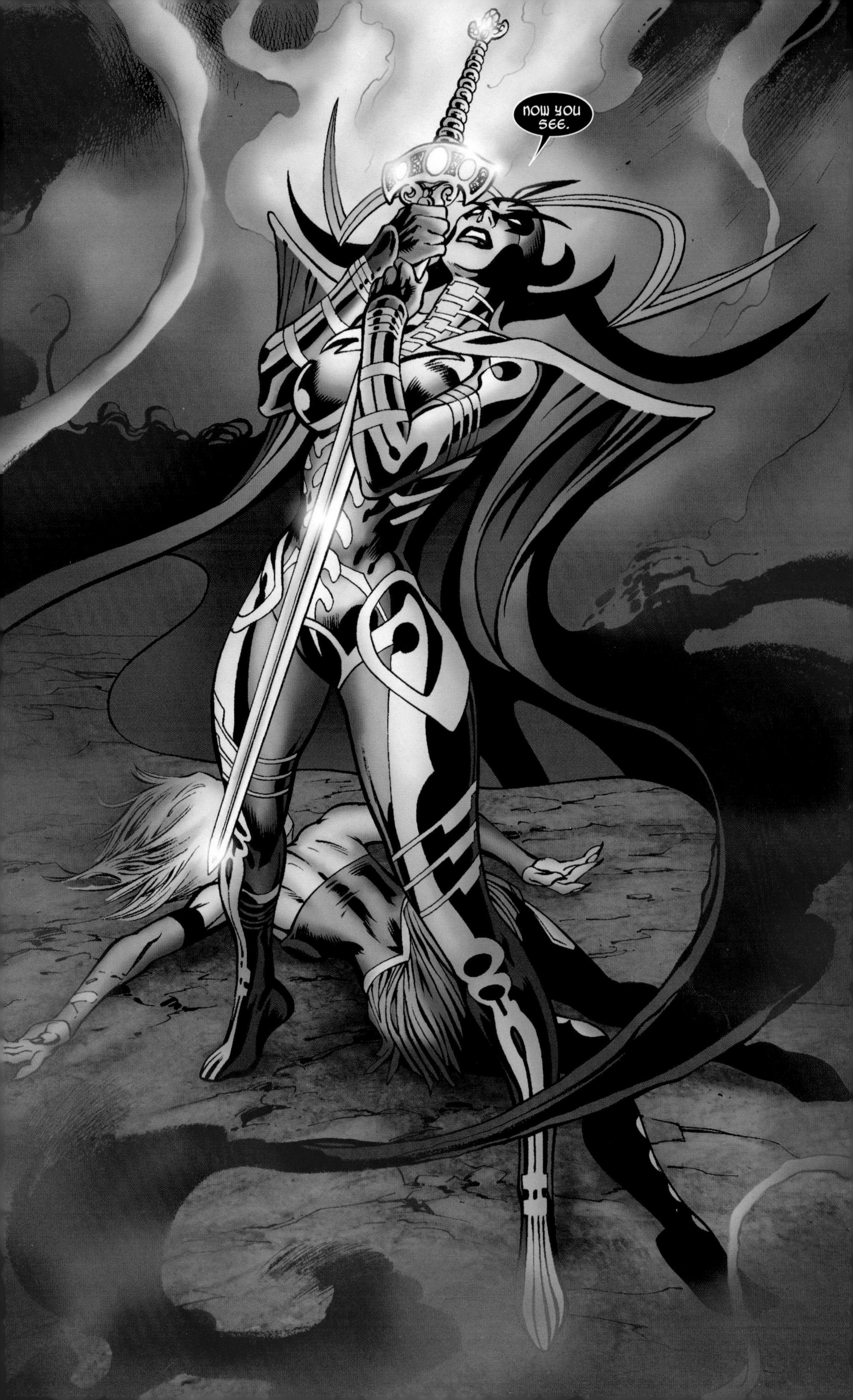
NOW YOU SEE.

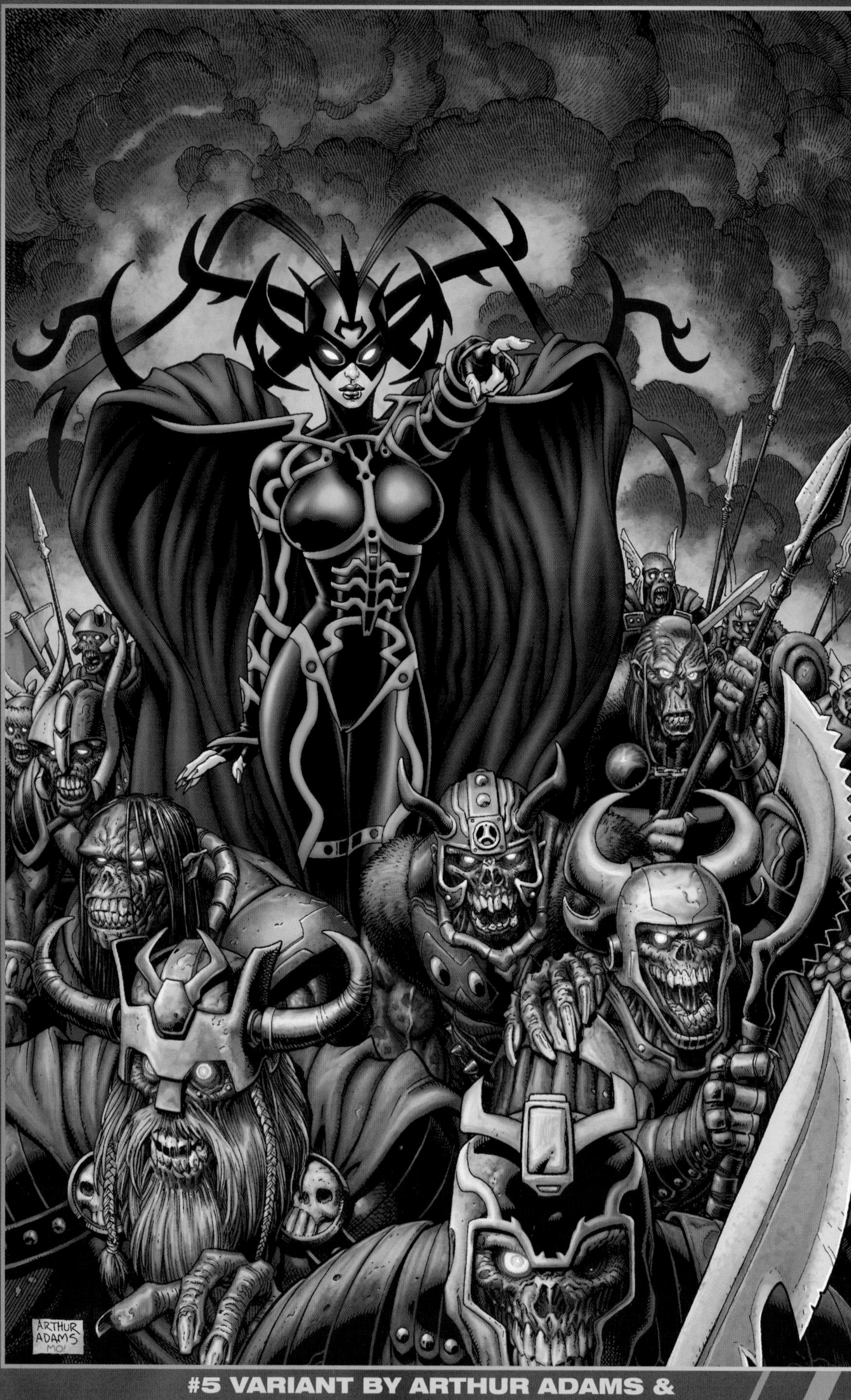
ARTHUR
ADAMS
MO!

#5 VARIANT BY ARTHUR ADAMS &
MORRY HOLLOWELL

5

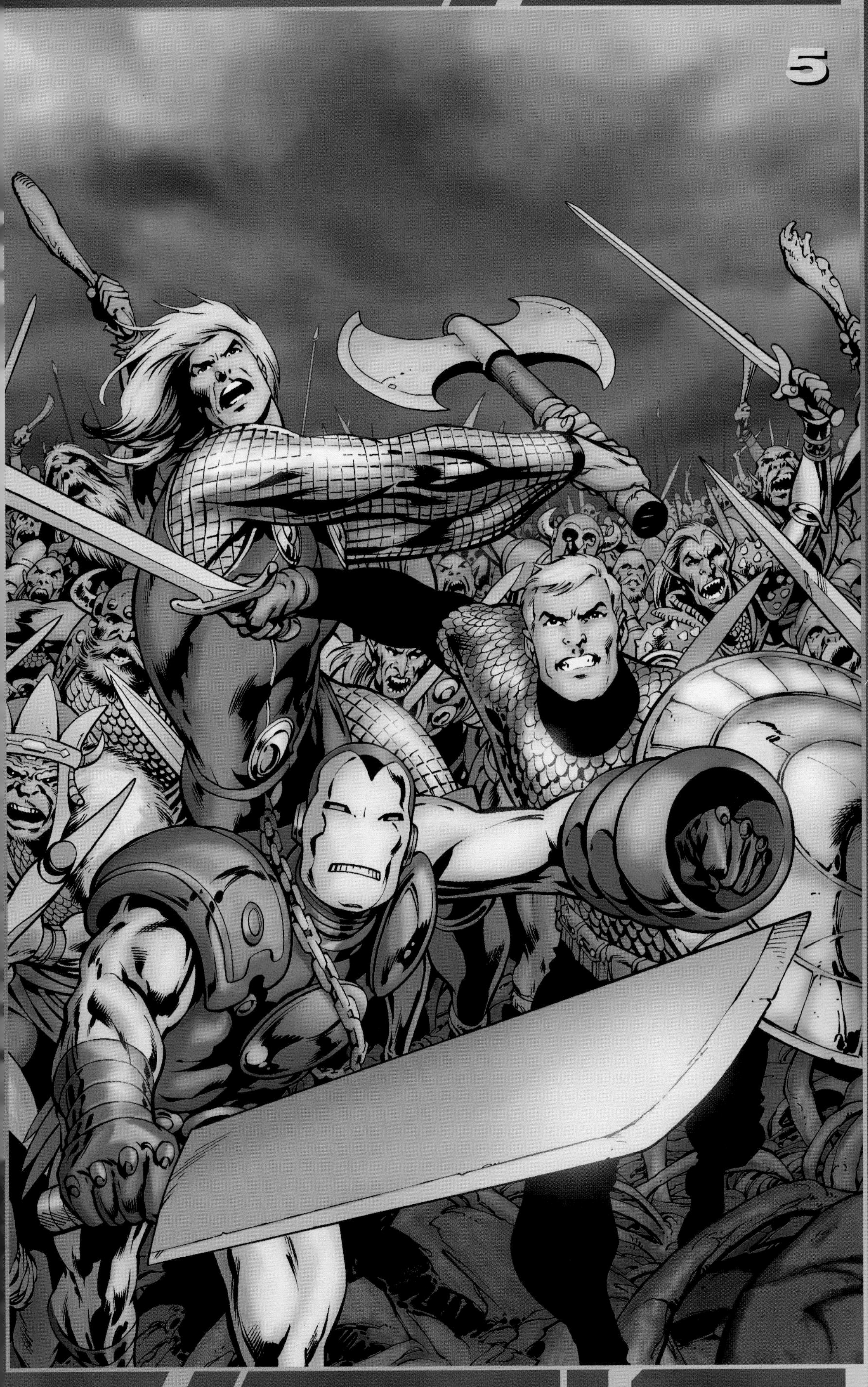

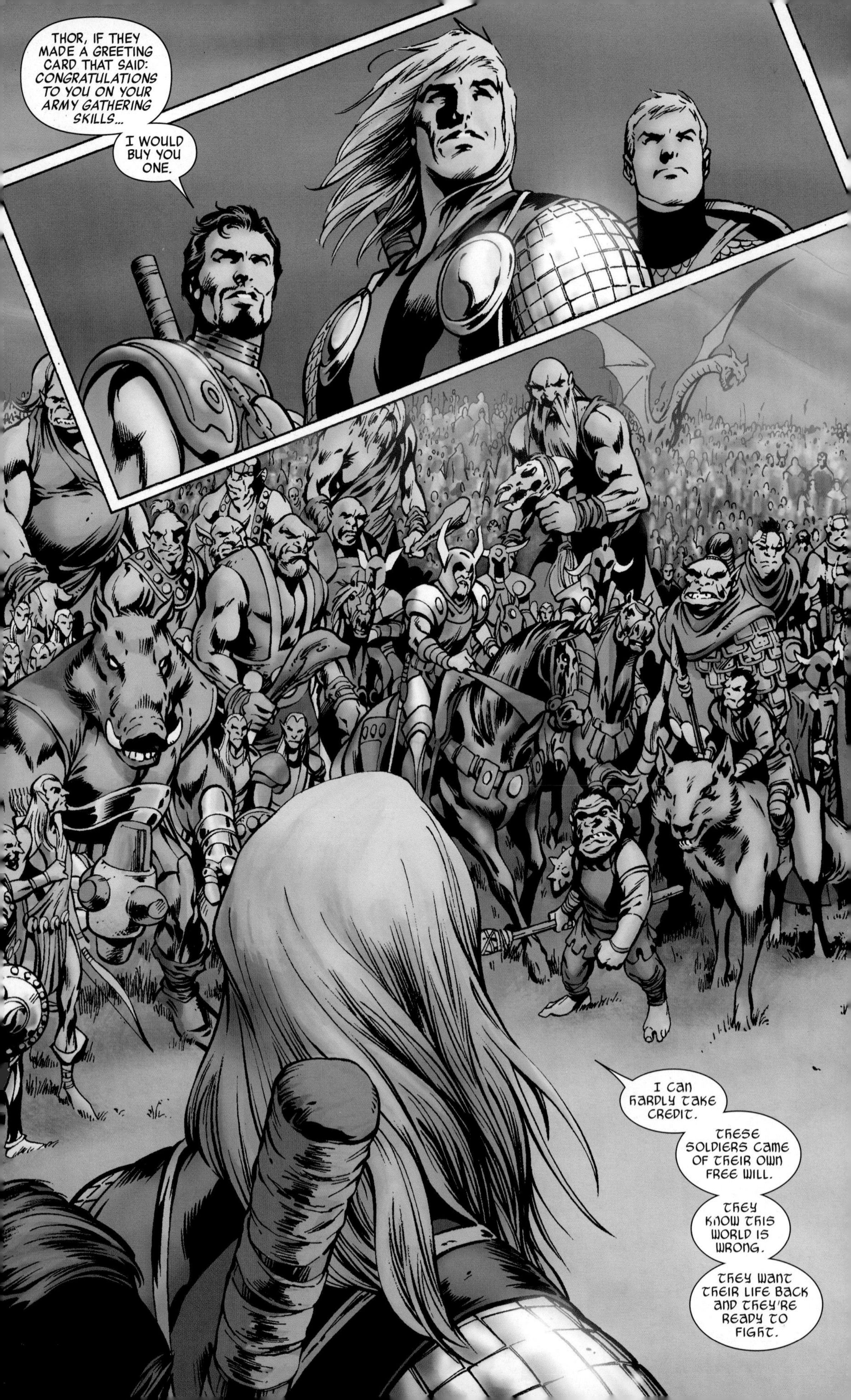
THOR, IF THEY MADE A GREETING CARD THAT SAID: CONGRATULATIONS TO YOU ON YOUR ARMY GATHERING SKILLS...
I WOULD BUY YOU ONE.
I CAN HARDLY TAKE CREDIT.
THESE SOLDIERS CAME OF THEIR OWN FREE WILL.
THEY KNOW THIS WORLD IS WRONG.
THEY WANT THEIR LIFE BACK AND THEY'RE READY TO FIGHT.

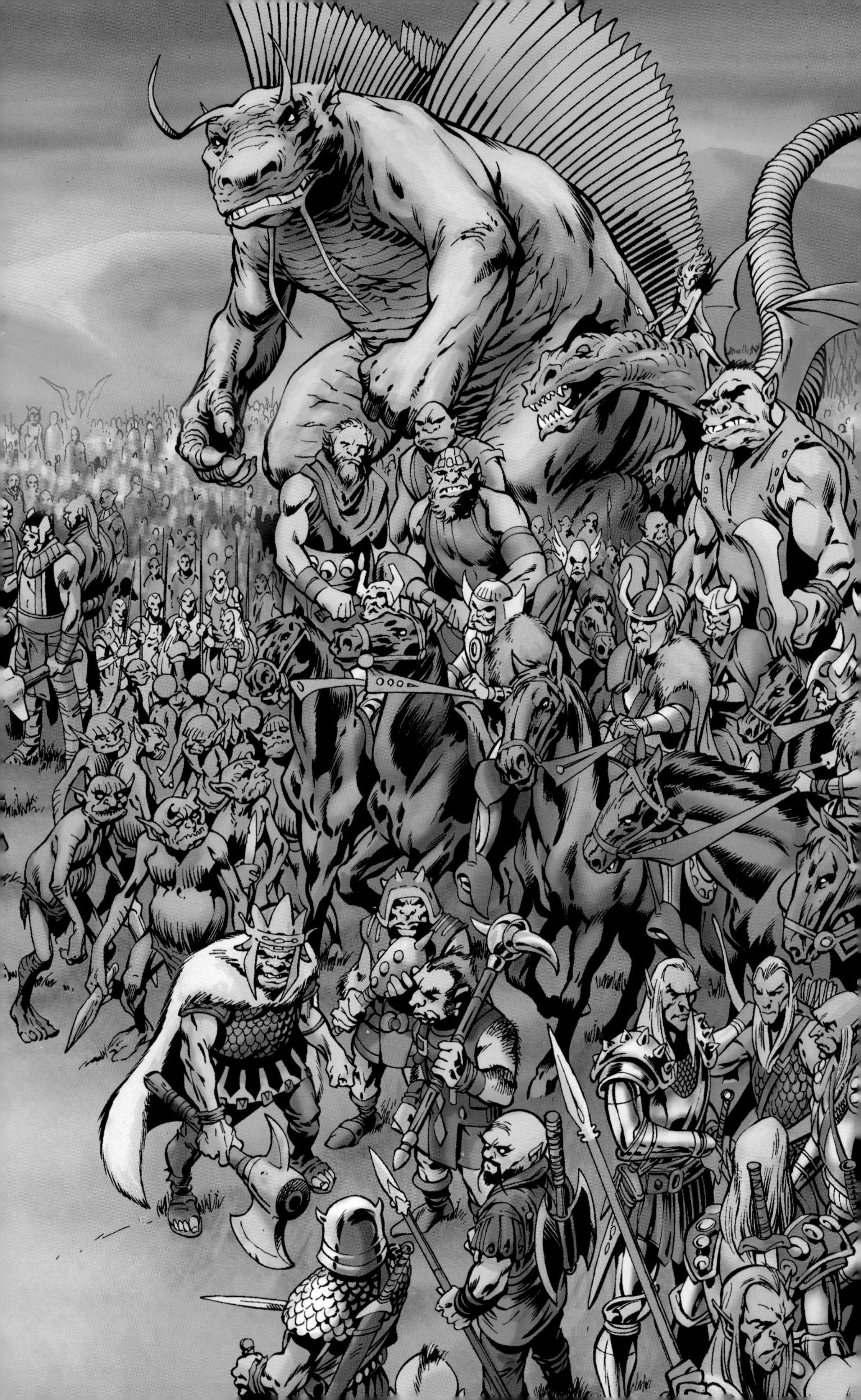

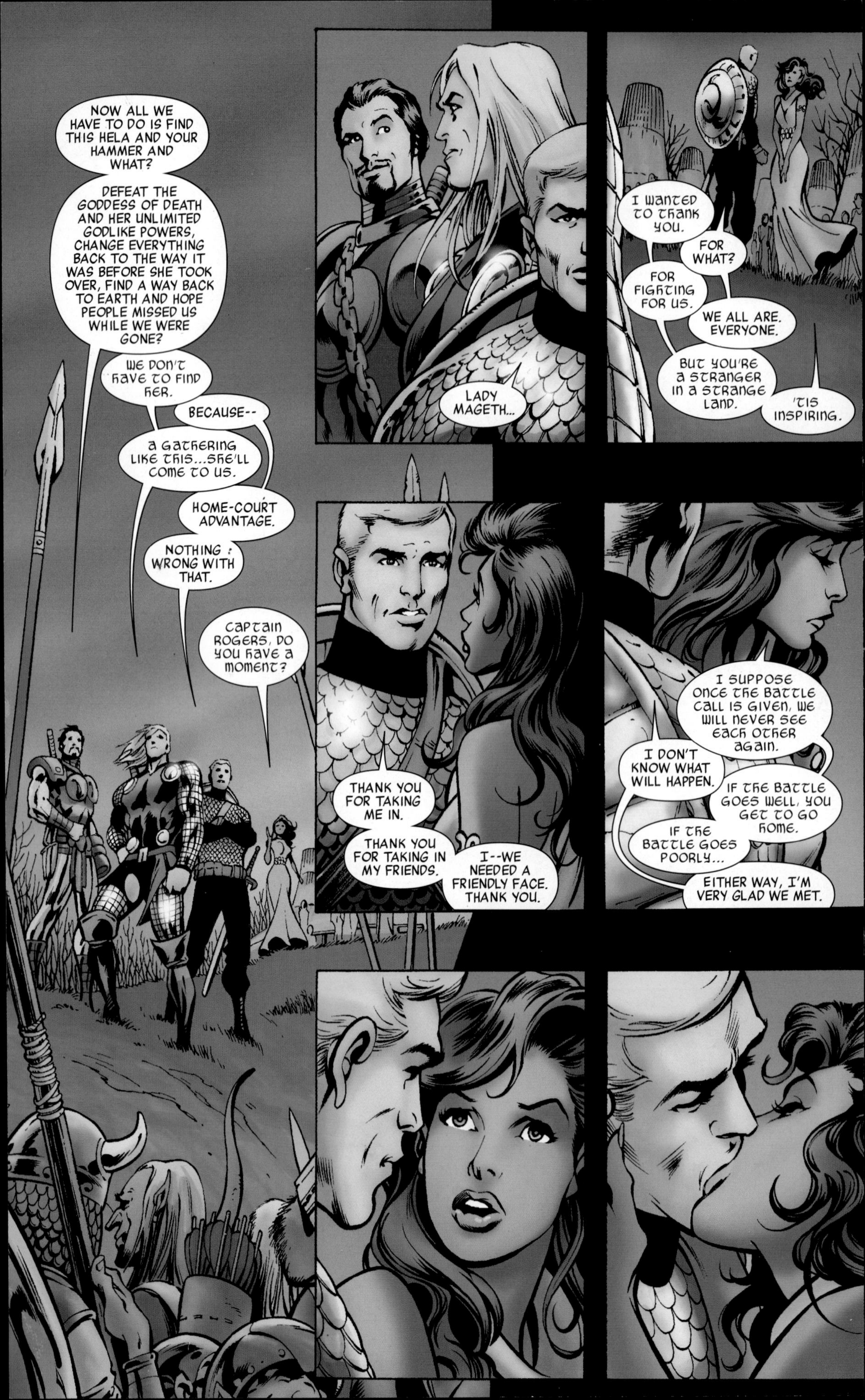
NOW ALL WE HAVE TO DO IS FIND THIS HELA AND YOUR HAMMER AND WHAT?
DEFEAT THE GODDESS OF DEATH AND HER UNLIMITED GODLIKE POWERS, CHANGE EVERYTHING BACK TO THE WAY IT WAS BEFORE SHE TOOK OVER, FIND A WAY BACK TO EARTH AND HOPE PEOPLE MISSED US WHILE WE WERE GONE?
WE DON'T HAVE TO FIND HER.
BECAUSE--
A GATHERING LIKE THIS...SHE'LL COME TO US.
HOME-COURT ADVANTAGE.
NOTHING WRONG WITH THAT.
CAPTAIN ROGERS, DO YOU HAVE A MOMENT?
LADY MAGETH...
I WANTED TO THANK YOU.
FOR WHAT?
FOR FIGHTING FOR US.
WE ALL ARE. EVERYONE.
BUT YOU'RE A STRANGER IN A STRANGE LAND.
'TIS INSPIRING.
THANK YOU FOR TAKING ME IN.
THANK YOU FOR TAKING IN MY FRIENDS.
I--WE NEEDED A FRIENDLY FACE. THANK YOU.
I SUPPOSE ONCE THE BATTLE CALL IS GIVEN, WE WILL NEVER SEE EACH OTHER AGAIN.
I DON'T KNOW WHAT WILL HAPPEN.
IF THE BATTLE GOES WELL, YOU GET TO GO HOME.
IF THE BATTLE GOES POORLY...
EITHER WAY, I'M VERY GLAD WE MET.

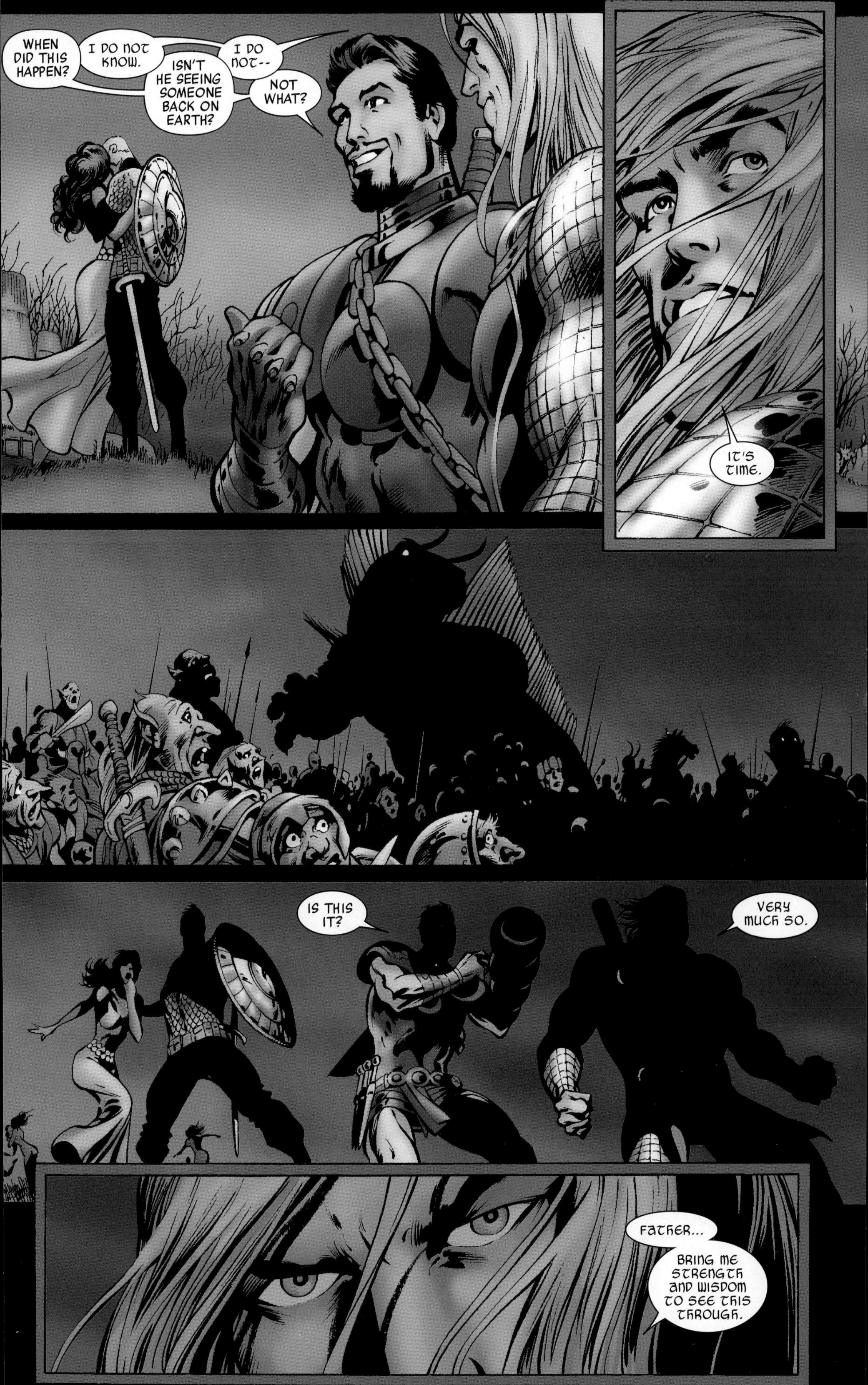
WHEN DID THIS HAPPEN?
I DO NOT KNOW.
ISN'T HE SEEING SOMEONE BACK ON EARTH?
I DO NOT--
NOT WHAT?
IT'S TIME.
IS THIS IT?
VERY MUCH SO.
FATHER...
BRING ME STRENGTH AND WISDOM TO SEE THIS THROUGH.

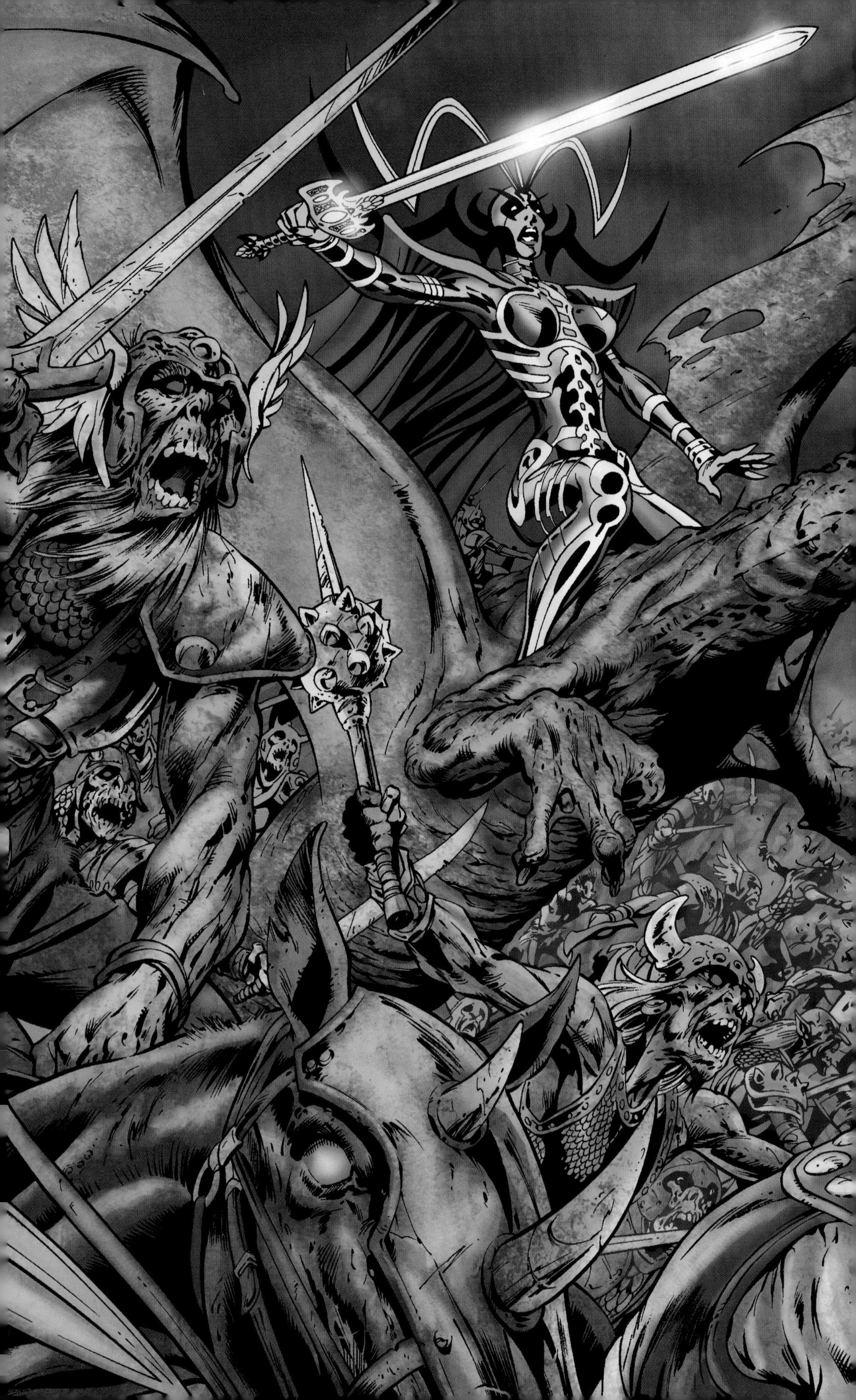

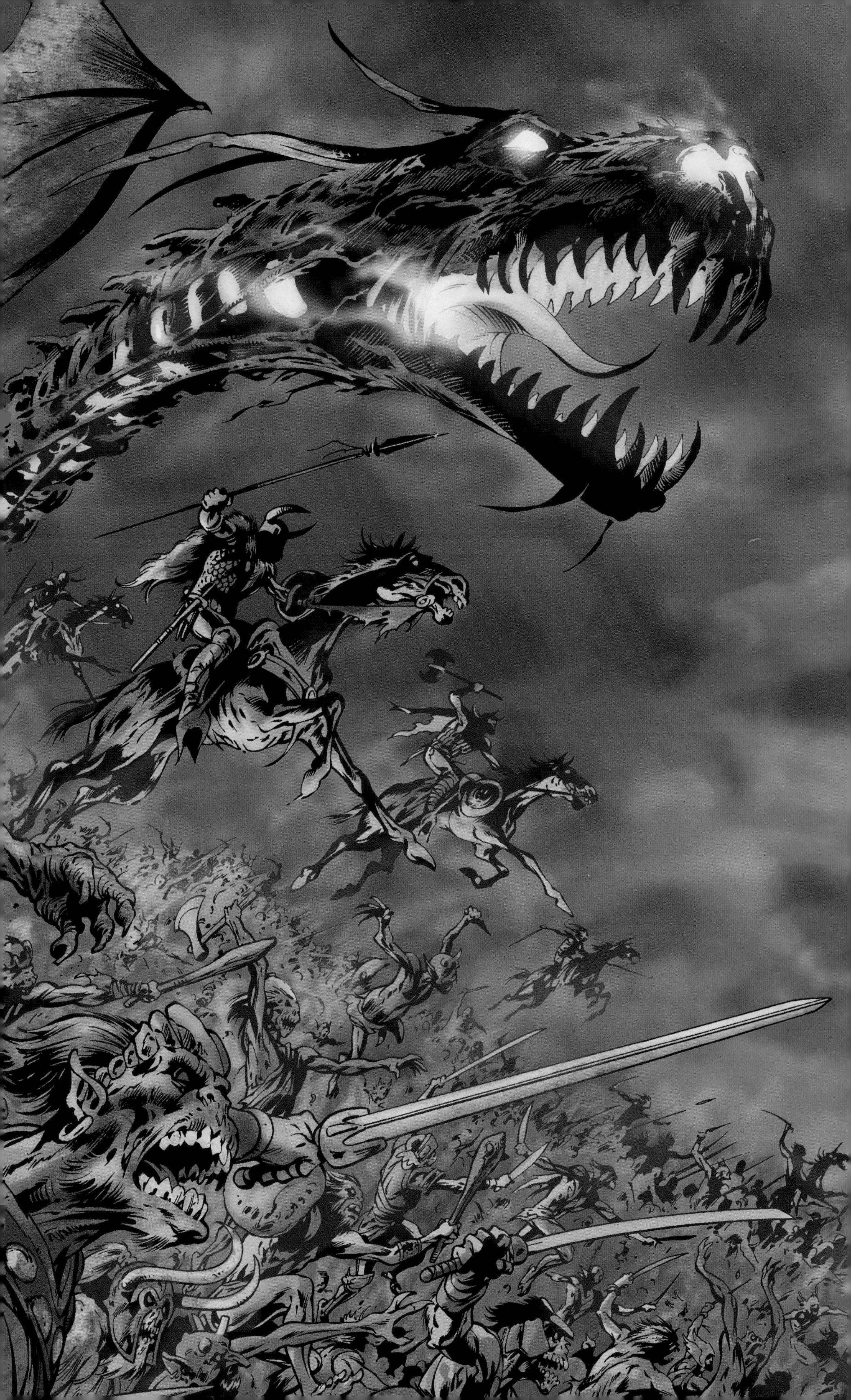

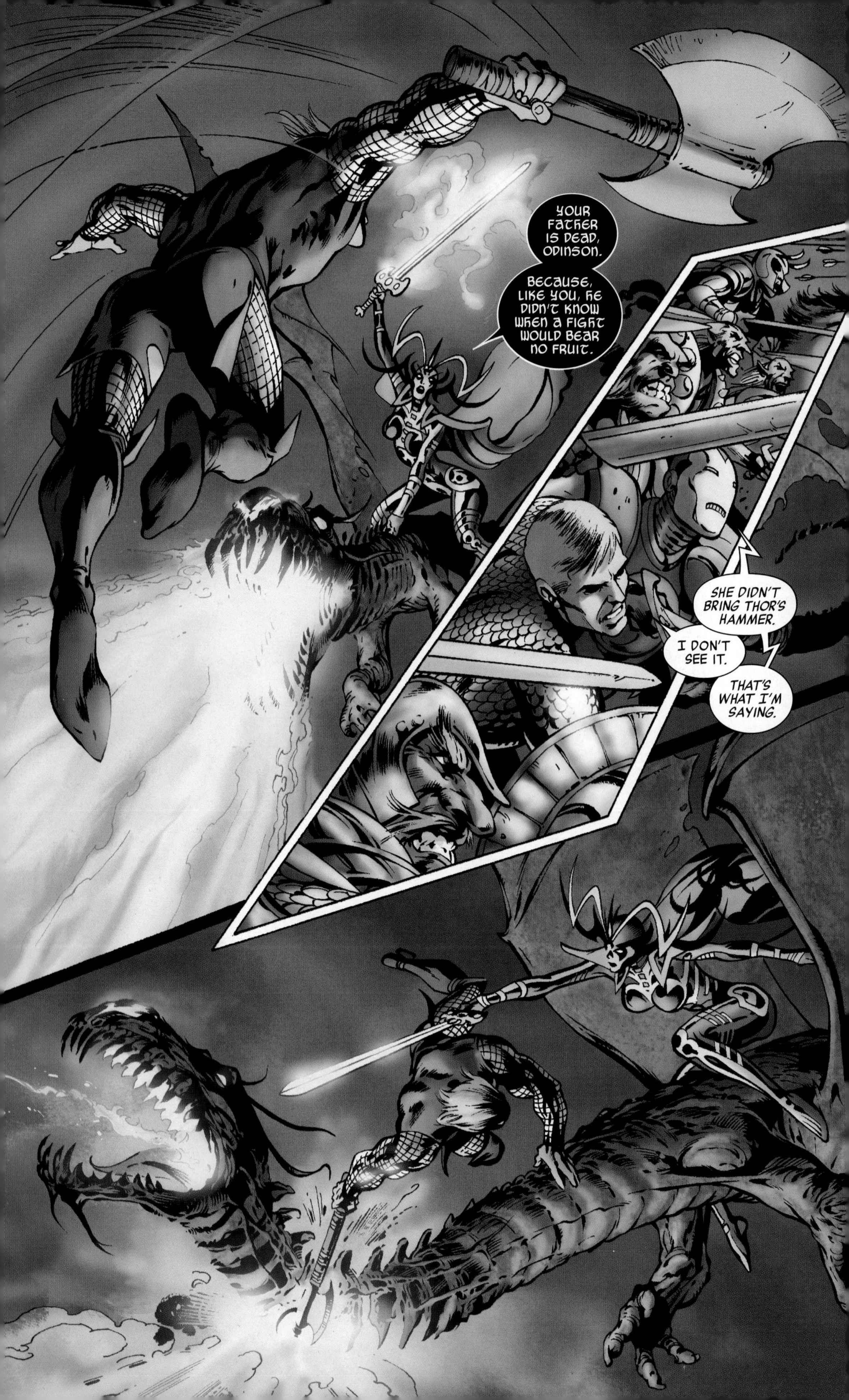
YOUR FATHER IS DEAD, ODINSON.
BECAUSE, LIKE YOU, HE DIDN'T KNOW WHEN A FIGHT WOULD BEAR NO FRUIT.
SHE DIDN'T BRING THOR'S HAMMER.
I DON'T SEE IT.
THAT'S WHAT I'M SAYING.

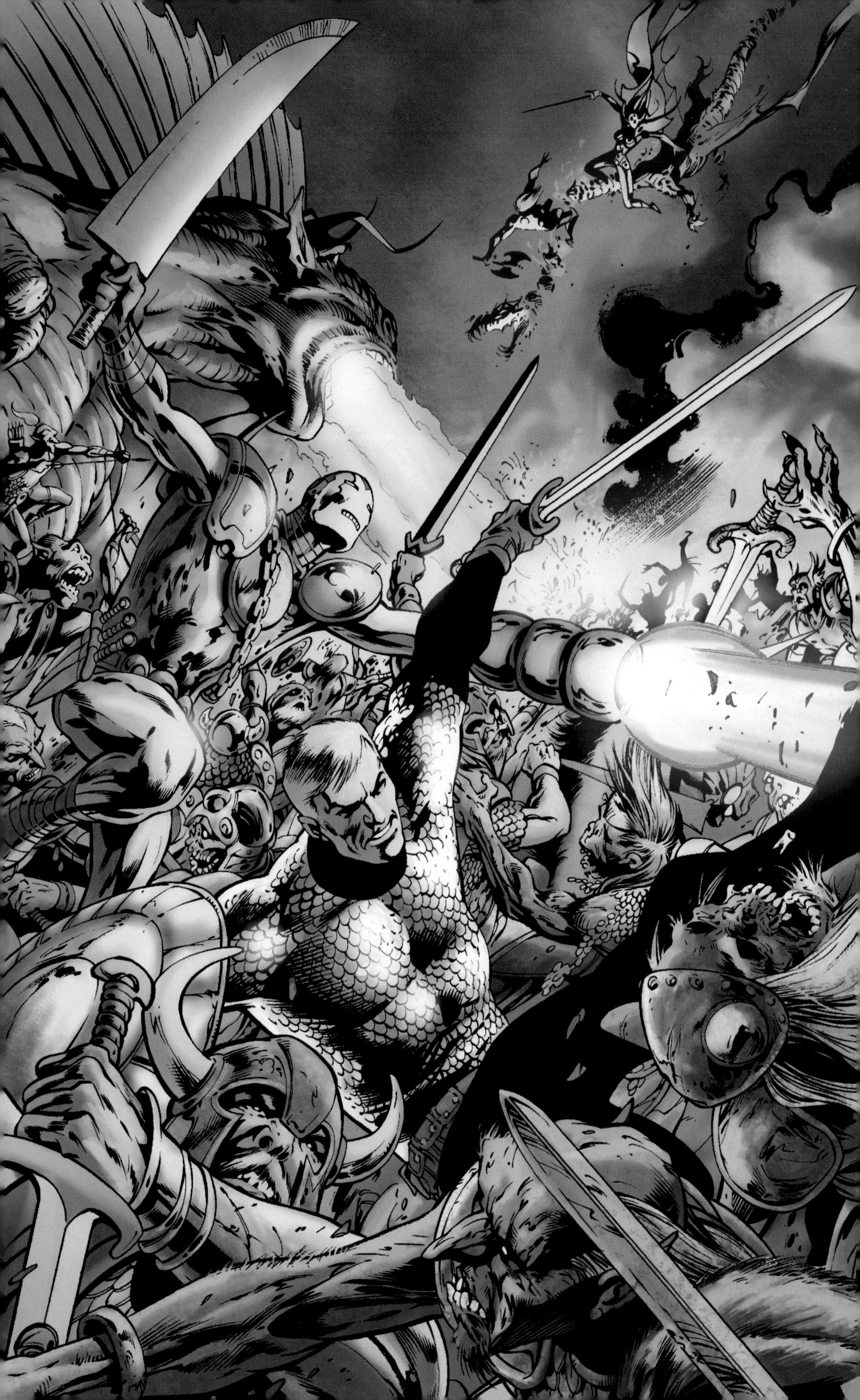

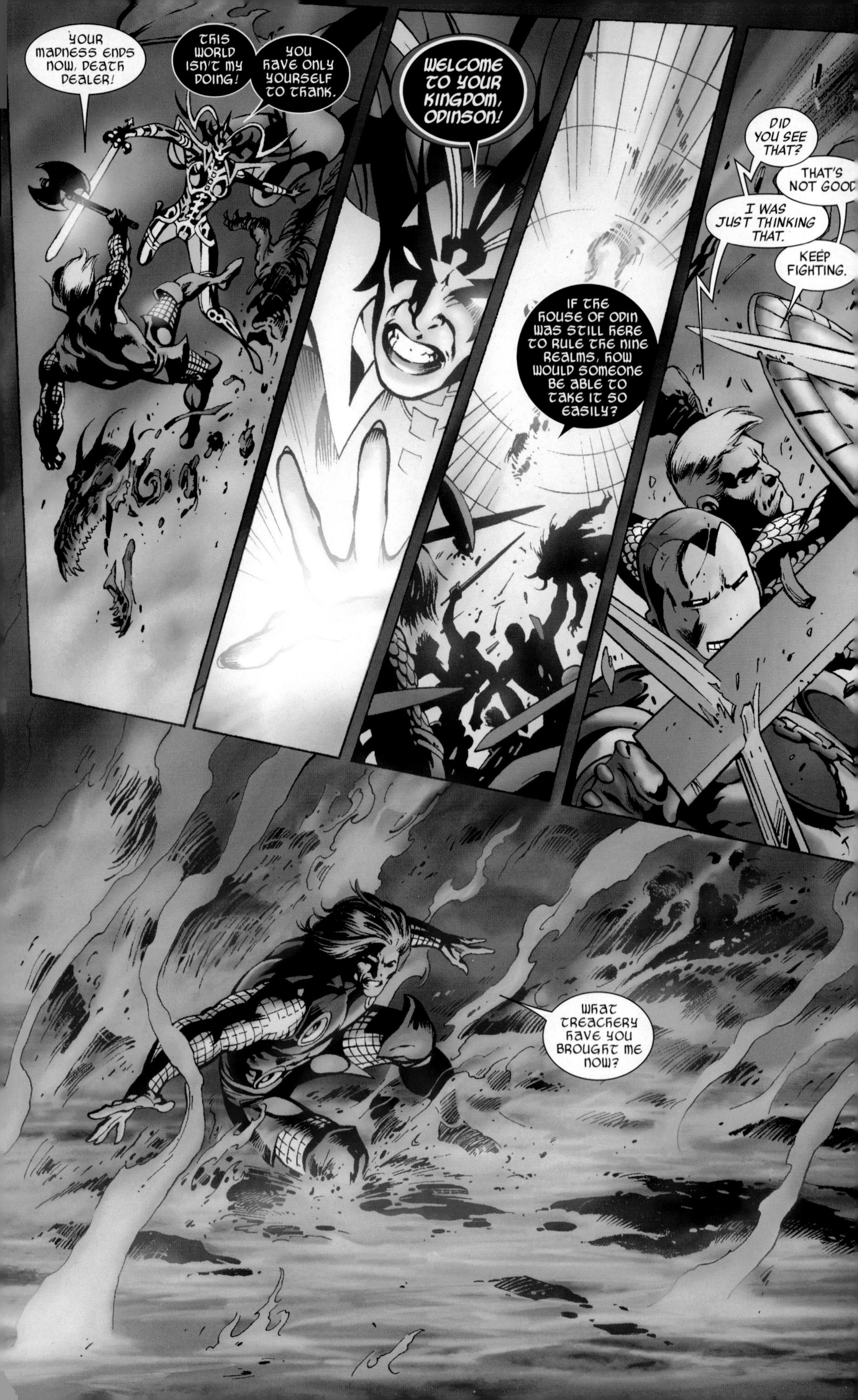
YOUR MADNESS ENDS NOW, DEATH DEALER!
THIS WORLD ISN'T MY DOING!
YOU HAVE ONLY YOURSELF TO THANK.
WELCOME TO YOUR KINGDOM, ODINSON!
IF THE HOUSE OF ODIN WAS STILL HERE TO RULE THE NINE REALMS, HOW WOULD SOMEONE BE ABLE TO TAKE IT SO EASILY?
DID YOU SEE THAT?
THAT'S NOT GOOD
I WAS JUST THINKING THAT.
KEEP FIGHTING.
WHAT TREACHERY HAVE YOU BROUGHT ME NOW?

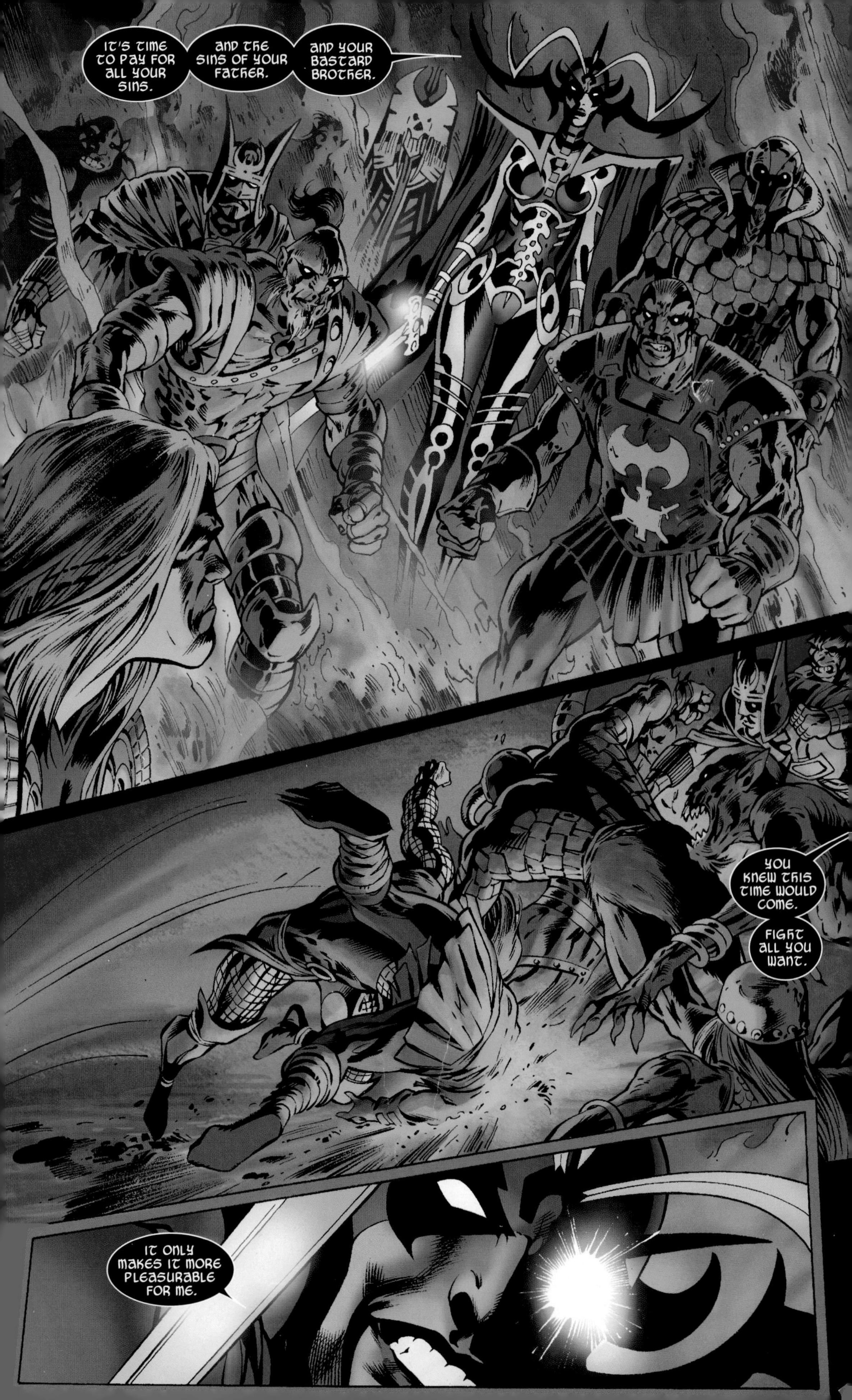
IT'S TIME TO PAY FOR ALL YOUR SINS.
AND THE SINS OF YOUR FATHER.
AND YOUR BASTARD BROTHER.
YOU KNEW THIS TIME WOULD COME.
FIGHT ALL YOU WANT.
IT ONLY MAKES IT MORE PLEASURABLE FOR ME.

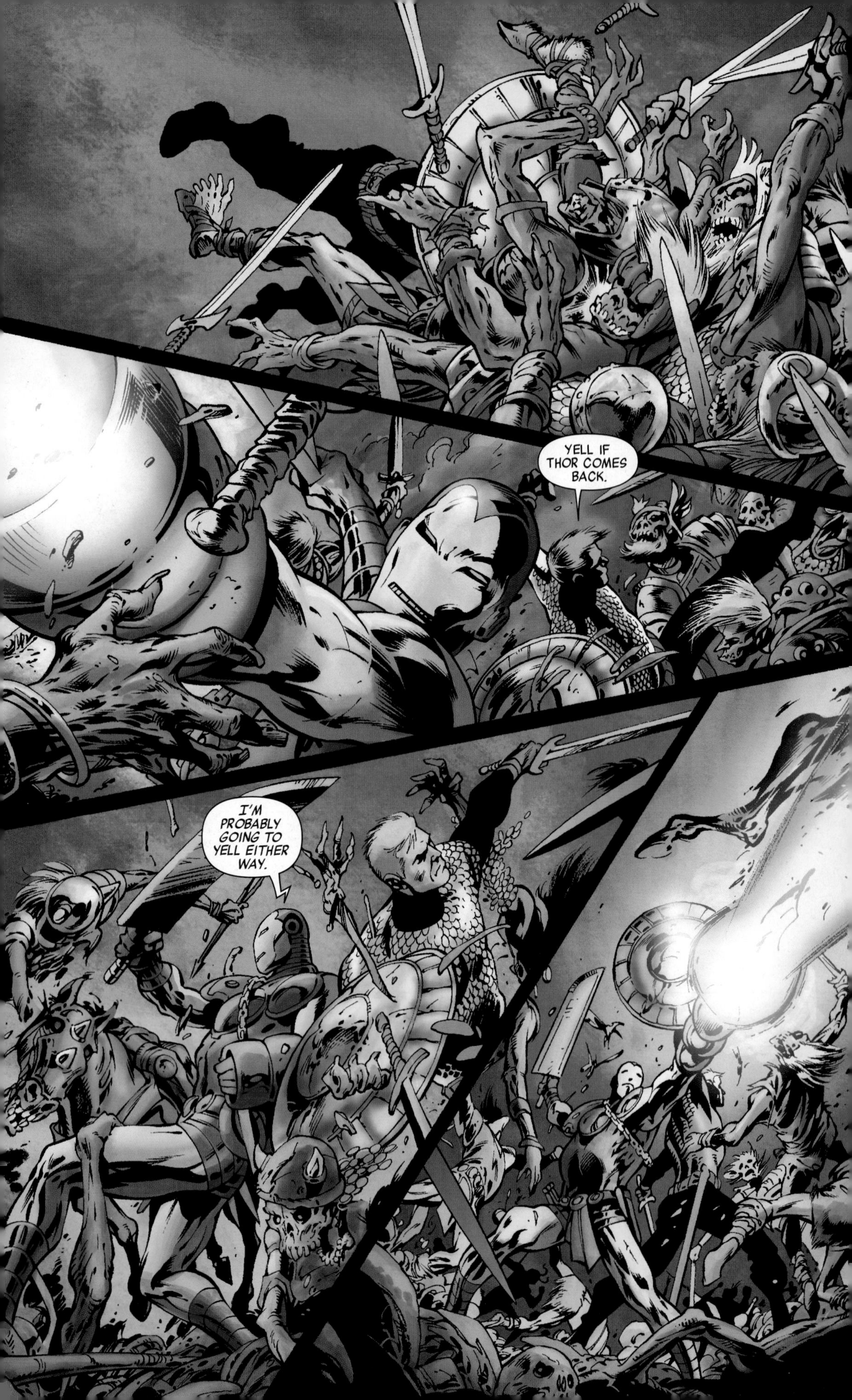
YELL IF THOR COMES BACK.
I'M PROBABLY GOING TO YELL EITHER WAY.

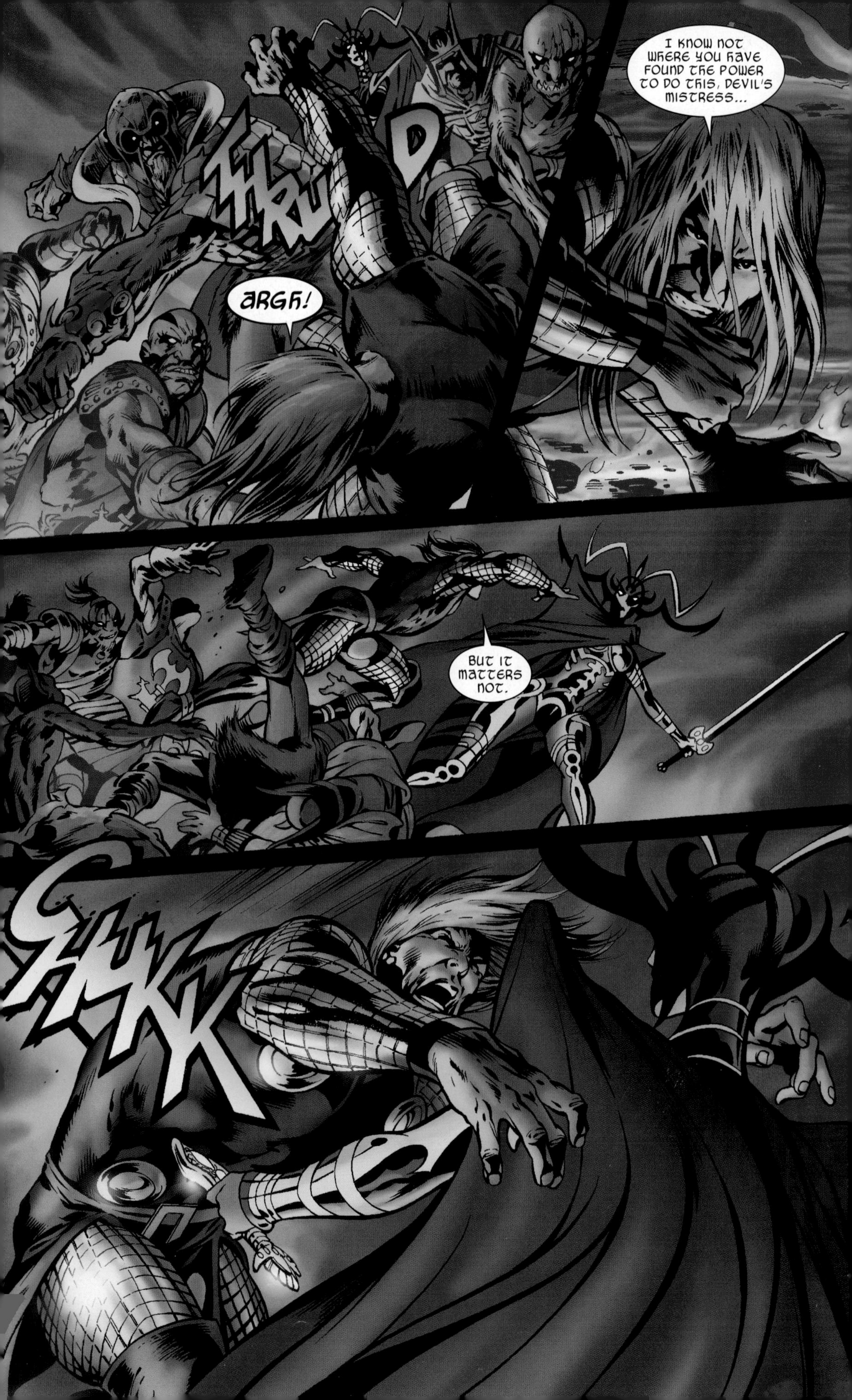
THRUDD
I KNOW NOT WHERE YOU HAVE FOUND THE POWER TO DO THIS, DEVIL'S MISTRESS...
ARGH!
BUT IT MATTERS NOT.
CHUKK

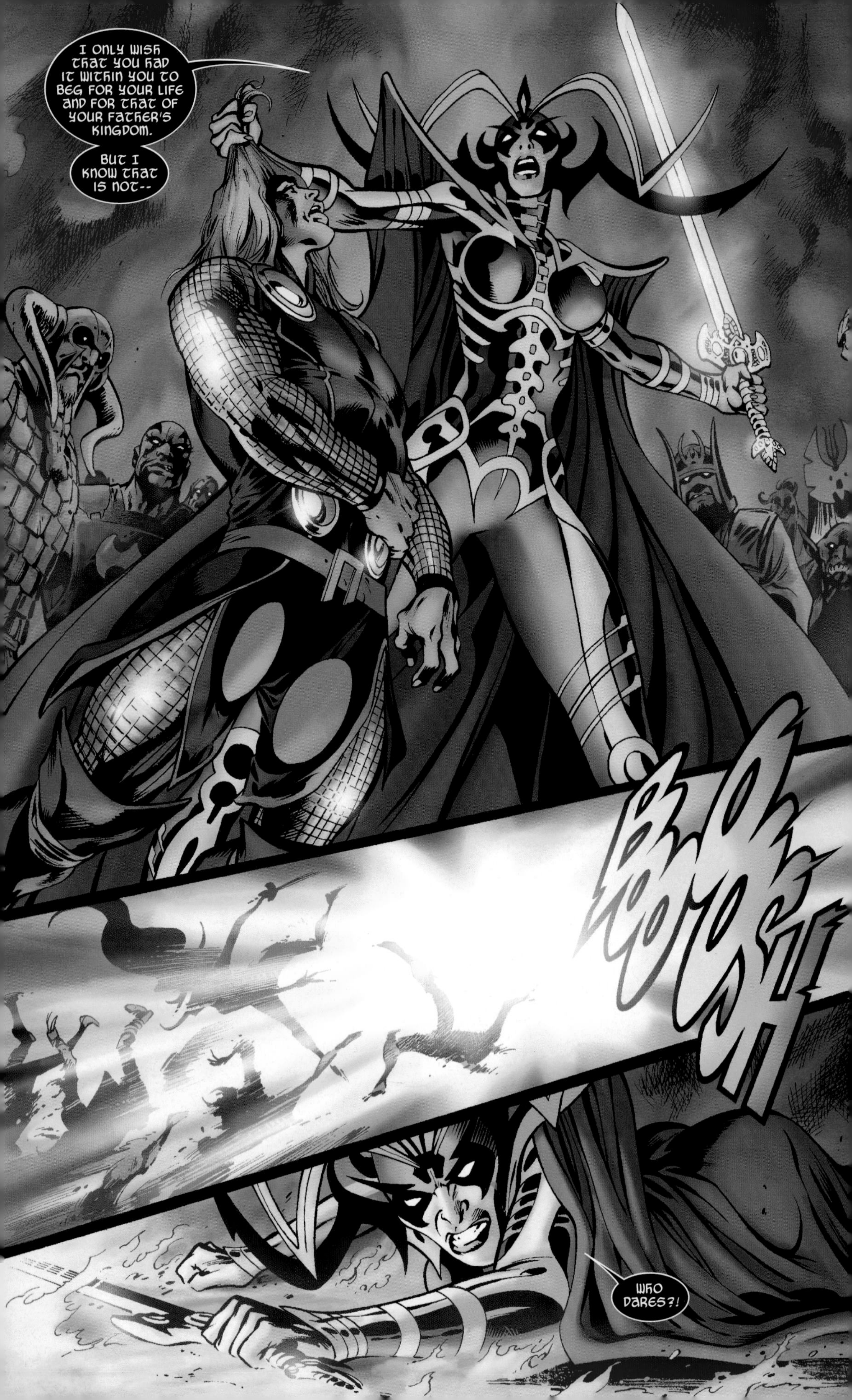
I ONLY WISH THAT YOU HAD IT WITHIN YOU TO BEG FOR YOUR LIFE AND FOR THAT OF YOUR FATHER'S KINGDOM.
BUT I KNOW THAT IS NOT--
BOOOOOSH
WHO DARES?!

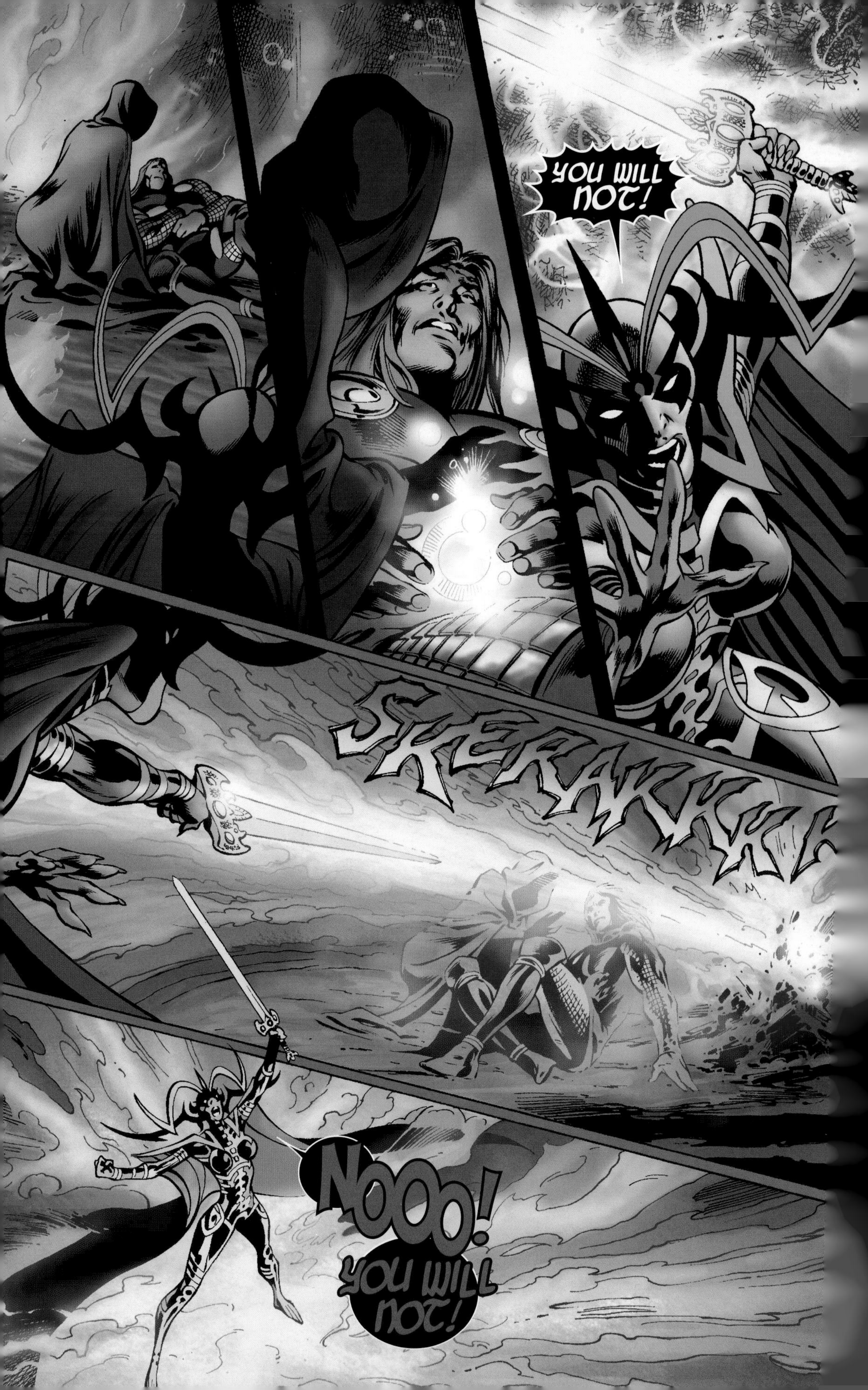
YOU WILL NOT!
SKERAKKKK
NOOO! YOU WILL NOT!

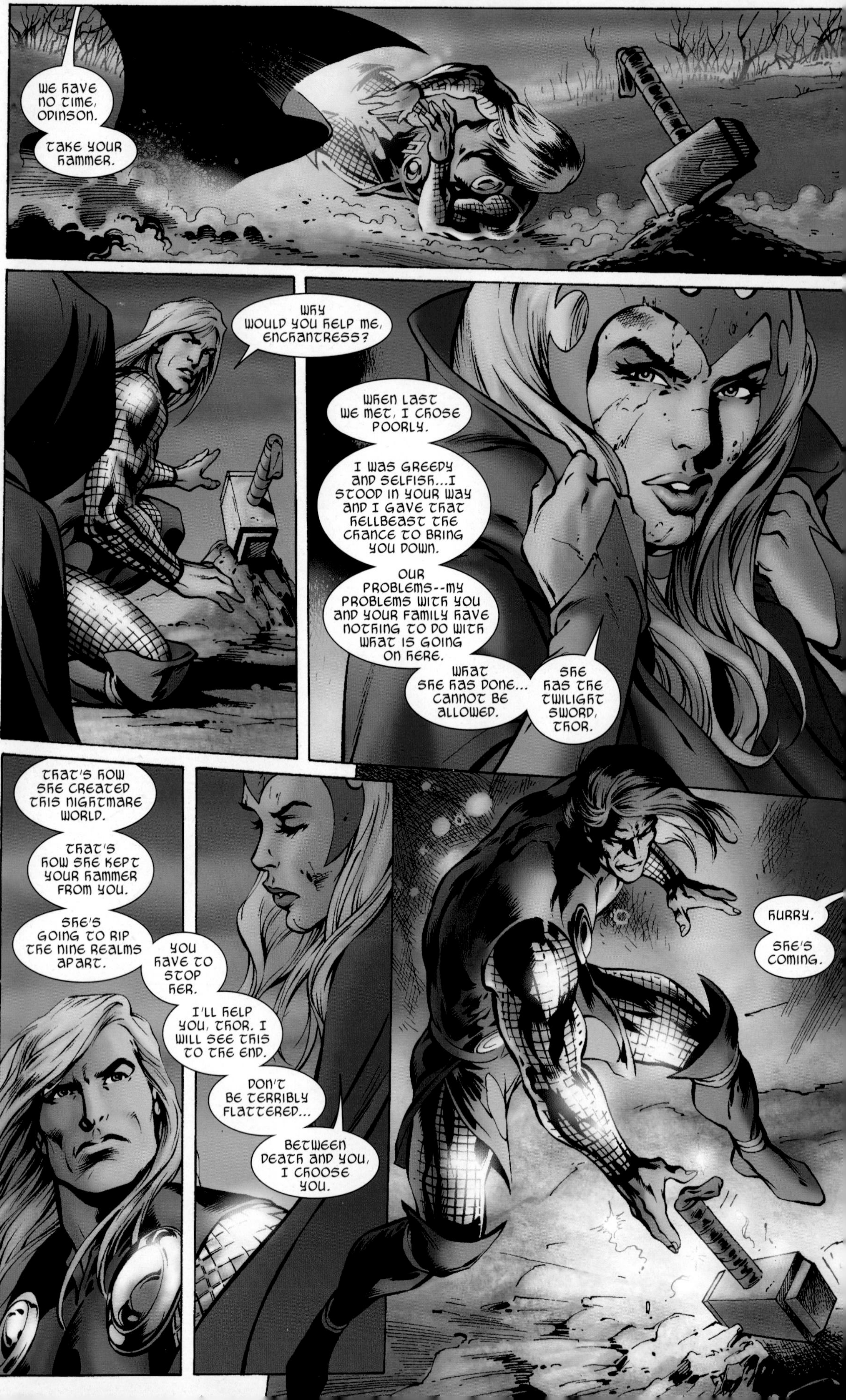
WE HAVE NO TIME, ODINSON.
TAKE YOUR HAMMER.
WHY WOULD YOU HELP ME, ENCHANTRESS?
WHEN LAST WE MET, I CHOSE POORLY.
I WAS GREEDY AND SELFISH...I STOOD IN YOUR WAY AND I GAVE THAT HELLBEAST THE CHANCE TO BRING YOU DOWN.
OUR PROBLEMS--MY PROBLEMS WITH YOU AND YOUR FAMILY HAVE NOTHING TO DO WITH WHAT IS GOING ON HERE.
WHAT SHE HAS DONE... CANNOT BE ALLOWED.
SHE HAS THE TWILIGHT SWORD, THOR.
THAT'S HOW SHE CREATED THIS NIGHTMARE WORLD.
THAT'S HOW SHE KEPT YOUR HAMMER FROM YOU.
SHE'S GOING TO RIP THE NINE REALMS APART.
YOU HAVE TO STOP HER.
I'LL HELP YOU, THOR. I WILL SEE THIS TO THE END.
DON'T BE TERRIBLY FLATTERED...
BETWEEN DEATH AND YOU, I CHOOSE YOU.
HURRY.
SHE'S COMING.

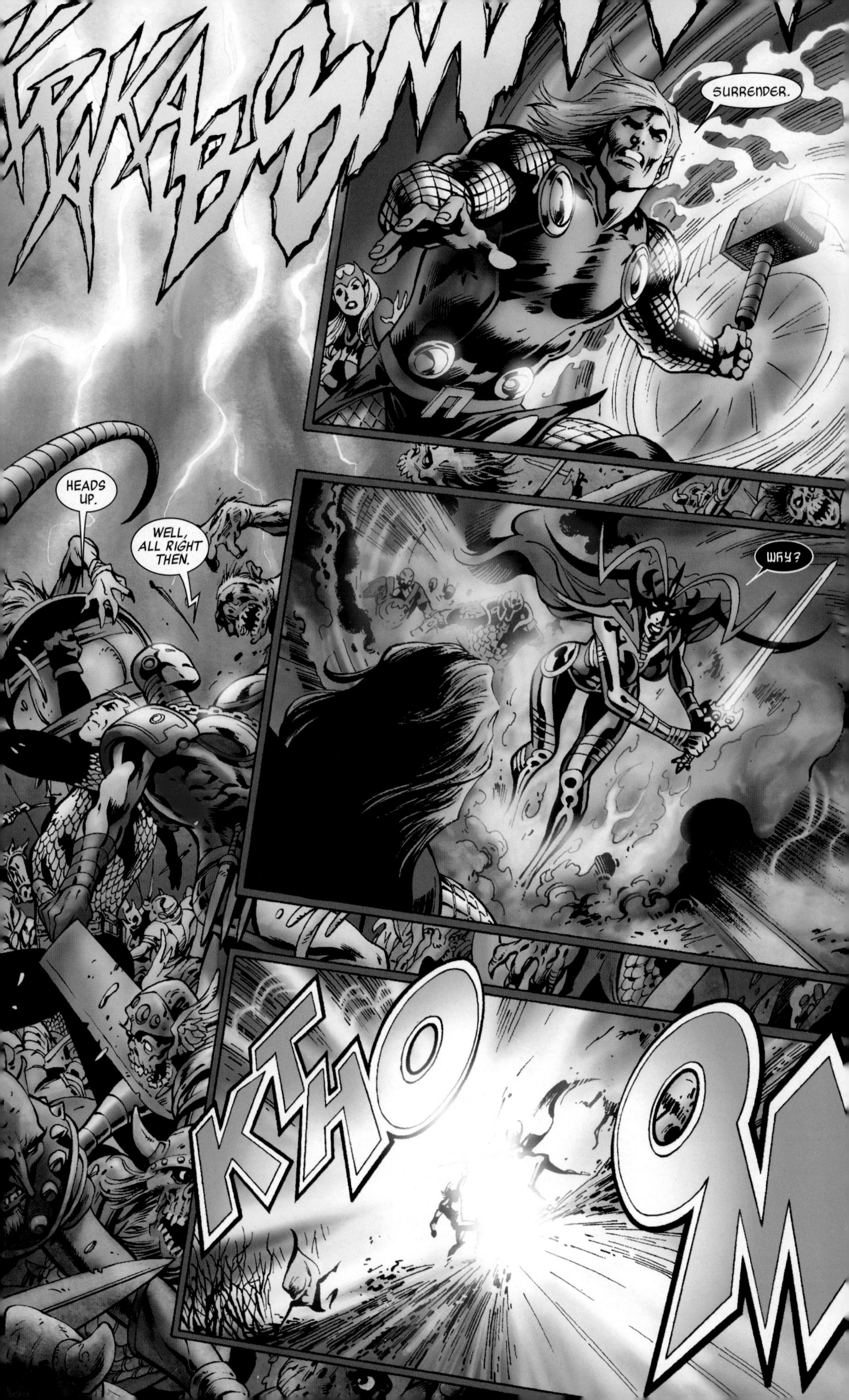
KRAKABOOM
SURRENDER.
HEADS UP.
WELL, ALL RIGHT THEN.
WHY?
KTHOOM

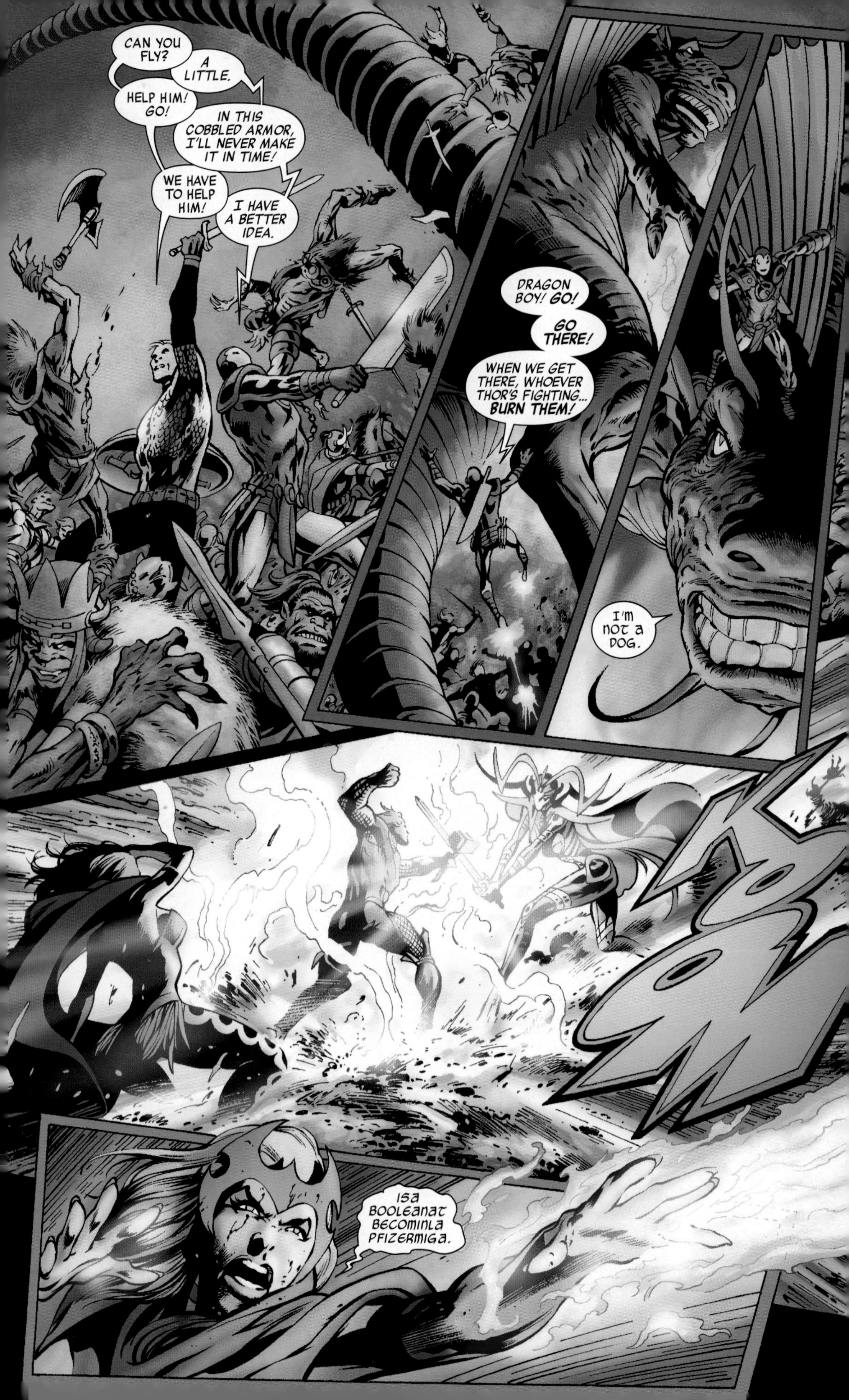

CAN YOU FLY?
A LITTLE.
HELP HIM! GO!
IN THIS COBBLED ARMOR, I'LL NEVER MAKE IT IN TIME!
WE HAVE TO HELP HIM!
I HAVE A BETTER IDEA.
DRAGON BOY! GO!
GO THERE!
WHEN WE GET THERE, WHOEVER THOR'S FIGHTING... BURN THEM!
I'M NOT A DOG.
ISA BOOLEANAT BECOMINLA PFIZERMIGA.

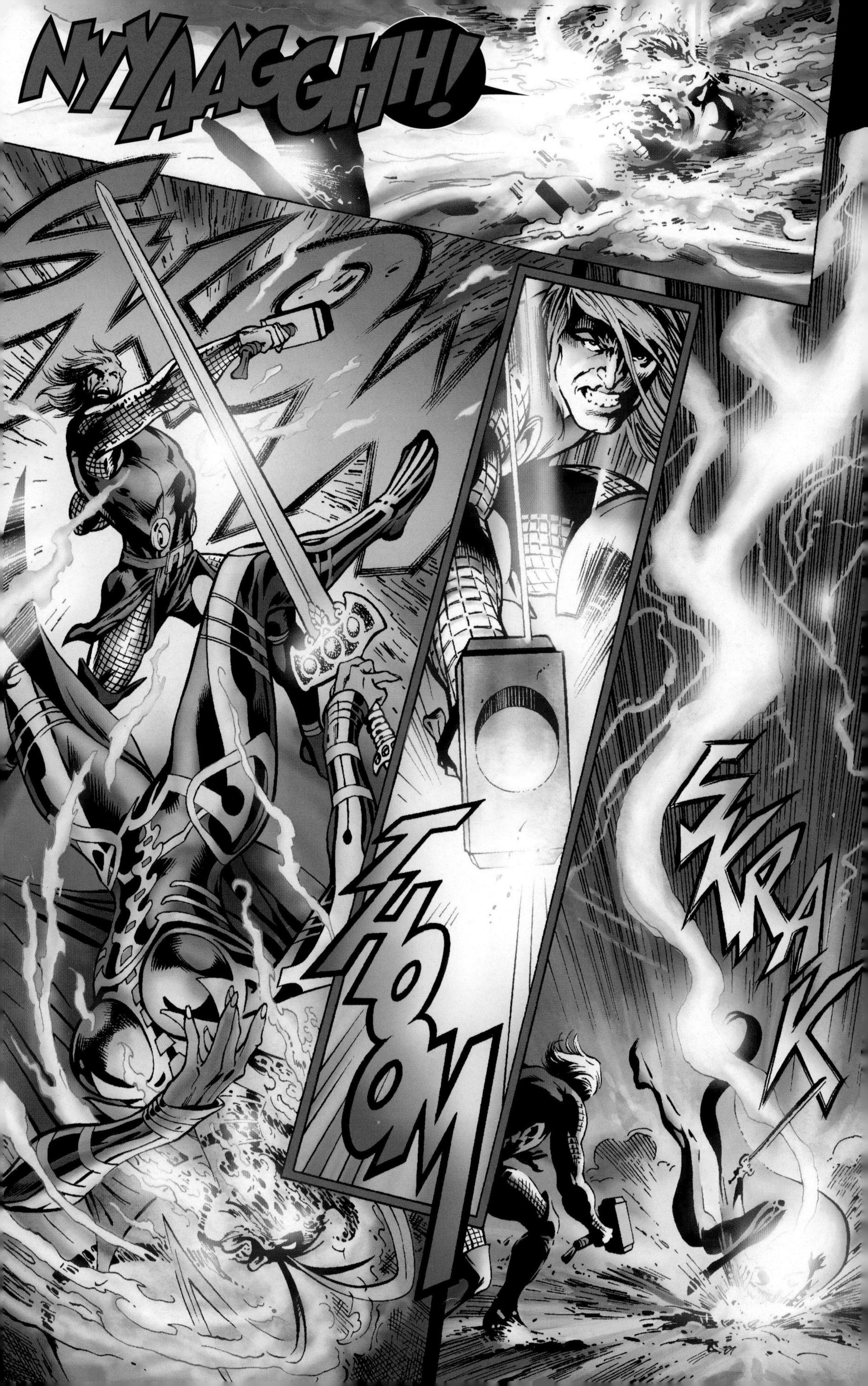
NYYAAGGHH!
THOOM
SKRAK

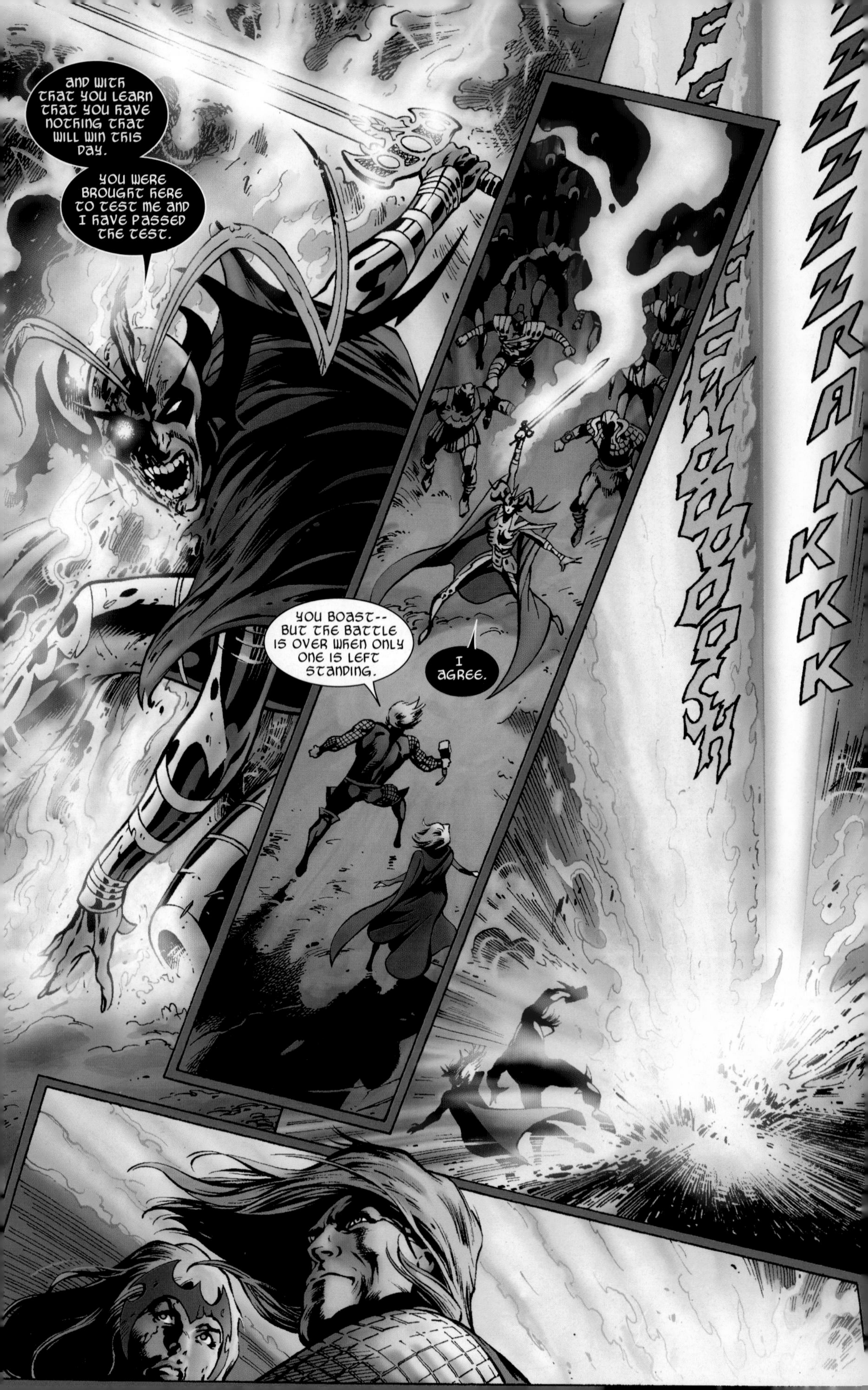
AND WITH THAT YOU LEARN THAT YOU HAVE NOTHING THAT WILL WIN THIS DAY.
YOU WERE BROUGHT HERE TO TEST ME AND I HAVE PASSED THE TEST.
YOU BOAST-- BUT THE BATTLE IS OVER WHEN ONLY ONE IS LEFT STANDING.
I AGREE.
FZZZZRAKKKKK
FWOOOOOOOM

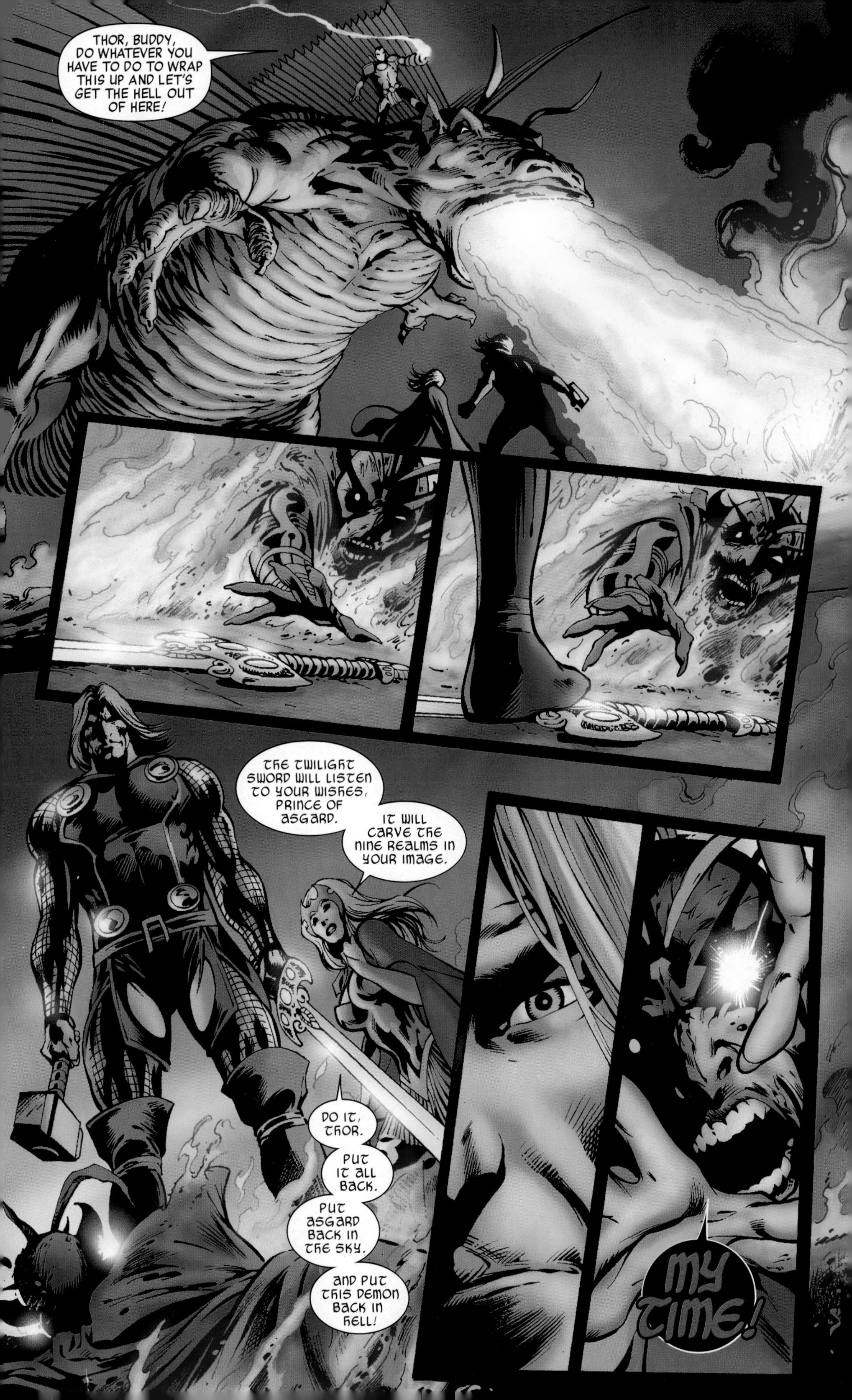

THOR, BUDDY, DO WHATEVER YOU HAVE TO DO TO WRAP THIS UP AND LET'S GET THE HELL OUT OF HERE!
THE TWILIGHT SWORD WILL LISTEN TO YOUR WISHES, PRINCE OF ASGARD.
IT WILL CARVE THE NINE REALMS IN YOUR IMAGE.
DO IT, THOR.
PUT IT ALL BACK.
PUT ASGARD BACK IN THE SKY.
AND PUT THIS DEMON BACK IN HELL!
MY TIME!

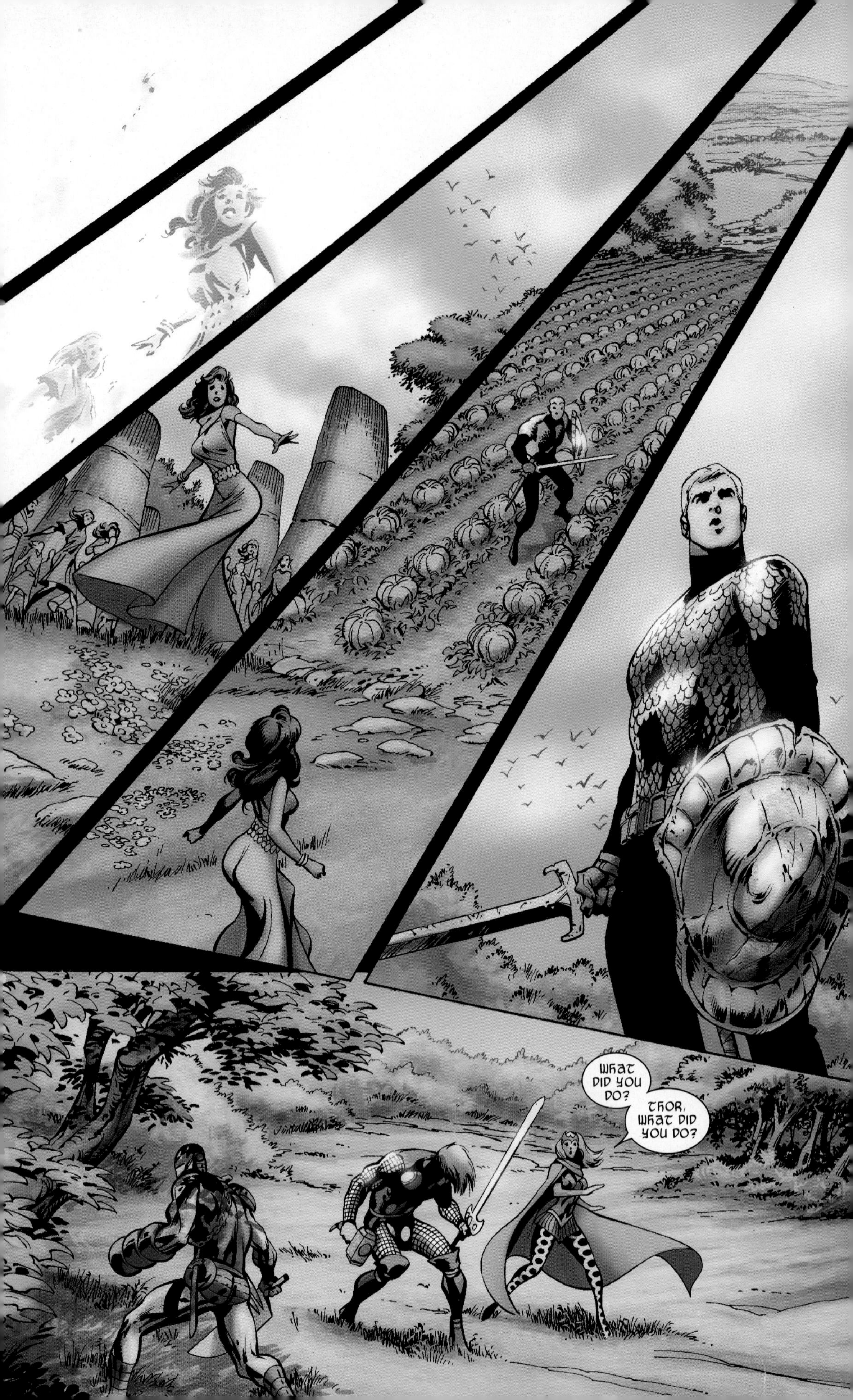
WHAT DID YOU DO?
THOR, WHAT DID YOU DO?

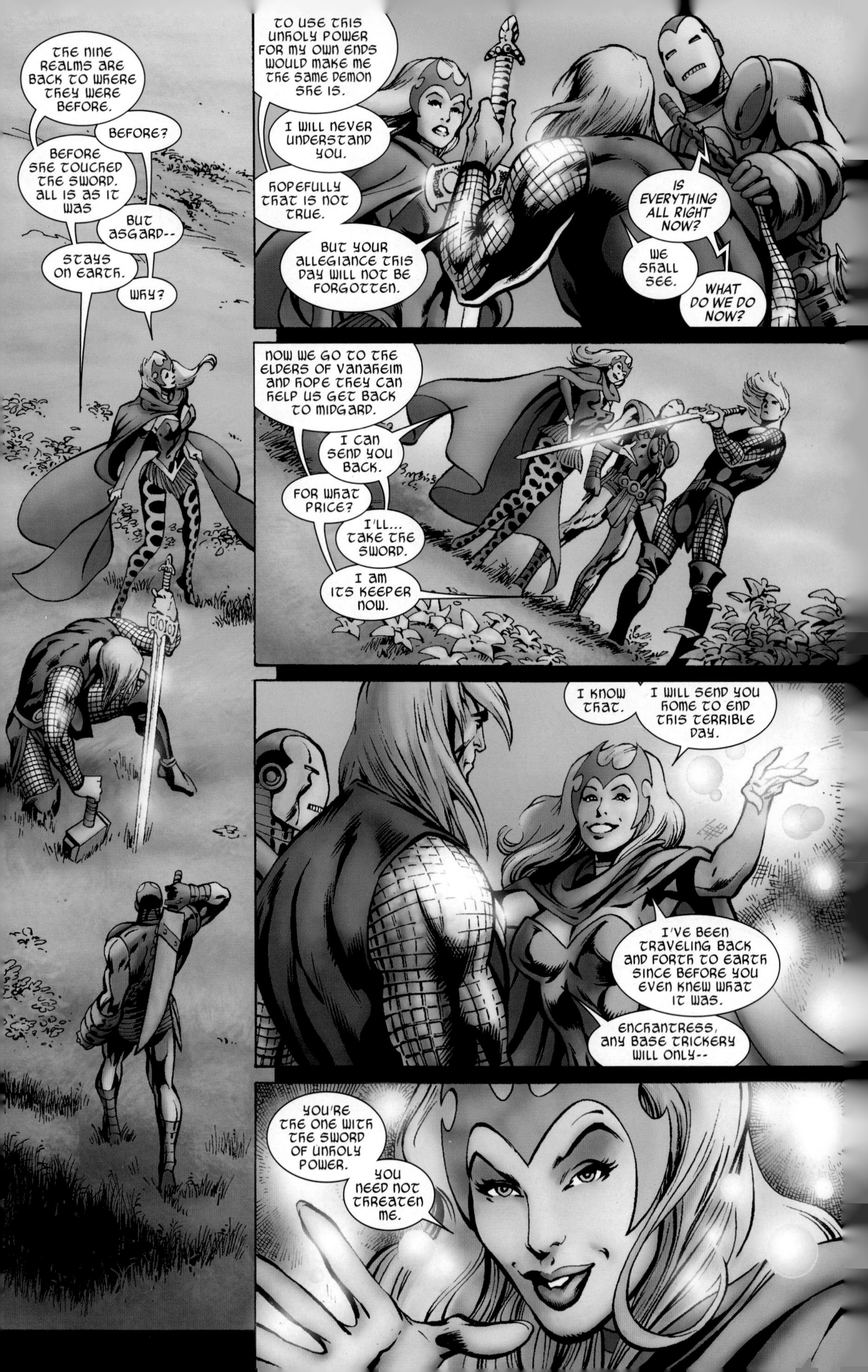
THE NINE REALMS ARE BACK TO WHERE THEY WERE BEFORE.
BEFORE?
BEFORE SHE TOUCHED THE SWORD. ALL IS AS IT WAS
BUT ASGARD--
STAYS ON EARTH.
WHY?
TO USE THIS UNHOLY POWER FOR MY OWN ENDS WOULD MAKE ME THE SAME DEMON SHE IS.
I WILL NEVER UNDERSTAND YOU.
HOPEFULLY THAT IS NOT TRUE.
BUT YOUR ALLEGIANCE THIS DAY WILL NOT BE FORGOTTEN.
IS EVERYTHING ALL RIGHT NOW?
WE SHALL SEE.
WHAT DO WE DO NOW?
NOW WE GO TO THE ELDERS OF VANAHEIM AND HOPE THEY CAN HELP US GET BACK TO MIDGARD.
I CAN SEND YOU BACK.
FOR WHAT PRICE?
I'LL... TAKE THE SWORD.
I AM ITS KEEPER NOW.
I KNOW THAT.
I WILL SEND YOU HOME TO END THIS TERRIBLE DAY.
I'VE BEEN TRAVELING BACK AND FORTH TO EARTH SINCE BEFORE YOU EVEN KNEW WHAT IT WAS.
ENCHANTRESS, ANY BASE TRICKERY WILL ONLY--
YOU'RE THE ONE WITH THE SWORD OF UNHOLY POWER.
YOU NEED NOT THREATEN ME.

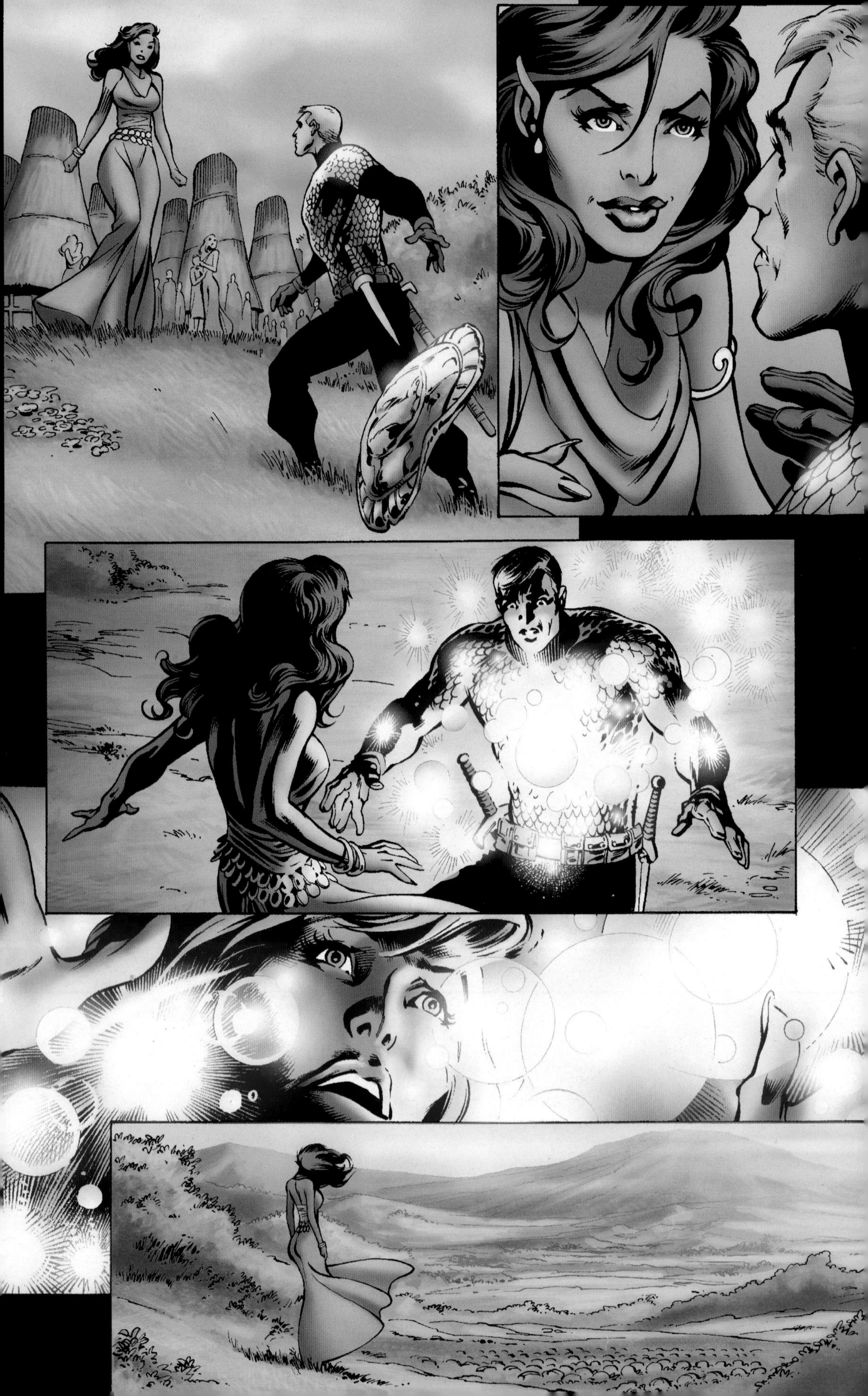

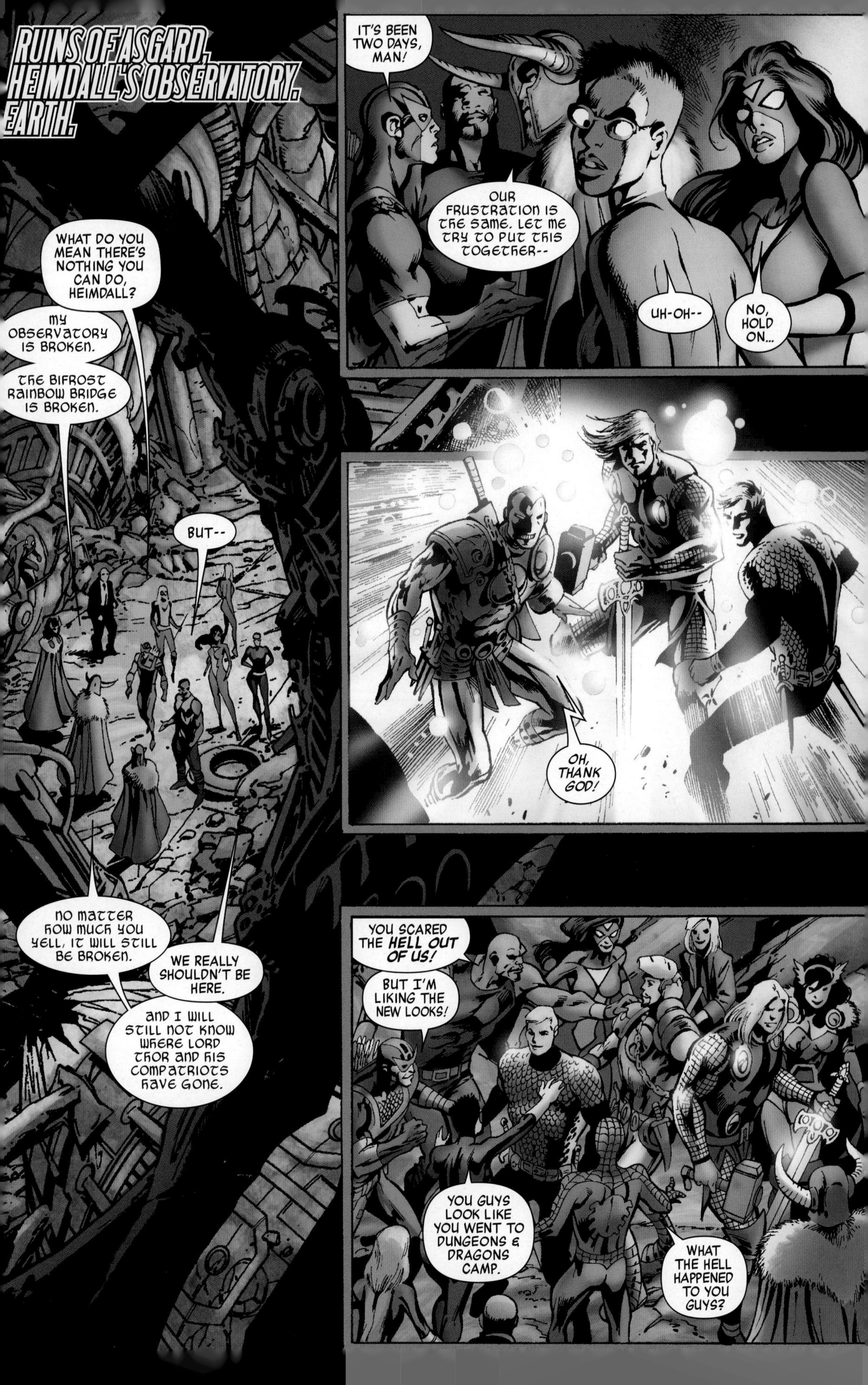
RUINS OF ASGARD, HEIMDALL'S OBSERVATORY. EARTH.
WHAT DO YOU MEAN THERE'S NOTHING YOU CAN DO, HEIMDALL?
MY OBSERVATORY IS BROKEN.
THE BIFROST RAINBOW BRIDGE IS BROKEN.
BUT--
NO MATTER HOW MUCH YOU YELL, IT WILL STILL BE BROKEN.
WE REALLY SHOULDN'T BE HERE.
AND I WILL STILL NOT KNOW WHERE LORD THOR AND HIS COMPATRIOTS HAVE GONE.
IT'S BEEN TWO DAYS, MAN!
OUR FRUSTRATION IS THE SAME. LET ME TRY TO PUT THIS TOGETHER--
UH-OH--
NO, HOLD ON...
OH, THANK GOD!
YOU SCARED THE HELL OUT OF US!
BUT I'M LIKING THE NEW LOOKS!
YOU GUYS LOOK LIKE YOU WENT TO DUNGEONS & DRAGONS CAMP.
WHAT THE HELL HAPPENED TO YOU GUYS?

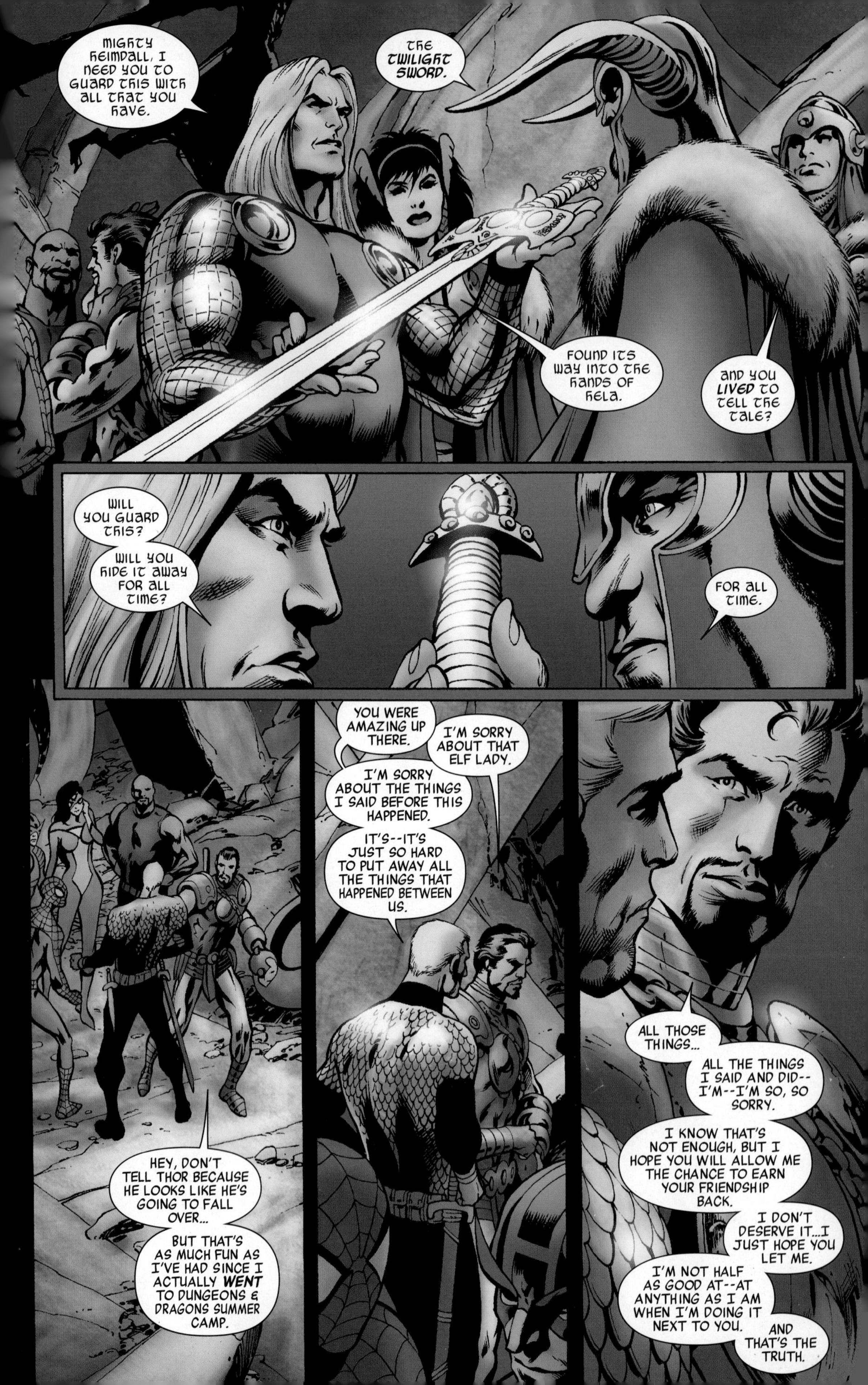
MIGHTY HEIMDALL, I NEED YOU TO GUARD THIS WITH ALL THAT YOU HAVE.
THE TWILIGHT SWORD.
FOUND ITS WAY INTO THE HANDS OF HELA.
AND YOU LIVED TO TELL THE TALE?
WILL YOU GUARD THIS?
WILL YOU HIDE IT AWAY FOR ALL TIME?
FOR ALL TIME.
HEY, DON'T TELL THOR BECAUSE HE LOOKS LIKE HE'S GOING TO FALL OVER...
BUT THAT'S AS MUCH FUN AS I'VE HAD SINCE I ACTUALLY WENT TO DUNGEONS & DRAGONS SUMMER CAMP.
YOU WERE AMAZING UP THERE.
I'M SORRY ABOUT THAT ELF LADY.
I'M SORRY ABOUT THE THINGS I SAID BEFORE THIS HAPPENED.
IT'S--IT'S JUST SO HARD TO PUT AWAY ALL THE THINGS THAT HAPPENED BETWEEN US.
ALL THOSE THINGS...
ALL THE THINGS I SAID AND DID--I'M--I'M SO, SO SORRY.
I KNOW THAT'S NOT ENOUGH, BUT I HOPE YOU WILL ALLOW ME THE CHANCE TO EARN YOUR FRIENDSHIP BACK.
I DON'T DESERVE IT...I JUST HOPE YOU LET ME.
I'M NOT HALF AS GOOD AT--AT ANYTHING AS I AM WHEN I'M DOING IT NEXT TO YOU.
AND THAT'S THE TRUTH.

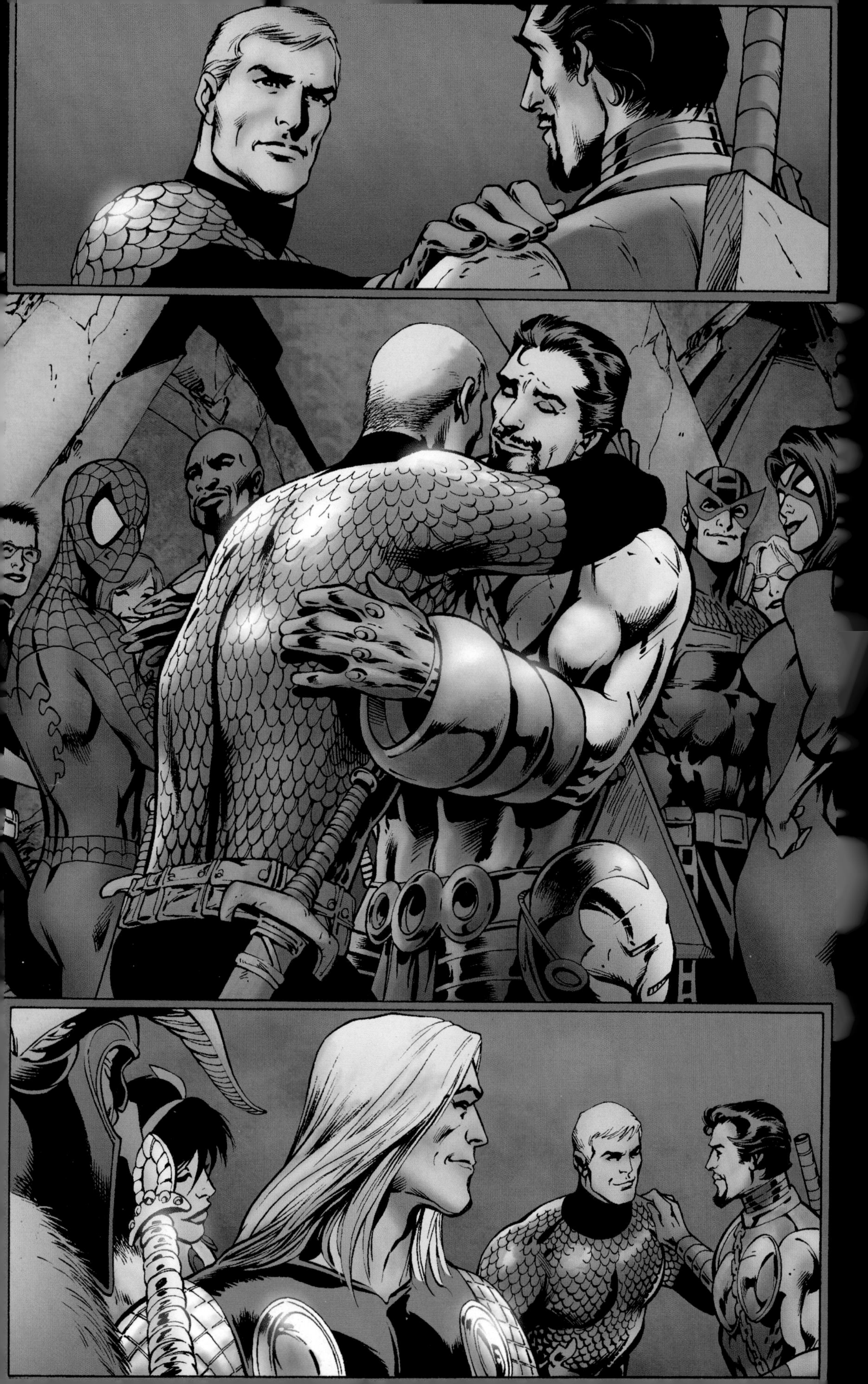

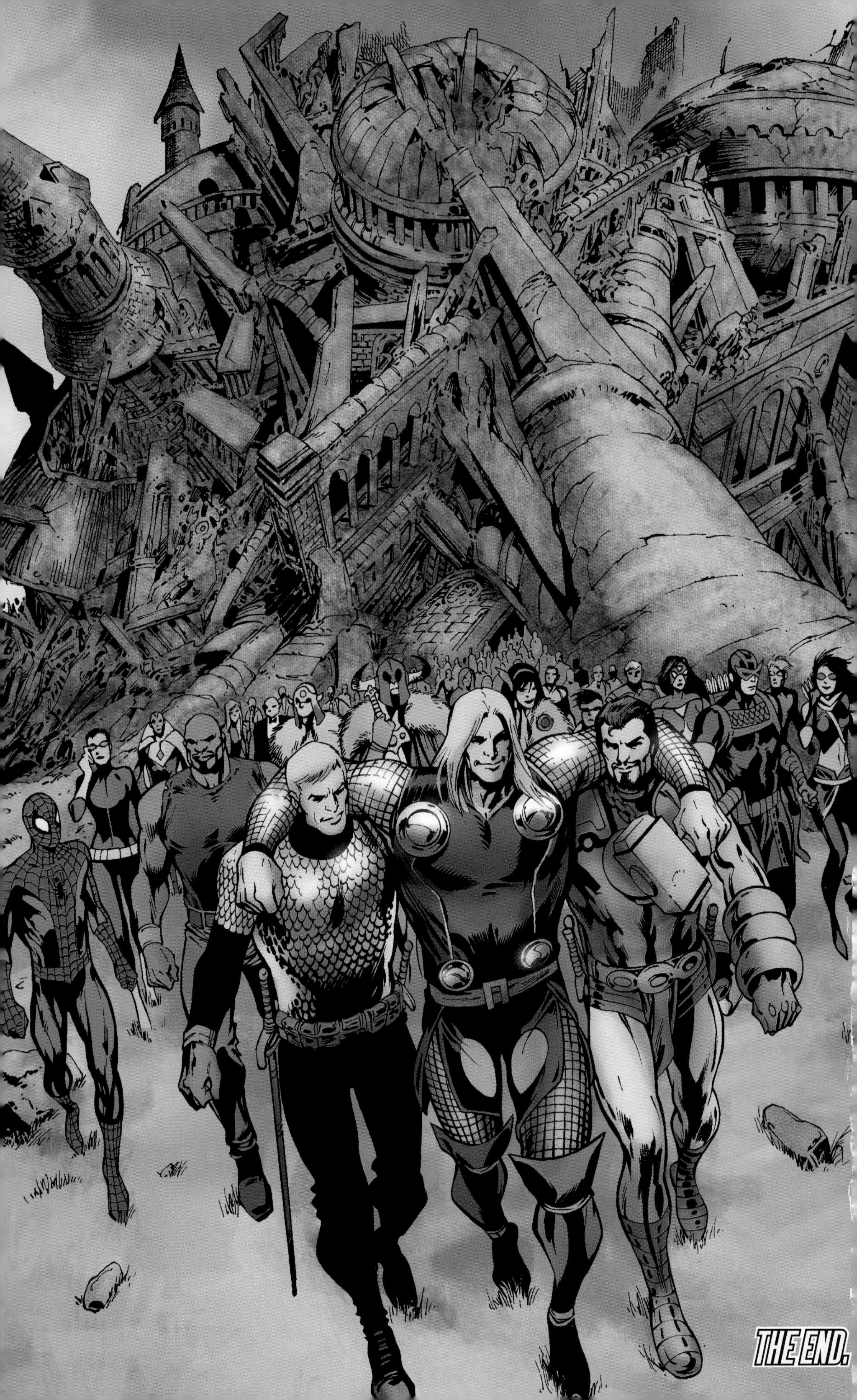
THE END.